COMHAIRLE CHON
LEABHARLANNA CHON

Economics

an **A-Z** guide

OTHER ECONOMIST BOOKS

Guide to Analysing Companies
Guide to Business Modelling
Guide to Business Planning
Guide to Economic Indicators
Guide to the European Union
Guide to Financial Management
Guide to Financial Markets
Guide to Investment Strategy
Guide to Management Ideas and Gurus
Guide to Organisation Design
Guide to Project Management
Numbers Guide
Style Guide

Book of Obituaries
Brands and Branding
Business Consulting
Business Miscellany
Business Strategy
Dealing with Financial Risk
Economics
Emerging Markets
The Future of Technology
Headhunters and How to Use Them
Mapping the Markets
Successful Strategy Execution
The City

Directors: an A–Z Guide
Investment: an A–Z Guide
Negotiation: an A–Z Guide

Pocket World in Figures

Economics

an A–Z guide

Matthew Bishop

THE ECONOMIST IN ASSOCIATION WITH
PROFILE BOOKS LTD

Published by Profile Books Ltd
3A Exmouth House, Pine Street, London EC1R 0JH

Developed from titles previously published as *Pocket Economics* and
Essential Economics

Designed by Sue Lamble
Typeset in EcoType by MacGuru Ltd
info@macguru.org.uk

Printed in the UK by CPI Bookmarque, Croydon, CRO 4TD

A CIP catalogue record for this book is available
from the British Library

ISBN 978 1 84668 166 0

Mixed Sources
Product group from well-managed
forests and other controlled sources
www.fsc.org   Cert no. TT-COC-002227
FSC   © 1996 Forest Stewardship Council

Contents

Introduction

The aim of this book is to explain economics and its most important ideas, and to demystify the most important economic terms and concepts. It is intended to be practical, rather than provide a comprehensive tour of economic theory. It focuses on the economics that affects jobs and prices and trade, that raises voices in boardrooms and bars and among politicians and pundits, in short, the economics that touches and shapes everyday life.

The book starts with an essay that examines the nature of economics and the challenges it must rise to if it is to be relevant in a fast-changing world. Following this is an A–Z of jargon, terms and concepts. In this section words in SMALL CAPITALS usually indicate a cross-reference to a separate entry, although readers should note that abbreviations that may not have a separate entry are also in small capitals. As is inevitable with a book of this nature, the entries draw heavily, and with gratitude, on the work of others. This includes many articles published in *The Economist* and previous Economist guides to economics.

Economics at the crossroads

For economics, these truly are the best of times and the worst of times. On the one hand, the dismal science (as Victorian writer Thomas Carlyle christened it) has never been more fashionable. Books about it top the best-seller lists, ranging from heavyweight tomes about macroeconomic policy – such as the memoirs of Alan Greenspan, former chairman of America's Federal Reserve bank, who once seemed to have the fate of the global economy in his hands – to populist books using economics to explain the weirdness of every day life, such as *Freakonomics*, by Steven Dubner and Steven Levitt.

On the other hand – and as an American president, Harry Truman, once complained, "all my economists say, 'on one hand ... on the other'" – the financial crisis that began in the summer of 2007 and the economic slowdown and recession that followed it shook confidence in what had become widely held economic truths. Over the previous quarter of a century, as market-oriented policies spread around the world after the fall of communism, there had been growing confidence among economists, and the politicians and policymakers who relied upon them, that macroeconomic policies could tame the traditional cycle of boom and bust, increasing prosperity around the world while keeping inflation and unemployment low.

That conventional wisdom has been shattered. Nor is it just macroeconomics that has been forced to be rethought and reinvented. The micro foundations of economics have also been shaken in recent years by evidence that in reality people do not behave as the rational, self-interested individuals – so-called *homo economicus* – on whom mainstream economic theories are based. This makes it more important than ever to understand the essentials of economics and how to use it; which questions it can answer with confidence, and which it cannot.

What is economics?

"Economics is what economists do," reckoned Jacob Viner, a leading 20th-century economist. That may not be a helpful definition, especially if another American president, Ronald Reagan, was right when he described economists as unworldly "people, who see something work in practice and wonder if it would work in theory". More helpfully, the authors of *Freakonomics* say that economics, at its root, is "the study of incentives: how people get what they want, or need, especially when other people want or need the same thing". This notion of people competing for the same thing points to what is probably the most useful definition of economics: "the study of how society uses its scarce resources" or, more snappily, "the science of choices". Without scarcity – of land, labour, raw materials, capital, entrepreneurial spirit, time – there would be no need to make choices about how to use those things to greatest effect, and thus no need for economics. At its best, economics helps people to make the right choices; at least, it shows them the most efficient way to use scarce resources in the process of achieving their goals.

There is nothing dismal about that. The more efficiently scarce things are used, the less they are wasted and the greater is the likelihood that people achieve their goals. True, choosing to do one thing means choosing not to do another. Perhaps the most important rule in economics is that every choice, every decision to do one thing rather than another, has a cost. Pointing this out can make economists seem to be professional party-poopers. Nobody tucking into a slap-up meal enjoys being reminded that there is no such thing as a free lunch. Yet an economic concept known as opportunity cost – which asks "What are you giving up to do this?" (in the case of lunch, at the very least time you could spend elsewhere) – is the key to making efficient choices.

Humans are optimistic creatures at heart and generally concentrate on the upside and underplay the downside. When economists talk about opportunity cost, they are not accentuating the negative for its own sake. They are taking a hard look at the downside of any choice to ensure, before going ahead, that the upside really is as desirable as it seems.

Some critics say that what makes economics truly dismal is that it reduces the whole of life to questions about money. It does not. Economics is about how to maximise a person's or a society's "welfare", not merely their financial wealth. Welfare, or "utility", is economic jargon for happiness or satisfaction, which even economists understand can come from many things besides money. Some economic theories have included in the definition of welfare the satisfaction individuals get from their family, or religion, or charitable giving and other forms of self-sacrifice, or from living on a healthy planet. True, economists do sometimes make the mistake of talking about money and welfare as if they are the same thing. This may be because changes in the amount of money an individual or society has are easy to measure, and changes in financial wealth do often move in step with changes in welfare.

That is why for most of the past century, the best-known economic theories and the economists who came up with those theories have focused on how to generate economic growth, and to do so fast enough to provide employment for all who want it but not so fast that it results in excessive price inflation. How best to do this has long been a source of controversy among economists, with rival schools of thought holding sway at different times – often years after their theories were first developed and the problems they had addressed were long gone. (A British economist, John Maynard Keynes, who gave his name to one of the rival schools, Keynesianism, famously complained that "even the most practical man of affairs is usually in the thrall of the ideas of some long-dead economist".)

Keynesianism, which saw governments as responsible through their spending for maintaining enough demand in the economy to keep unemployment low, was dominant in the decades after the second world war. During the 1960s, economists thought the "Phillips Curve" proved that policymakers could make a choice between higher inflation and lower unemployment, and lower inflation and higher unemployment. Subsequent experience showed that the seemingly clear relationship between unemployment and inflation had been at most a short-term phenomenon rather than an iron law of economics. Then, when inflation and then stagflation (high inflation, high unemployment and lacklustre economic growth) came to be seen as the leading economic problem facing the world, neoclassical economics dominated, with an emphasis on keeping inflation low through controlling the amount of money in the economy, while promoting growth and thus lowering unemployment by allowing a greater role for market forces.

The return of big government

Now the pendulum seems to be swinging again, as the credit crunch that began in 2007 led into recession and, in turn, to efforts by governments in many countries to revive economic growth through new Keynesian spending programmes. These were introduced with much less confidence of success than the first time. In part, this was because the early Keynesian era ended badly. Yet it was also because the leading economic thinkers and policymakers of the past quarter of a century had become increasingly certain that they were mastering economic management, through a combination of lightly regulated markets, automatic counter-cyclical fiscal policy and setting interest rates according to medium-term targets for inflation. Yet suddenly, in the eyes of many people, including some of these leaders themselves, they were revealed as emperors wearing no clothes.

If it is much debated whether or not economics is dismal, its claims to be a science are even more controversial. The failure of Keynesian demand management in the 1970s highlighted the limitations of economic policymakers who believed they could keep both unemployment and inflation low by precise policies of "fine tuning". The credit crunch and its aftermath highlighted severe flaws in financial economics, which was the basis of the scientific-sounding "financial engineering" used by economists on Wall Street and in the City of London to create derivatives and other financial instruments that, economic theory said, would make the capital markets perform more efficiently.

Flick through an academic journal of economics, and you will find page after page of mathematical equations and sophisticated analyses of data. Economic forecasters spend much of their time crunching numbers using powerful computers, all of which seems scientific enough. Many economists think their work is on a par with that of their counterparts in physical sciences such as chemistry and physics. Yet much of economics falls short of what qualifies as true science.

Good science requires theory that is capable of being proved wrong and vigorous testing to see whether it is supported by the facts. How does economics measure up? Consider some of the big macroeconomic policy questions on which the advice of economists is sought. How can inflation be lowered and full employment be created? Why is one country richer than another? Not even the leading economic theories on such questions can be tested in the thorough way that, say, a chemist would test a theory about how one chemical will react with another.

An economy is highly complex. It is hard to tell if the various forces influencing unemployment or inflation are really the ones suggested by theory. Macroeconomic policy is implemented under conditions of great uncertainty about the future. If things go wrong, or even if they go well, it will rarely be clear if a policy was right (or wrong) or merely lucky (or unlucky).

True scientists, such as chemists, would find out by rerunning the experiment many times. The events on which macroeconomic theory is based cannot be replicated, at least with the precision and frequency that would generate enough data to reach rock solid conclusions. With historical events, such as the high unemployment of the 1930s, the hyper-inflation of the 1970s, or even the credit-crunch of 2007, there is no way to repeat an experiment by starting all over again with a different set of economic policies to see how things would have turned out. Besides, even if they could be repeated, because people's behaviour often changes, they might not act in the same way second time around. Even the best macroeconomic theories fall short of the sort of "hard" scientific theories people are happy to trust with their lives when they step into an aircraft or have a hip replacement.

So macroeconomic advice should always come with a health warning. The failure of the latest attempt to abolish the economic cycle of boom and bust, like those before it, was yet more proof of what economists should have known all along.

Unlike macroeconomics, the core rules of market economics have been tested in thousands of different markets, in many different places, at many different times. They do not work every time. But mostly they hold true. Take, for example, the laws of supply and demand. In a free market, if you put up your price, the chances are you will sell less. Lower your price, and you can expect to sell more. When the market is not allowed to work its magic, the scarce resources are often allocated inefficiently. They are used to make produce that does not properly satisfy demand, and the price mechanism is often replaced by rationing and illegal black markets or other corruption.

Indeed, markets can often do a better job than government when it comes to efficiently allocating scarce resources. When Adam Smith, the 18th-century "father of economics", said that the market economy works as if an "invisible hand" guides the actions of individuals to combine for the common good, this is what he meant. It was the growing recognition of the virtues of market economics that from around 1980 drove the huge shift in economic policy around the world that is now under fire.

This emphasised a "micro-macro" approach based on promoting markets and the conditions that enable markets to work well. Many government-owned firms were privatised and government-controlled markets deregulated. Competition was promoted, increasing choice in the marketplace, and tax rates cut to give people a greater financial incentive to sell their skills in the market. Trade barriers were lowered, making it easier for markets to cross national borders. To lower unemployment, instead of enthusing about using demand management as the main, best way to prevent a downturn in the economic cycle, economists instead sought to encourage workers to become more employable by removing regulations that discouraged employers from hiring and by urging, and even paying, people to increase their human capital, particularly through education. The need to revive the global economy after it slowed alarmingly in 2008 led governments, academics and the public alike to question much of this prevailing economic policy consensus.

It is likely to take years of debate before a new consensus on macroeconomic policy emerges. Although the role of government spending, regulation and ownership (including of large stakes in major banks) is likely to be bigger than in the previous era, the principal uncertainty is whether bigger government will also be smarter government. The danger is that the failings of the first era of big-government Keynesianism will be repeated. But perhaps governments will learn from those failings and appreciate those things that worked well during the subsequent more market-oriented era. (Indeed, even in the so-called free market era, it was clear that markets do not work well in the absence of the rule of law and good government. At a minimum, there is a need for clear, legally protected private property rights, helping participants in markets to know that their trades are legally watertight, which makes them more likely to trade.)

Much may depend on whether governments find ways to harness the creativity of the private sector, rather than crowd it out through unimaginative public spending. For example, increased infrastructure spending is a key element of many fiscal stimulus plans; but there are big differences in the extent to which governments use competitive processes to design and award infrastructure projects. Another question is whether governments impose so much regulation on the financial sector that it loses its ability to do the risk-taking essential to wealth creation.

Trade has already become a battleground for this new era, as protectionists who were vocal but largely ineffective in the past quarter of a century see the recent financial crisis and slowdown as an opportunity to erect barriers to trade – or, as some of them prefer to describe it, to make the trading system "fairer". Most economists believe that, on balance, free trade is beneficial to everyone concerned, but that did not stop a protectionist backlash in the 1930s helping to turn economic slowdown into the Great Depression. Could it happen again?

Some recent developments in economics have helped to revive the belief that government should intervene far more to shape the decisions taken by individuals in markets. Traditionally, economists have typically described the thought processes of homo sapiens as more like that of Star Trek's half-Vulcan, half-human Spock – strictly logical, centred on a clearly defined goal and apparently free from the unsteady influences of emotion or irrationality – than the uncertain, error-prone groping with which most of us are familiar. Of course, a large part of human behaviour does fit the rational pattern so beloved of economists, but much of it does not.

Economists are now waking up to this fact. A wind of change is blowing some human spirit back into the ivory towers where economic theory is made. There is a growing school of economists who are drawing on a vast range of behavioural traits identified by experimental psychologists, which amount to a frontal assault on the whole idea that people, individually or as a group, mostly act rationally. For instance, bubbles and crashes seem to be the result of people being swayed by the mood of the crowd, rather than by careful, rational decision-making. A new field of economics that draws on neuroscience has been born in the past decade, called neuroeconomics, which also challenges the traditional assumption in economics of a rational decision-maker, *homo economicus*.

Increasingly, economists are starting to develop theories based on behavioural economics and neuroeconomics by which government can use incentives or other techniques to help people take more rational economic decisions. This new approach has been called "liberal paternalism", as it combines liberal free markets with a paternalistic state. It remains to be seen if these new approaches will work in practice, but it is likely to be an area of great debate and experimentation by economists.

Saving the world

How best to reduce poverty will remain an important question for economists. The rise of inequality that accompanied the market-oriented policies introduced from the 1980s, while in some respects exaggerated by critics of those policies, was reviving calls for action, such as higher taxes on the rich, even before the credit crisis of 2007 and its economic aftermath. The market-oriented policies had been introduced largely because of two concerns: first, that taxing the rich heavily may discourage them from wealth creation; and second, that giving money to the poor can destroy market incentives to self-help and make the recipient of aid dependent on the giver.

Economists increasingly debate whether absolute poverty should be regarded as quite different from relative poverty. They point out that relative poverty can increase even when, thanks to economic growth, absolute poverty is falling. Is an increase in the number of people in relative poverty as a result of rising income inequality worth worrying about if absolute poverty is falling? So far, there is little consensus among economists. There is more agreement that to stop inequality increasing would require much greater government intervention than reducing absolute poverty, and that such intervention might reduce the rate of economic growth. Likewise, most economists agree that the world's poorest countries could get richer by being more open to international trade, enforcing sensibly drafted laws, encouraging private property and educating their people. However, there is growing debate about the proper sequencing of the introduction of different macro and micro policies during the process of transition from bad to good policy. There is growing evidence of the dangers of doing the right things in the wrong order.

The relationship between democracy and economic growth has become increasingly controversial among economists. Some see it as one of the foundations of successful economic policy, not least because political freedom usually (if not always) goes hand-in-hand with economic freedom. But the strong economic performance of China, despite its continuing undemocratic government, has led a growing number of economists to make the case for economic growth without democracy, so-called "authoritarian capitalism".

Another increasingly important battleground for economists will be protecting the environment, and above all, figuring out what to do about climate change and its consequences. Environmentalists are wrong when they argue that economics only values economic growth (it does not) and is thus inherently anti-environmental. But they are right to point out that, in practice, the statistic most often used to indicate whether economic welfare is rising or falling is a purely monetary measure, GDP, and that better measures of economic success or failure, that take environmental and other non-monetary factors into account, are needed.

Nevertheless, in recent decades, countries with the highest levels of GDP have generally made the greatest progress in reducing environmental damage – with the notable exception of climate change. Many environmentalists argue that governments should tackle the problem by banning "undesirable" economic activity. Yet economists have been some of the leading advocates of market-based alternatives, which they believe are more efficient. For instance, there have been attempts to reduce the carbon emissions that contribute to climate change by issuing tradable rights to pollute, which in an efficient market should end up in the hands of the companies that produce the most economic wealth for each "unit" of pollution. However, these have so far not worked well in practice. They will ultimately require global agreement on a scheme which addresses all carbon emissions worldwide, which will require politicians to be convinced of their economic merits as well as the urgency of tackling the problem. And some economists reckon a tax on carbon is a better bet than a tradable emissions system.

Yet another challenge will be to understand the economic implications of the information revolution now under way, notably through the spread of the internet. Inadequate information, and the high cost of getting better information, has long been one of the main causes of market failure, and of government economic policy mistakes. Possibly, the ready availability of information will enable government policy to be much more effective than in the past. Certainly, that is what advocates of liberal paternalism believe. If so, the role of the free market's invisible hand in allocating scarce resources might decline again. It is more likely that better information will mean less market failure, and thus less need for government intervention, including in areas such as education and health care.

Whether they are trying to improve public services or help individuals and firms do better in the private sector, economists will need to understand better why some markets work more efficiently than others and some not at all. Existing theories do not answer well enough a long list of important questions. What is the most efficient way to set prices, or to change them? Why do firms exist in the forms they do? Does it make sense for companies to spend so much money on advertising and brand building? What is the best way to generate innovation? How can financial markets in shares, bonds, currencies, and so on be made to work more efficiently? In particular, what might be done to stop or better manage the consequences of financial bubbles? What are the circumstances in which government actions to deal with market failure go wrong? And so on. With so many interesting and important questions to grapple with, no wonder economics is more fashionable than ever.

A–Z

Absolute advantage

This is the simplest yardstick of economic performance. If one person, firm or country can produce more of something with the same amount of effort and resources, they have an absolute advantage over other producers. Being the best at something does not mean that doing that thing is the best way to use your scarce economic resources. The question of what to specialise in – and how to maximise the benefits from international trade – is best decided according to COMPARATIVE ADVANTAGE. Both absolute and comparative advantage may change significantly over time.

Adaptive expectations

A theory of how people form their views about the future that assumes they do so using past trends and the errors in their own earlier predictions. Contrast with RATIONAL EXPECTATIONS.

Advance market commitment

In February 2007, a new form of incentive for INNOVATION was launched by the GOVERNMENTS of the UK, Canada, Italy, Norway and Russia in PUBLIC-PRIVATE partnership with the charitable Bill & Melinda Gates Foundation. They promised $1.5 billion to buy a vaccine to protect against pneumococcal disease which could potentially save the lives of 5.4m children by 2030. The idea was that by guaranteeing that there would be DEMAND for the vaccine, this advance market commitment (AMC) made it far more likely that the vaccine would be developed by one or more pharmaceutical companies. Without the AMC, which is a legally binding government-backed contract, those companies considered it too risky to devote (enough) money to developing the vaccine. This is expected to be the first of many AMCs.

Adverse selection

When you do business with people you would be better off avoiding this. It is one of two main sorts of MARKET FAILURE often associated with INSURANCE. The other is MORAL HAZARD. Adverse selection can be a problem when there is ASYMMETRIC INFORMATION between the seller of insurance and the buyer; in particular, insurance will often not be profitable when buyers have better information about their RISK of claiming than does the seller. Ideally, insurance premiums should be set according to the risk of a randomly selected person in the insured slice of the POPULATION (55-year-old male smokers, say). In practice, this means the AVERAGE risk of that group.

When there is adverse selection, people who know they have a higher risk of claiming than the average of the group will buy the insurance, whereas those who have a below-average risk may decide it is too expensive to be worth buying. In this case, premiums set according to the average risk will not be sufficient to cover the claims that eventually arise, because among the people who have bought the policy more will have above-average risk than below-average risk. Putting up the premium will not solve this problem, for as the premium rises the insurance policy will become unattractive to more of the people who know they have a lower risk of claiming. One way to reduce adverse selection is to make the purchase of insurance compulsory, so that those for whom insurance priced for average risk is unattractive are not able to opt out.

Advertising

Many FIRMS advertise their goods or SERVICES, but are they wasting economic resources? Some economists reckon that advertising merely manipulates consumer tastes and creates desires that would not otherwise exist. By increasing product differentiation and encouraging BRAND loyalty, advertising may make consumers less PRICE sensitive, moving the market further from PERFECT COMPETITION towards imperfect competition (see MONOPOLISTIC COMPETITION) and increasing the ability of firms to charge more than MARGINAL cost. Heavy spending on advertising may also create a BARRIER TO ENTRY, as a firm entering the market would have to spend a lot on advertising too.

However, some economists argue that advertising is economically valuable because it increases the flow of INFORMATION in the economy and reduces the ASYMMETRIC INFORMATION between the seller and the consumer. This intensifies competition, as consumers can be made aware quickly when there is a better deal on offer.

Agency costs

These can arise when somebody (the principal) hires somebody else (the agent) to carry out a task and the interests of the agent conflict with the interests of the principal. An example of such principal–agent problems comes from the relationship between the shareholders who own a public company and the managers who run it. The owners would like managers to run the firm in ways that maximise the value of their SHARES, whereas the managers' priority may be, say, to build a business empire through rapid expansion and MERGERS AND ACQUISITIONS, which may not increase their firm's share PRICE.

One way to reduce agency costs is for the principal to monitor what the agent does to make sure it is what he has been hired to do. But this can be costly, too. It may be impossible to define the agent's job in a way that can be monitored effectively. For instance, it is hard to know whether a manager who has expanded a firm through an acquisition that reduced its share price was pursuing his own empire-building interests or, say, was trying to maximise shareholder value but was unlucky.

Another way to lower agency costs, especially when monitoring is too expensive or too difficult, is to make the interests of the agent more like those of the principal. For instance, from the early 1990s, an increasingly popular way to minimise the agency costs arising from the separation of ownership and management of public companies was to pay managers partly with shares and share options in the company. This, it was hoped, would give the managers a powerful incentive to act in the interests of the owners by maximising shareholder value. But even this did not turn out to be a perfect solution. Unless the rules governing when shares and options are awarded or sold are set with great care, they can create new agency costs rather than eliminate them. Some managers with lots of share options have engaged in accounting fraud in order to increase the value of those options long enough for them to cash some of them in, but to the detriment of their firm and its other shareholders. See, for example, ENRON.

Agflation

Rising FOOD PRICES.

Agriculture

Farming around the world continues to become more productive while generally accounting for a smaller share of employment and NATIONAL INCOME, although in some poor countries it remains the sector on which the country and its people depend.

Farming, forestry and fishing in 1913 accounted for 28% of employment in the United States, 41% in France and 60% in Japan, but only 12% in the UK. Now the proportion of the workforce employed in such activities has dropped below 6% in these and most other industrialised countries.

The total value of international trade in agriculture has risen steadily. But the global agriculture market remains severely distorted by trade barriers and government SUBSIDY, such as the EUROPEAN UNION's Common AGRICULTURAL POLICY. The rapid rise in recent years of the use of biofuels, often subsidised by GOVERNMENTS, has further distorted agricultural markets, leading to significantly higher FOOD PRICES.

Agricultural policy

Countries often provide support for their farmers using trade barriers and subsidy because, for example:

- domestic AGRICULTURE, even if it is inefficient by world standards, can be an INSURANCE policy in case it becomes difficult (as it does, for example, in wartime) to buy agricultural produce from abroad;
- farmers' groups have proved adept at lobbying;
- politicians have sought to slow the depopulation of rural areas;
- agricultural PRICES can be volatile, as a result of unpredictable weather, among other things;
- financial support can provide a safety net in unexpectedly severe market conditions;
- biofuels are seen as a desirable alternative to fossil fuels given the need to curb climate change.

Broadly, GOVERNMENTS have tried two methods of subsidising agriculture. The first, used in the United States during the 1930s and in the UK before it joined the EUROPEAN UNION, is to top up farmers' incomes if they fall below a level deemed acceptable. Farmers may be required to set aside some of their land in return for this support. The second is to guarantee a minimum level of farm prices by buying up surplus SUPPLY and storing or destroying it if prices would otherwise fall below the guaranteed levels. This was the approach adopted by the EU when it set up its Common Agricultural Policy. To keep down the direct cost of this subsidy the EU used trade barriers, including import levies, to minimise COMPETITION to EU farmers from produce available more cheaply on world agriculture markets. More recent American farm-support policy has combined income top-ups and some guaranteed prices.

As most governments have become more committed to international trade, such agricultural policies have come under increasing attack, although the FREE TRADE rhetoric has often run far ahead of genuine reform. In 2006, rich countries together spent $268 billion supporting their farmers, more than six times what they spent on INTERNATIONAL AID. Finding a way to end agricultural support had become by far the biggest remaining challenge for those trying to negotiate global free trade.

However, FOOD PRICES have been rising sharply, with particularly painful consequences for poor consumers in DEVELOPING COUNTRIES, where there have been a growing number of food riots. Two of the causes of this AGFLATION are rising prosperity in developing countries, which has lead to greater DEMAND for meat (animals require more grain to produce a meal than if the diner simply ate grain), and farmers switching land from food to biofuel production. This has led to a renewed interest in finding ways to raise agricultural PRODUCTIVITY, perhaps through a new "green revolution" similar to that which saved an estimated billion lives (mostly) in Asia during the second half of the 20th century.

Aid

See INTERNATIONAL AID.

Altruism

It is often alleged that altruism is inconsistent with economic rationality, which assumes that people behave selfishly. Certainly, much economic analysis is concerned with how individuals behave, and *homo economicus* (ECONOMIC MAN) is usually assumed to act in his or her self-interest. However, self-interest does not necessarily mean selfish. Some economic models in the fields of BEHAVIOURAL ECONOMICS and NEUROECONOMICS assume that self-interested individuals behave altruistically because they get some benefit, or UTILITY, from doing so. For instance, it may make them feel better about themselves, or be a useful INSURANCE policy against social unrest, say. Some economic models go further and relax the traditional assumption of fully rational behaviour by simply assuming that people sometimes behave altruistically, even if this may be against their self-interest. Either way, there is much economic literature about CHARITY, INTERNATIONAL AID, PUBLIC SPENDING and redistributive TAXATION.

Amortisation

The running down or payment of a loan by instalments. An example is a repayment mortgage on a house, which is amortised by making monthly payments that over a pre-agreed period of time cover the value of the loan plus INTEREST. With loans that are not amortised, the borrower pays only interest during the period of the loan and then repays the sum borrowed in full.

Animal spirits

The colourful name that KEYNES gave to one of the essential ingredients of economic prosperity: confidence. According to Keynes, animal spirits are a particular sort of confidence, "naive optimism". He meant this in the sense that, for entrepreneurs in particular, "the thought of ultimate loss which often overtakes pioneers, as experience undoubtedly tells us and them, is put aside as a healthy man puts aside the expectation of death". Where these animal spirits come from is something of a mystery. Certainly, attempts by politicians and others to talk up confidence by making optimistic noises about economic prospects have rarely done much good.

Antitrust

GOVERNMENT policy for dealing with MONOPOLY. Antitrust laws aim to stop abuses of MARKET POWER by big companies and, sometimes, to prevent corporate MERGERS AND ACQUISITIONS that would create or strengthen a monopolist. There have been big differences in antitrust policies both among countries and within the same country over time. This has reflected different ideas about what constitutes a monopoly and, where there is one, what sorts of behaviour are abusive.

In the United States, monopoly policy has been built on the Sherman Antitrust Act of 1890. This prohibited contracts or conspiracies to restrain trade or, in the words of a later act, to monopolise commerce. In the early 20th century this law was used to reduce the economic power wielded by so-called "robber barons", such as J.P. Morgan and John D. Rockefeller, who dominated much of American industry through huge trusts that controlled companies' voting SHARES. Du Pont chemicals, the railroad companies and Rockefeller's Standard Oil, among others, were broken up. In the 1970s the Sherman Act was turned (ultimately without success) against IBM, and in 1982 it secured the break-up of AT&T's nation-wide telecoms monopoly.

In the 1980s a more LAISSEZ-FAIRE approach was adopted, underpinned by economic theories from the CHICAGO SCHOOL. These theories said that the only justification for antitrust intervention should be that a lack of COMPETITION harmed consumers, and not that a firm had become, in some ill-defined sense, too big. Some monopolistic activities previously targeted by antitrust authorities, such as PREDATORY PRICING and exclusive marketing agreements, were much less harmful to consumers than had been thought in the past. They also criticised the traditional method of identifying a monopoly, which was based on looking at what percentage of a market was served by the biggest firm or FIRMS, using a measure known as the HERFINDAHL-HIRSCHMAN INDEX. Instead, they argued that even a market dominated by one firm need not be a matter of antitrust concern, provided it was a CON-TESTABLE MARKET.

In the 1990s American antitrust policy became somewhat more interventionist. A high-profile lawsuit was launched against Microsoft in 1998. The giant software company was found guilty of anti-competitive behaviour, which was said to slow the pace of INNOVATION. However, fears that the firm would be broken up, signalling a far more interventionist American antitrust policy, proved misplaced. Microsoft was not severely punished.

In the UK, antitrust policy was long judged according to what policymakers decided was in the public interest. At times this approach was comparatively permissive of mergers and acquisitions; at others it was less so. However, in the mid-1980s the UK followed the American lead in basing antitrust policy on whether changes in competition harmed consumers. Within the rest of the EUROPEAN UNION several big countries pursued policies of building up national champions, allowing chosen firms to enjoy some monopoly power at home which could be used to make them more effective competitors abroad. Only during the 1990s did the European Commission become increasingly active in antitrust policy, mostly seeking to promote competition within the EU.

In 2000, the EU controversially blocked a merger between two American firms, GE and Honeywell; the deal had already been approved by America's antitrust regulators. Subsequently, it also levied large fines on Microsoft, which some economists said reflected a more stringent definition of antitrust than America's. These controversies highlighted an important issue. As GLOBALISATION increases, the relevant market for judging whether market power exists or is being abused will increasingly cover far more territory than any one single economy. Indeed, there may be a need to establish a global antitrust watchdog, perhaps under the auspices of the WORLD TRADE ORGANISATION.

Appreciation

A rise in the value of an ASSET and the opposite of DEPRECIATION. When the value of a currency rises relative to another, it appreciates.

Arbitrage

Buying an ASSET in one market and simultaneously selling an identical asset at a higher PRICE. Sometimes these will be identical assets in different markets, for instance, SHARES in a company listed on both the London Stock Exchange and New York Stock Exchange. Often the assets being arbitraged will be identical in a more complicated way; for example, they will be different sorts of financial securities that are each exposed to identical risks. According to the EFFICIENT MARKET HYPOTHESIS, arbitrage is possible only when there is inefficiency in the market – and arbitrage is a process that makes markets more efficient.

Some kinds of arbitrage are completely risk-free – this is pure arbitrage. For instance, if EUROS are available more cheaply in dollars in London than in New York, arbitrageurs (also known as arbs) can make a risk-free PROFIT by buying euros in London and selling an identical amount of them in New York. Opportunities for pure arbitrage have become rare in recent years, partly because of the GLOBALISATION of financial markets. Among other things, this has reduced opportunities for regulatory arbitrage, which takes advantage of differences in financial regulations between countries. Today, most of what is called arbitrage, much of it done by HEDGE FUNDS, involves assets that have some similarities but are not identical. This is not pure arbitrage and, on occasions, it can be extremely risky.

Arbitrage pricing theory

This is one of two influential economic theories of how ASSETS are priced in the FINANCIAL MARKETS. The other is the CAPITAL ASSET PRICING MODEL. ARBITRAGE pricing theory says that the PRICE of a financial asset reflects a few key RISK factors, such as the expected rate of INTEREST and how the price of the asset changes relative to the price of a portfolio of assets. If the price of an asset happens to diverge from what the theory says it should be, arbitrage by investors should bring it back into line.

Asian crisis

During 1997–98, many East Asian economies suffered a severe financial and economic crisis. This had big consequences for the global FINANCIAL MARKETS, which had become increasingly exposed to the promise that Asia had seemed to offer. The crisis destroyed wealth on a massive scale and sent absolute POVERTY shooting up. In the banking system alone, corporate loans equivalent to around half of one year's GDP went bad – a destruction of savings on a scale more usually associated with a full-scale war. The precise cause of the crisis remains a matter of debate. Fingers have been pointed at the CURRENCY PEG adopted by some countries and at the reduction of CAPITAL CONTROLS in the years before the crisis. Some blamed economic CONTAGION. The crisis brought an end to a then widespread belief that there was a distinct "Asian way" of capitalism that might prove just as successful as capitalism in the United States or Europe. Instead, critics turned their fire on Asian cronyism, ill-disciplined banking and lack of TRANSPARENCY.

In the years following the crisis, most of the countries involved introduced reforms designed to increase transparency and improve the health of the banking system, although some (such as South Korea) went much further than others (such as Indonesia). Many Asian GOVERNMENTS built up large RESERVES of foreign currencies to protect themselves against a repeat of this crisis. Some economists believe this gave rise to a SAVINGS glut, which contributed to the BUBBLES that contributed to the global economic crisis that began in 2007 by making CAPITAL available too cheaply.

Asset-backed securities

See SECURITISATION.

Assets

Things that have earning power or some other value to their owner.

Asymmetric information

When somebody knows more than somebody else. Such asymmetric information can make it difficult for the two people to do business together, which is why economists, especially those practising GAME THEORY, are interested in it. Transactions involving asymmetric (or private) information are everywhere. A GOVERNMENT selling broadcasting licences does not know what buyers are prepared to pay for them; a lender does not know how likely a borrower is to repay; a used-car seller knows more about the quality of the car being sold than do potential buyers. This kind of asymmetry can distort people's incentives and result in significant inefficiencies.

Asymmetric shock

When something unexpected happens that affects one economy (or part of an economy) more than the rest. This can create big problems for policymakers if they are trying to set a MACROECONOMIC POLICY that works for both the area affected by the SHOCK and the unaffected area. For instance, some economic areas may be OIL exporters and thus highly dependent on the PRICE of oil, but other areas are not. If the oil price plunges, the oil-dependent area would benefit from policies designed to boost DEMAND that might be unsuited to the needs of the rest of the economy. This may be a constant problem for those responsible for setting the INTEREST RATE for the EURO given the big differences – and different potential exposures to shocks – among the economies within the EURO ZONE.

Auctions

Going, going, gone. Holding an auction can be an extremely efficient way for a seller to set the PRICE of its products, especially if it does not have much INFORMATION about how much people may be willing to pay for them. Auctions fascinate economists, especially those who specialise in GAME THEORY. They have long been a feature of the sale of art and antiques in the rooms of FIRMS such as Sotheby's and Christie's. But in recent years they have played a growing role in other parts of the economy, ranging from the allocation of government-controlled broadcasting bandwidth to the awarding of work to subcontractors by GOVERN-MENTS and big FIRMS using competitive tendering, and even more recently the sale of goods over the internet.

An English auction is the most familiar. Bidders compete to offer higher prices and drop out until only one remains. In a Dutch auction, the auctioneer calls out a high price then keeps lowering it until there is a buyer. There are various forms of sealed bid auctions. In a first price sealed bid, each buyer submits a price in a sealed envelope and all bids are opened simultaneously, with the highest offer winning.

In a second price Vickrey auction, named after Nobel Prize-winning economist William Vickrey, bidders submit sealed bids without knowing the bids of others in the auction. The highest bidder wins, but only pays the amount of the second highest bid. This gives bidders an incentive to bid the true value of the goods.

An English, Dutch or Vickrey auction will work well for a seller if there is more than one serious bidder, as COMPETITION will ensure that the price is set at the level at which it is not worth more to any other bidder but the winner. Indeed, in a competitive auction the successful bidder may end up offering more than what is being auctioned is actually worth. This is known as the WINNER'S CURSE.

Which method will generate the best price for the seller

depends on how many bidders take part and how well informed they are. Unfortunately for the seller, this information is not always available before the auction takes place.

Austrian economics

A brand of NEO-CLASSICAL ECONOMICS established in Vienna during the late 19th century and the first half of the 20th century. It was strongly opposed to Marxism and, more broadly, to the use of economic theories to justify GOVERNMENT intervention in the economy. Prominent members included Friedrich HAYEK and Ludwig von Mises. It gave birth to the definition of economics as the science of studying human behaviour as a relationship between ends and scarce means that have alternative uses. Austrian economic thinking was characterised by attributing all economic activity, including the behaviour of apparently impersonal institutions, to the wishes and actions of individuals. It did this by examining choices in terms of their OPPORTUNITY COST (that is, what is the next best use of resources to that which is being considered?) and by analysing the impact of timing on decision-making.

Hayek correctly predicted the failure of Soviet-style central planning. His ideas are said to have inspired many of the free-market reforms carried out during the 1980s in the United States under Ronald Reagan and in the UK under Margaret Thatcher.

Autarky

The idea that a country should be self-sufficient and not take part in international trade. The experience of countries that have pursued this Utopian ideal by substituting domestic production for IMPORTS is an unhappy one. No country has been able to produce the full range of goods demanded by its POPULATION at competitive PRICES. Indeed, those that have tried to do so have condemned themselves to inefficiency and comparative POVERTY, compared with countries that engage in international trade.

Authoritarian capitalism

See CAPITALISM.

Average

A number that is calculated to summarise a group of numbers. The most commonly used average is the mean, the sum of the numbers divided by however many numbers there are in the group. The median is the middle value in a group of numbers ranked in order of size. The mode is the number that occurs most often in a group of numbers. Take the following group of numbers:

1, 2, 2, 9, 12, 13, 17
The mean is $56 \div 7 = 8$
The median is 9
The mode is 2

Backwardation

When a COMMODITY is valued more highly in a spot market (that is, when it is for delivery today) than in a futures market (for delivery at some point in the future). Normally, INTEREST costs mean that futures PRICES are higher than SPOT PRICES, unless the markets expect the price of the commodity to fall over time, perhaps because there is a temporary bottleneck in SUPPLY. When spot prices are lower than futures prices it is known as contango.

Balance of payments

The total of all the MONEY coming into a country from abroad less all of the money going out of the country during the same period. This is usually broken down into the current account and the CAPITAL account. The current account includes:

- VISIBLE TRADE (known as merchandise trade in the United States), which is the value of EXPORTS and IMPORTS of physical goods;
- INVISIBLE TRADE, which is receipts and payments for SERVICES, such as banking or ADVERTISING, and other intangible goods, such as copyrights, as well as cross-border DIVIDEND and INTEREST payments;
- private TRANSFERS, such as money sent home as REMITTANCES by expatriate workers;
- official transfers, such as INTERNATIONAL AID.

The capital account includes:

- long-term capital flows, such as money invested in foreign

FIRMS, and profits made by selling those investments and bringing the money home;

■ short-term capital flows, such as money invested in foreign currencies by international speculators, and funds moved around the world for business purposes by multinational companies. These short-term flows can lead to sharp movements in exchange rates, which bear little relation to what currencies should be worth judging by fundamental measures of value such as PURCHASING POWER PARITY.

As bills must be paid, ultimately a country's accounts must balance (although because real life is never that neat a balancing item is usually inserted to cover up the inconsistencies).

"Balance of payments crisis" is a politically charged phrase. But a country can often sustain a current-account DEFICIT for many years without its economy suffering, because any deficit is likely to be tiny compared with the country's NATIONAL INCOME and wealth. Indeed, if the deficit is caused by firms importing technology and other capital goods from abroad, which will improve their PRODUCTIVITY, the economy may benefit. A deficit that has to be financed by the public sector may be more problematic, particularly if the public sector faces limits on how much it can raise taxes or borrow or has few financial RESERVES. For instance, when the Russian government failed to pay the interest on its foreign debt in August 1998 it found it impossible to borrow any more money in the international FINANCIAL MARKETS. Nor was it able to increase taxes in its collapsing economy or to find anybody within Russia willing to lend it money. That truly was a balance of payments crisis.

In the early years of the 21st century, the current-account deficit of the United States grew to over 5% of its GDP, making its economy increasingly (and, to some economists, worryingly) reliant on foreign credit, particularly from China and OIL-rich Arab countries.

Balanced budget

When total public-sector spending equals total GOVERNMENT INCOME during the same period from taxes and charges for public SERVICES. Politicians in some countries, such as the United States, have argued that government should be required to run a balanced budget in order to have sound public finances. However, there is no economic reason why public borrowing need necessarily be bad. For instance, if the DEBT is used to invest in things that will increase the GROWTH rate of the economy – INFRASTRUCTURE, say, or education – it may be justified, especially because a government can typically borrow more cheaply than other borrowers. It may also make more economic sense to try to balance the budget on average over an entire economic cycle, with public-sector deficits boosting the economy during RECESSIONS and surpluses stopping it overheating during booms, than to balance it every year.

Bank

Starting out as places that would guard your MONEY, banks became the main source of CREDIT CREATION. From the 1980s onwards, borrowers increasingly turned for loans to the FINANCIAL MARKETS and to non-savings institutions, such as credit-card companies and consumer-finance FIRMS. This reduced the profitability of traditional bank lending and led many banks to enter new areas of business, such as selling INSURANCE policies and mutual funds. Traditional banks also began to sell parcels of their loans in the financial markets by a process called SECURITISATION. This process broke down dramatically in the summer of 2007, as a CREDIT CRUNCH hit both the banking system and the financial markets, with severe consequences for the global economy.

What the most efficient split is between bank lending and

other sorts of lending was debatable even before the credit crunch. Economists argued endlessly about whether an economy such as the United States, in which firms have relied more heavily on the EQUITY and DEBT markets than on banks to fund their INVESTMENT, functions better than one such as, say, Germany, in which banks have traditionally been the main source of corporate finance.

Banks come in many different forms. Commercial banks, also known as retail banks, cater directly for the general public and lend to (mostly small and medium-sized) firms. In the past, they did so largely through a network of bank branches, although increasingly these are giving way to ATMs, the telephone and the internet. Wholesale banks largely transact with other banks and financial institutions. Investment banks, also known as merchant banks, concentrate on raising money for companies from private investors or in the financial markets, by finding buyers for their equity and corporate BONDS. Universal banks do most or all of the above including, through bancassurance, selling insurance. These banks have long been a feature of continental European economies. However, in the United States financial laws such as the Glass-Steagall Act separated different forms of banking from each other and kept banks out of the insurance business. These laws were abolished in 1999, although during the preceding couple of decades regulators effectively dismantled them by changing the way they were applied. Even so, because of these and other laws, which for many years stopped banks from operating across state borders, the United States has far more lending institutions than other countries. In 2003 there were over four lending institutions per 100,000 people, compared with fewer than one per 100,000 in the UK and France.

The credit crunch that began in 2007 was associated with widespread distress in the banking system. Many banks failed, or came close to failure, and GOVERNMENTS in many countries intervened in an attempt to stabilise the FINANCIAL SYSTEM.

Billions of dollars were pumped into banks to help them achieve the CAPITAL ADEQUACY RATIO required by regulators. Leading investment banks became commercial banks, accepting closer oversight in exchange for additional government support. In several countries, including the United States and the UK, governments acquired shares in leading banks, which in combination with more intense REGULATION amounted to the NATIONALISATION of banking in the eyes of some economists. The full consequences of this dramatic change are unlikely to be clear for many years.

Bankruptcy

When a court judges that a debtor is unable to make the payments owed to a CREDITOR. How bankrupts are treated can affect economic GROWTH. If bankrupts are punished too severely, would-be entrepreneurs may be discouraged from taking the financial risks needed to make the most of their ideas. That is why limited liability is a crucial element of modern CAPITALISM. However, letting off defaulting debtors too readily may discourage potential creditors because of MORAL HAZARD.

America's bankruptcy code, in particular its Chapter 11 protection for FIRMS from their creditors, is particularly friendly to troubled borrowers, allowing them to borrow more money and giving them time to work out their problems. Some other countries quickly close down a bankrupt firm, and try to repay its DEBTS by selling off any ASSETS it has.

Barriers to entry (or exit)

How FIRMS keep out COMPETITION – an important source of INCUMBENT ADVANTAGE. There are four main categories of barriers:

- A firm may own a crucial resource, such as an OIL well, or it may have an exclusive operating licence, for instance, to broadcast on a particular radio wavelength, or some INTELLECTUAL PROPERTY, such as PATENTS.

- A big firm with ECONOMIES OF SCALE may have a significant competitive advantage because it can produce a large OUTPUT at lower costs than can a smaller potential rival.

- An incumbent firm may make it hard for a would-be entrant by incurring huge SUNK COSTS, spending lots of MONEY on things such as ADVERTISING, which any rival must match to compete effectively but which have no value if the attempt to compete should fail.

- Powerful firms can discourage entry by raising exit costs, for example by making it an industry norm to hire workers on long-term contracts, which make firing an expensive process.

Barter

Paying for goods or SERVICES with other goods or services, instead of with MONEY. It is often popular when the quality of money is low or uncertain, perhaps because of high INFLATION or counterfeiting, or when people are ASSET-rich but cash-poor, or when TAXATION or extortion by criminals is high. Little wonder, then, that barter became popular in Russia during the late 1990s.

Basel 1 and 2

An attempt to reduce the number of BANK failures by tying a bank's CAPITAL ADEQUACY RATIO to the riskiness of the loans it makes. For instance, there is less chance of a loan to a GOVERNMENT going bad than a loan to, say, a start-up business, so the bank should not have to hold as much CAPITAL in reserve against the first loan as against the second. The first attempt to do this worldwide was by the Basel committee for international banking supervision in 1988. However, its system of judging the relative riskiness of different loans was crude. For instance, it penalised banks no more for making loans to a fly-by-night software company in Thailand than to Microsoft; no more for loans to South Korea, bailed out by the IMF in 1998, than to Switzerland. In 1998, "Basel 2" was proposed, using much more sophisticated risk classifications. However, controversy over these new classifications, and the cost to banks of administering the new approach, led to several delays to the introduction of Basel 2. Following the onset in 2007 of the CREDIT CRUNCH and banking crisis, it was expected that further reforms to the Basel framework would be necessary.

Basis point

One one-hundredth of a PERCENTAGE POINT. Small movements in the INTEREST RATE, the exchange rate and BOND YIELDS are often described in terms of basis points. If a bond yield moves from 5.25% to 5.45%, it has risen by 20 basis points.

Behavioural economics

A branch of ECONOMICS that concentrates on explaining the economic decisions people make in practice, especially when these conflict with what conventional economic theory predicts they will do. Behaviourists try to augment or replace traditional ideas of economic rationality (*homo economicus*) with decision-making models borrowed from psychology. According to psychologists, people are disproportionately influenced by a fear of feeling regret and will often forgo benefits even to avoid only a small risk of feeling they have failed. They are also prone to cognitive dissonance, often holding on to a belief plainly at odds with new evidence, usually because the belief has been held and cherished for a long time. Then there is anchoring: people are often overly influenced by outside suggestion. People apparently also suffer from status quo bias: they are willing to take bigger gambles to maintain the status quo than they would be to acquire it in the first place. They are also prone to procrastination.

Traditional UTILITY theory assumes that people make individual decisions in the context of the big picture. But psychologists have found that they generally compartmentalise, often on superficial grounds. They then make choices about things in one particular mental compartment without taking account of the implications for things in other compartments.

There is lots of evidence that people are persistently and irrationally overconfident. They are also vulnerable to hindsight bias: once something happens they overestimate the extent to which they could have predicted it. Many of these traits are captured in PROSPECT THEORY, which is at the heart of much of behavioural economics. In recent years, there has been growing interest in how individual biases in behaviour aggregate into the mass irrationality of CROWDS, including the formation of financial BUBBLES.

Bear

An investor who thinks that the PRICE of a particular security or class of SECURITIES (SHARES, say) is going to fall; the opposite of a BULL.

Beta

Part of an economic theory for valuing financial SECURITIES and calculating the COST OF CAPITAL, known as the CAPITAL ASSET

PRICING MODEL, beta measures the sensitivity of the PRICE of a particular ASSET to changes in the market as a whole. If a company's SHARES have a beta of 0.8 it implies that on average the share price will change by 0.8% if there is a 1% change in the market. There is a long-running debate about whether a beta calculated from a security's past relationship with the market actually predicts how that relationship will behave in future, leading some doubting economists to claim that beta is "dead".

Big Mac index

Devised by Pam Woodall of *The Economist* in 1986 as a light-hearted guide to whether currencies are at their "correct" level. The Big Mac index is based on one of the oldest concepts in international ECONOMICS, PURCHASING POWER PARITY (PPP), the notion that a dollar, say, should buy the same amount in all countries. In the LONG RUN, argue PPP fans, currencies should move towards the exchange rate which equalises the PRICES of an identical basket of goods and SERVICES in each country. In this case, the basket is a McDonald's Big Mac, which is produced in more than 100 countries. The Big Mac PPP is the exchange rate that would leave hamburgers costing the same in the United States as elsewhere. Comparing actual exchange rates with the Big Mac rate indicates whether a currency is undervalued or overvalued. Some studies have found that the Big Mac index is often a better predictor of currency movements than more theoretically rigorous models.

Black economy

If you pay your cleaner or builder in cash, or for some reason neglect to tell the taxman that you were paid for a service rendered, you participate in the black or underground economy. Such transactions do not normally show up in the figures for GDP, so the black economy may mean that a country is much richer than the official data suggest. In the United States and the UK, the black economy adds an estimated 5–10% to GDP; in Italy, it may add 30%. As for Russia, in the late 1990s estimates of the black economy ranged as high as 50% of GDP.

Black-Scholes

A formula for pricing financial options. Its invention allowed a previously undreamed-of precision in the pricing of options (which had hitherto been done using crude rules of thumb), and probably made possible the explosive growth in the markets for options and other DERIVATIVES that took place after the formula became widely used in the early 1970s. Myron Scholes and Robert Merton were awarded the NOBEL PRIZE IN ECONOMICS for their part in devising the formula; their co-inventor, Fischer Black (1938–95), was ineligible, having died. The CREDIT CRUNCH that began in 2007 prompted renewed questioning of the usefulness of the formula because of the role that wrongly priced derivatives played in the crisis.

Black swan

A high-impact, hard to predict and rare event. It was long assumed that swans are inevitably white, and thus a black swan was a met-aphor for something that could not exist. Then black swans were discovered in Australia in the 17th century, and the black swan came to represent an occurrence of the unexpected. This idea was most recently popularised by mathematician Nassim Nicholas Taleb in his 2006 book *The Black Swan*. He describes as black swans such things as the rise of the internet and the personal computer, the terrorist attacks in the United States on September

11th 2001, and the fact that the losses suffered by BANKS in the economic crisis that began in 2007 were many times greater than was predicted by their RISK models. He argued that most people prefer to ignore the possibility of black swans, as they like to believe the universe is orderly and predictable. He is especially critical of this sort of thinking by those economists responsible for modern finance theory, such as the EFFICIENT MARKET HYPOTH-ESIS, which has underpinned the rapid growth in the market for DERIVATIVES. Critics have argued that black swan is too imprecise a concept to be of any scientific value.

Bonds

"Gentlemen prefer bonds," punned Andrew Mellon, an American tycoon and Treasury secretary. A bond is an INTEREST-bearing SECURITY issued by GOVERNMENTS, companies and some other organisations. Bonds are an alternative way for the issuer to raise CAPITAL to selling SHARES or taking out a BANK loan. Like shares in listed companies, once they have been issued bonds may be traded on the open market. A bond's YIELD is the INTEREST RATE (or coupon) paid on the bond divided by the bond's market PRICE. Bonds are regarded as a lower-RISK INVESTMENT. Government bonds, in particular, are highly unlikely to miss their promised payments. Corporate bonds typically come with different RATINGS, reflecting their different RISK. Those issued by blue-chip companies, rated as "investment grade", are unlikely to default; this might not be the case with high-yield "junk" bonds issued by FIRMS with less healthy financials. (See YIELD CURVE.)

Boom and bust

See BUSINESS CYCLE.

Bottom of the pyramid

The billions of people, mostly in DEVELOPING COUNTRIES, who get by on no more than a few dollars a day. Mainstream FIRMS serving rich economies have tended to ignore people at the bottom of the pyramid, thinking that they have too little MONEY ever to be profitable customers. However, as economist C.K. Prahalad wrote in his 2004 book, *The Fortune at the Bottom of the Pyramid: Eradicating Poverty Through Profits*, there are lots of opportunities to make money by serving these people, and the process of serving them can help lift them out of POVERTY. Firms will often need to reinvent their business models to tap these markets, such as using different methods of distribution and lowering costs through a process he calls "frugal engineering".

Bounded rationality

A theory of human decision-making that assumes that people behave rationally, but only within the limits of the INFORMATION available to them. Because their information may be inadequate (bounded) they make take decisions that appear to be irrational according to traditional theories about *homo economicus* (ECONOMIC MAN). (See also BEHAVIOURAL ECONOMICS.)

Brand

The stalking-horse for international CAPITALISM. A focus for all the worries about environmental damage, human-rights abuses and sweated labour that opponents of GLOBALISATION like to put on their placards. A symbol of America's corporate power, since most of the world's best-known brands, from Coca-Cola to Nike, are American. That is the case against.

Many economists regard brands as a good thing, however. A

brand provides a guarantee of reliability and quality. Consumer trust is the basis of all brand values. So companies that own the brands have an immense incentive to work to retain that trust. Brands have value only where consumers have choice. The arrival of foreign brands, and the emergence of domestic brands, in former communist and other poorer countries points to an increase in COMPETITION from which consumers gain. Because a strong brand often requires expensive ADVERTISING and good marketing, it can raise both PRICE and BARRIERS TO ENTRY. But not to insuperable levels: brands fade as tastes change; if quality is not maintained, neither is the brand.

Bretton Woods

A conference held at Bretton Woods, New Hampshire, in 1944, which designed the structure of the international monetary system after the second world war and set up the IMF and the WORLD BANK. It was agreed that the EXCHANGE RATES of IMF members would be pegged to the dollar, with a maximum variation of 1% either side of the agreed rate. Rates could be adjusted more sharply only if a country's BALANCE OF PAYMENTS was in fundamental DISEQUILIBRIUM. In August 1971 economic troubles and the cost of financing the Vietnam war led the American president, Richard Nixon, to devalue the dollar. This shattered confidence in the fixed exchange rate system and by 1973 all the main currencies were floating freely, at rates set mostly by MARKET FORCES rather than GOVERNMENT fiat.

The growing economic clout of DEVELOPING COUNTRIES, which had little say in the original Bretton Woods process, and the global governance failures revealed by the economic crisis that began in 2007, led to calls for a fundamental redesign of the global economic framework and institutions. The shorthand for this was a "new Bretton Woods".

BRIC

Shorthand for fast-growing DEVELOPING COUNTRIES. In 2001 Jim O'Neill, chief economist of Goldman Sachs, came up with the acronym BRIC for the next four countries it expected to enter the economic big league: Brazil, Russia, India and China.

Bubble

When the PRICE of an ASSET rises far higher than can be explained by fundamentals, such as the INCOME likely to derive from holding the asset. The *Chicago Tribune* of April 13th 1890, writing about the then mania in real-estate prices, described "men who bought property at prices they knew perfectly well were fictitious, but who were prepared to pay such prices simply because they knew that some still greater fool could be depended on to take the property off their hands and leave them with a profit". Such behaviour is a feature of all bubbles.

Famous bubbles include tulip mania in Holland during the 17th century, when the prices of tulip bulbs reached unheard of levels, and the South Sea Bubble in Britain a century later, although there have been many others since, including the dotcom bubble in internet company SHARES that burst in 2000, and the bubble in HOUSE PRICES which, when it burst in 2007, helped to trigger a CREDIT CRUNCH.

Economists argue about whether bubbles are the result of the irrational behaviour of CROWDS (perhaps coupled with exploitation of the gullible masses by some savvy speculators) or, instead, are the result of rational decisions by people who have only limited INFORMATION about the fundamental value of an asset and thus for whom it may be quite sensible to assume the market price is sound. Whatever their cause, bubbles do not last forever and often end not with a pop but with a crash.

Budget

An annual procedure to decide how much PUBLIC SPENDING there should be in the year ahead and what mix of TAXATION, charging for SERVICES and borrowing should finance it. The budgeting process differs enormously from one country to another. In the United States, for example, the president proposes a budget in February for the fiscal year starting the following October, but this has to be approved by Congress. By the time a final decision has to be made, ideally no later than September, there are often three competing versions: the president's latest proposal, one from the Senate and another from the House of Representatives. What finally emerges is the result of last-minute negotiations. Occasionally, delays in agreeing the budget have led to the temporary closure of some federal government offices. Contrast this with the UK, where most of what the government proposes is usually approved by Parliament, and some changes take effect as soon as they are announced (subject to subsequent parliamentary vote).

Bull

An investor who expects the PRICE of a particular security to rise; the opposite of a BEAR.

Business confidence

How the people who run companies feel about their organisations' prospects. In many countries, surveys measure AVERAGE business confidence. These can provide useful signs about the current condition of the economy, because companies often have INFORMATION about consumer demand sooner than GOVERNMENT statisticians do.

Business cycle

Boom and bust. The long-run pattern of economic GROWTH and RECESSION. According to the Centre for International Business Cycle Research at Columbia University, between 1854 and 1945 the AVERAGE expansion lasted 29 months and the average contraction 21 months. Since the second world war, however, expansions have lasted almost twice as long, an average of 50 months, and contractions have shortened to an average of only 11 months. Over the years, economists have produced numerous theories of why economic activity fluctuates so much, none of them particularly convincing. A Kitchin cycle supposedly lasted 39 months and was caused by fluctuations in companies' inventories. The Juglar cycle would last 8–9 years as a result of changes in INVESTMENT in plant and machinery. Then there was the 20-year Kuznets cycle, allegedly driven by house-building, and, perhaps the best-known theory of them all, the 50-year KONDRATIEFF WAVE.

HAYEK tangled with KEYNES over what caused the business cycle, and won the NOBEL PRIZE IN ECONOMICS for his theory that variations in an economy's OUTPUT depended on the sort of CAPITAL it had. Taking a quite different tack, in the late 1960s Arthur Okun, an economic adviser to presidents Kennedy and Johnson, proclaimed that the business cycle was "obsolete". A year later, the American economy was in recession. Again, in the late 1990s, some economists claimed that technological INNOVATION and GLOBALISATION meant that the business cycle was a thing of the past. Alas, they were soon proved wrong.

Buyer's market

A market in which SUPPLY seems plentiful and PRICES seem low; the opposite of a SELLER'S MARKET.

Cannibalise

Eating people is wrong. Eating your own business may not be. FIRMS used to be reluctant to launch new products and SERVICES that competed with what they were already doing, as the new thing would eat into (cannibalise) their existing business. In today's innovative, technology-intensive economy, however, a willingness to cannibalise is more often seen as a good thing. This is because INNOVATION often takes the form of what economists call creative destruction (see SCHUMPETER), in which a superior new product destroys the market for existing products. In this environment, the best course of action for successful firms that want to avoid losing their market to a rival with an innovation may be to carry out the creative destruction themselves.

Capacity

The amount a company or an economy can produce using its current equipment, workers, CAPITAL and other resources at full tilt. Judging how close an economy is to operating at full capacity is an important ingredient of MONETARY POLICY, for if there is not enough spare capacity to absorb an increase in DEMAND, PRICES are likely to rise instead. Measuring an economy's OUTPUT GAP – how far current OUTPUT is above or below what it would be at full capacity – is difficult, if not impossible, which is why even the best-intentioned CENTRAL BANK can struggle to keep down INFLATION. When there is too much spare capacity, however, the result can be DEFLATION, as FIRMS and employees cut their prices and wage demands to compete for whatever demand there may be.

Capital

MONEY or ASSETS put to economic use, the life-blood of CAPITAL-ISM. Economists describe capital as one of the four essential ingredients of economic activity, the factors of production, along with LAND, LABOUR and ENTERPRISE. Production processes that use a lot of capital relative to labour are CAPITAL INTENSIVE; those that use comparatively little capital are LABOUR INTENSIVE. Capital takes different forms. A firm's assets are known as its capital, which may include fixed capital (machinery, buildings, and so on) and working capital (stocks of raw materials and part-finished products, as well as money, that are used up quickly in the production process). Financial capital includes money, BONDS and SHARES. HUMAN CAPITAL is the economic wealth or potential contained in a person, some of it endowed at birth, the rest the product of training and education, if only in the university of life. The invisible glue of relationships and institutions that holds an economy together is its SOCIAL CAPITAL.

Capital adequacy ratio

The ratio of a BANK'S CAPITAL to its total ASSETS, required by regulators to be above a minimum ("adequate") level so that there is little RISK of the bank going bust. How high this minimum level is may vary according to how risky a bank's activities are. (See BASEL 1 AND 2.)

Capital asset pricing model

A method of valuing ASSETS and calculating the COST OF CAPITAL (for an alternative, see ARBITRAGE PRICING THEORY). The capital asset pricing model (CAPM) has come to dominate modern finance.

The rationale of the CAPM can be simplified as follows. Investors can eliminate some sorts of RISK, known as RESIDUAL RISK or alpha, by holding a diversified portfolio of assets (see MODERN PORTFOLIO THEORY). These alpha risks are specific to an individual asset, for example the risk that a company's managers will turn out to be no good. Some risks, such as that of a global RECESSION, cannot be eliminated through diversification. So even a basket of all of the SHARES in a stockmarket will still be risky. People must be rewarded for investing in such a risky basket by earning RETURNS on average above those that they can get on safer assets, such as TREASURY BILLS. Assuming investors diversify away alpha risks, how an investor values any particular asset should depend crucially on how much the asset's PRICE is affected by the risk of the market as a whole. The market's risk contribution is captured by a measure of relative VOLATILITY, BETA, which indicates how much an asset's price is expected to change when the overall market changes.

Safe investments have a beta close to zero; economists call these assets risk free. Riskier investments, such as SHARES, should earn a premium over the risk-free rate. How much is calculated by the AVERAGE premium for all assets of that type, multiplied by the particular asset's beta.

But does the CAPM work? It all comes down to beta, which some economists have found of dubious use. They think the CAPM may be an elegant theory that is no good in practice. Yet it is the most widely used method for calculating the cost of capital.

Capital controls

GOVERNMENT-imposed restrictions on the ability of CAPITAL to move in or out of a country. Examples include limits on foreign INVESTMENT in a country's FINANCIAL MARKETS, on direct investment by foreigners in businesses or property, and on domestic residents' investments abroad. Until the 20th century capital controls were uncommon, but many countries then imposed them. Following the end of the second world war only Switzerland, Canada and the United States adopted open capital regimes. Other rich countries maintained strict controls and many made them tougher during the 1960s and 1970s. This changed in the 1980s and early 1990s, when most developed countries scrapped their capital controls.

The pattern was more mixed in DEVELOPING COUNTRIES. Latin American countries imposed lots of them during the debt crisis of the 1980s then scrapped most of them from the late 1980s onwards. Asian countries began to loosen their widespread capital controls in the 1980s and did so more rapidly during the 1990s.

In developed countries, there were two main reasons why capital controls were lifted: free markets became more fashionable and financiers became adept at finding ways around the controls. Developing countries later discovered that foreign capital could play a part in financing domestic investment, from roads in Thailand to telecoms systems in Mexico, and, furthermore, that financial capital often brought with it valuable HUMAN CAPITAL. They also found that capital controls did not work and had unwanted side-effects. Latin America's controls in the 1980s failed to keep much money at home and also deterred foreign investment.

The ASIAN CRISIS and CAPITAL FLIGHT of the late 1990s revived interest in capital controls, as some Asian governments wondered whether lifting the controls had left them vulnerable to the whims of international speculators, whose money could flow out of a country as fast as it once flowed in, creating economic instability. Argentina moved aggressively to control capital flows in ways that made foreigners reluctant to invest there. There was also discussion of a "Tobin tax" on short-term capital movements, proposed by James TOBIN, a winner of the NOBEL PRIZE IN ECONOMICS. Even so, they mostly considered only limited controls on short-term capital movements, particularly movements out of a country, and did not reverse the broader 20-year-old process of global financial and economic LIBERALISATION. However, the global economic crisis that started in 2007 prompted some countries to consider a change of direction that potentially would reverse some aspects of GLOBALISATION and liberalisation.

Capital flight

When CAPITAL flows rapidly out of a country, usually because something happens which causes investors suddenly to lose confidence in its economy. (Strictly speaking, the problem is not so much the MONEY leaving, but rather that investors in general suddenly lower their valuation of all the country's ASSETS.) This is particularly worrying when the flight capital belongs to the country's own citizens. This is often associated with a sharp fall in the EXCHANGE RATE of the abandoned country's currency.

Capital gains

The PROFIT from the sale of a CAPITAL ASSET, such as a SHARE or a property. Capital gains are subject to TAXATION in most countries. Some economists argue that capital gains should be taxed lightly (if at all) compared with other sources of INCOME. They argue that the less tax is levied on capital gains, the greater is the incentive to put capital to productive use. Put another way, capital gains tax is effectively a tax on CAPITALISM. However, if capital gains are given too friendly a treatment by the tax authorities, accountants will no doubt invent all sorts of creative ways to disguise other income as capital gains.

Capital intensive

A production process that involves relatively large amounts of CAPITAL; the opposite of LABOUR INTENSIVE.

Capital markets

Markets in SECURITIES such as BONDS and SHARES. GOVERNMENTS and companies use them to raise longer-term CAPITAL from investors, although few of the millions of capital-market transactions every day involve the issuer of the security. Most trades are in the SECONDARY MARKETS, between investors who have bought the securities and other investors who want to buy them. Contrast with MONEY MARKETS, where short-term capital is raised.

Capitalism

The winner, at least for now, of the battle of economic "isms" – although it was badly bruised by the global economic crisis that began in 2007. Capitalism is a free-market system built on private ownership, in particular the idea that owners of CAPITAL have PROPERTY RIGHTS that entitle them to earn a PROFIT as a reward for putting their capital at RISK in some form of economic activity. Opinion (and practice) differs considerably among capitalist countries about what role the state should play in the economy. But everyone agrees that, at the very least, for capitalism to work the state must be strong enough to guarantee property rights. According to Karl MARX, capitalism contains the seeds of its own destruction, but so far this has proved a more accurate description of Marx's progeny, COMMUNISM.

Until recently, it had come to be believed that capitalism functioned best when associated with democracy, but as China started to grow fast by embracing capitalism without democracy, some economists argued that its "authoritarian capitalism" could work better than the democratic alternative. By contrast, they said, India's democracy may have hindered the development of its capitalism by overly restricting the ability of business people to act.

Capital structure

The composition of a company's mixture of DEBT and EQUITY financing. A firm's debt-equity ratio is often referred to as its GEARING. Taking on more debt is known as gearing up, or increasing leverage. In the 1960s, Franco Modigliani and Merton Miller (1923–2000) published a series of articles arguing that it did not matter whether a company financed its activities by issuing debt, or equity, or a mixture of the two. (For this they were awarded the NOBEL PRIZE IN ECONOMICS.) But, they said, this rule does not apply if one source of financing is treated more favourably by the taxman than another. In the United States, debt has long had tax advantages over equity, so their theory implies that American FIRMS should finance themselves with debt. Companies also finance themselves by using the PROFIT they retain after paying DIVIDENDS.

CAPM

See CAPITAL ASSET PRICING MODEL.

Cartel

An agreement between two or more FIRMS in the same industry to co-operate in fixing PRICES and/or carving up the market and restricting the amount of OUTPUT they produce. It is particularly common when there is an OLIGOPOLY. The aim of such collusion is to increase PROFIT by reducing COMPETITION. Identifying and breaking up cartels is an important part of the competition policy overseen by ANTITRUST watchdogs in most countries, although proving the existence of a cartel is rarely easy, as firms are usually not so careless as to put agreements to collude on paper. The desire to form cartels is strong. As Adam SMITH put it:

> **❝** People of the same trade seldom meet together, even for merriment and diversion, but the conversation ends in a conspiracy against the public or in some contrivance to raise prices.

Catch-up effect

In any period, the economies of countries that start off poor generally grow faster than the economies of countries that start off rich. As a result, the NATIONAL INCOME of poor countries usually catches up with the national income of rich countries. New technology may even allow DEVELOPING COUNTRIES to leap-frog over industrialised countries with older technology. This, at least, is the traditional economic theory. In recent years, there has been considerable debate about the extent and speed of convergence in reality.

One reason to expect catch-up is that workers in poor countries have little access to CAPITAL, so their PRODUCTIVITY is often low. Increasing the amount of capital at their disposal by only a small amount can produce huge gains in productivity. Countries with lots of capital, and as a result higher levels of productivity, would enjoy a much smaller gain from a similar increase in capital. This is one possible explanation for the much faster GROWTH of Japan and Germany, compared with the United States and the UK, after the second world war and the faster growth of several Asian "tigers", compared with developed countries, during the 1980s and most of the 1990s.

CDO

Short for collateralised debt obligation (see SECURITISATION).

CDS

Short for CREDIT DEFAULT SWAP.

Central bank

A guardian of the monetary system. A central BANK sets short-term INTEREST RATES and oversees the health of the FINANCIAL SYSTEM, including by assessing the soundness of banks and acting as LENDER OF LAST RESORT to banks that get into financial difficulties. The FEDERAL RESERVE, the central bank of the United States, was founded in 1913. The Bank of England, known affectionately as the "Old Lady of Threadneedle Street", was established in 1694, 26 years after the creation of the world's first central bank in Sweden. With the birth of the EURO in 1999, the MONETARY POLICY powers of the central banks of 11 European countries were transferred to a new EUROPEAN CENTRAL BANK, based in Frankfurt.

During the 1990s there was a trend to make central banks independent from political intervention in their day-to-day operations and allow them to set interest rates. Independent central banks should be able to concentrate on the long-term needs of an economy, whereas political intervention may be guided by the short-term needs of the GOVERNMENT. In theory, an independent central bank should reduce the risk of INFLATION. Some central banks are legally required to set interest rates so as to hit an explicit INFLATION TARGET. Politicians are often tempted to exploit a possible short-term trade-off between inflation and UNEMPLOYMENT, even though the long-term consequence of easing policy in this way is (most economists say) that the unemployment rate returns to what you started with and inflation is higher. An independent central bank, because it does not have to worry about persuading an electorate to vote for it, is more likely to act in the best LONG-RUN interests of the economy.

Central banks came under unprecedented stress during the economic crisis that began in 2007. They increased their intervention in the financial system by pumping huge sums of money into banks to improve their LIQUIDITY and, later, to keep them afloat. Lender of last resort support was extended to many financial FIRMS that did not previously have that protection. However, the decision not to extend lender of last resort status to Lehman Brothers, which led to the BANKRUPTCY of the Wall Street investment bank in September 2008, was criticised by many economists for making the economic crisis much worse. Central banks were also criticised by some economists for failing to act in the years before 2007 to prevent BUBBLES in ASSET prices which many blamed for the severity of the economic crisis after they burst.

    " *The economic repercussions of a stockmarket crash depend less on the severity of the crash itself than on the response of economic policymakers, particularly central bankers.*
Ben Bernanke, chairman of the Federal Reserve

Ceteris paribus

Other things being equal. Economists use this Latin phrase to cover their backs. For example, they might say that "higher INTEREST RATES will lead to lower INFLATION, *ceteris paribus*", which means that they will stand by their prediction about inflation only if nothing else changes apart from the rise in the interest rate.

Charity

"Bah! Humbug" was Scrooge's opinion of charitable giving. Some economists reckon charity goes against economic rationality. Some have argued that the popularity of charitable giving is proof that people are not economically rational. Others argue that it shows that ALTRUISM is something that people get pleasure (UTILITY) from, and so are willing to spend some of their INCOME on it. An interesting question is the extent to which the state is competing with private charity when it redistributes money from rich to poor or spends more on health care and whether this is inefficient. Starting in the late 1990s, there was a sharp rise in philanthropy by wealthy individuals and some big FIRMS. Their businesslike approach to giving is called PHILANTHROCAPITALISM.

Chicago School

A fervently free-market economic philosophy long associated with the University of Chicago. At times, especially in the decades after the second world war when KEYNESIAN ECONOMICS was the orthodoxy in much of the world, the Chicago School was regarded as a bastion of unworldly extremism. However, from the late 1970s it came to be regarded as mainstream by many and Chicago trained economists often played a crucial part in the implementation of policies of low INFLATION and market LIBERALISATION that swept the world during the 1980s and 1990s. By 2008, boasted the University of Chicago, some 25 of the 62 then winners of the NOBEL PRIZE IN ECONOMICS had been faculty members, students or researchers there.

Classical dichotomy

See MONETARY NEUTRALITY.

Classical economics

The dominant theory of economics from the 18th century to the 20th century, when it evolved into NEO-CLASSICAL ECONOMICS. Classical economists, who included Adam SMITH, David RICARDO and John Stuart Mill, believed that the pursuit of individual self-interest produced the greatest possible economic benefits for society as a whole through the power of the INVISIBLE HAND. They also believed that an economy is always in EQUILIBRIUM or moving towards it.

Equilibrium was ensured in the LABOUR market by movements in WAGES and in the CAPITAL market by changes in the rate of INTEREST. The INTEREST RATE ensured that total SAVINGS in an economy were equal to total INVESTMENT. In DISEQUILIBRIUM, higher interest rates encouraged more saving and less investment, and lower rates meant less saving and more investment. When the DEMAND for labour rose or fell, wages would also rise or fall to keep the workforce at FULL EMPLOYMENT.

In the 1920s and 1930s, John Maynard KEYNES attacked some of the main beliefs of classical and neo-classical economics, which became unfashionable. In particular, he argued that the rate of interest was determined or influenced by the speculative actions of investors in BONDS and that wages were inflexible downwards, so that if demand for labour fell, the result would be higher UNEMPLOYMENT rather than cheaper workers.

Closed economy

An economy that does not take part in international TRADE; the opposite of an OPEN ECONOMY. Today, about the only notable example left of a closed economy is North Korea (see AUTARKY).

Coase theorem

See EXTERNALITY.

Collateral

An ASSET pledged by a borrower that may be seized by a lender to recover the value of a loan if the borrower fails to meet the required INTEREST charges or repayments.

Collateralised debt obligation

See SECURITISATION.

Collusion

See CARTEL.

Command economy

When a GOVERNMENT controls all aspects of economic activity (see, for example, COMMUNISM).

Commodity

A comparatively homogeneous product that can typically be bought in bulk. It usually refers to a raw material – OIL, cotton, cocoa, silver – but can also describe a manufactured product used to make other things, for example, microchips used in personal computers. Commodities are often traded on commodity exchanges. Until around 2005, when the world started to experience what many economists regarded as a commodity BUBBLE, for decades, the AVERAGE PRICE of natural commodities fell steadily in REAL TERMS, in defiance of some predictions that growing consumption of non-renewables such as copper would force prices up. At times the oil price has risen sharply in real terms, most notably during the 1970s and between 2005 and 2008. This was caused not by the exhaustion of limited supplies but by rationing by the OPEC CARTEL, or war, or fear of it, particularly in the oil-rich Middle East, or – in the most recent case – by some combination of soaring global DEMAND and SPECULATION.

Commoditisation

The process of becoming a COMMODITY. Microchips, for example, started out as a specialised technical INNOVATION, costing a lot and earning their makers a high PROFIT on each chip. Now chips are largely homogeneous: the same chip can be used for many things, and any manufacturer willing to invest in some fairly standardised equipment can make them. As a result, COMPETITION is fierce and PRICES and profit margins are low. Some economists argue that in today's economy the faster pace of innovation will make the process of commoditisation increasingly common.

Common goods

See TRAGEDY OF THE COMMONS.

Communism

The enemy of CAPITALISM and now nearly extinct. Invented by Karl MARX, who predicted that feudalism and capitalism would be succeeded by the "dictatorship of the proletariat", during which the state would "wither away" and economic life would be organised to achieve "from each according to his abilities, to each according to his needs". The Soviet Union was the most prominent attempt to put communism into practice and the result was conspicuous failure, although some modern followers of Marx reckon that the Soviets missed the point.

Comparative advantage

Paul Samuelson, one of the 20th century's greatest economists, once remarked that the principle of comparative advantage was the only big idea that ECONOMICS had produced that was both true and surprising. It is also one of the oldest theories in economics, usually ascribed to David RICARDO. The theory underpins the economic case for FREE TRADE. But it is often misunderstood or misrepresented by opponents of free trade. It shows how countries can gain from trading with each other even if one of them is more efficient – it has an ABSOLUTE ADVANTAGE – in every sort of economic activity. Comparative advantage is about identifying which activities a country (or firm or individual) is most efficient at doing.

To see how this theory works imagine two countries, Alpha and Omega. Each country has 1,000 workers and can make two goods, computers and cars. Alpha's economy is far more productive than Omega's. To make a car, Alpha needs 2 workers, compared with Omega's 4. To make a computer, Alpha uses 10 workers, compared with Omega's 100. If there is no trade, and in each country half the workers are in each industry, Alpha produces 250 cars and 50 computers and Omega produces 125 cars and 5 computers.

What if the two countries specialise? Although Alpha makes both cars and computers more efficiently than Omega (it has an absolute advantage), it has a bigger edge in computer-making. So it now devotes most of its resources to that industry, employing 700 workers to make computers and only 300 to make cars. This raises computer output to 70 and cuts car production to 150. Omega switches entirely to cars, turning out 250.

World output of both goods has risen. Both countries can consume more of both if they trade, but at what PRICE? Neither will want to import what it could make more cheaply at home. So Alpha will want at least 5 cars per computer, and Omega will not give up more than 25 cars per computer. Suppose the terms of trade are fixed at 12 cars per computer and 120 cars are exchanged for 10 computers. Then Alpha ends up with 270 cars and 60 computers, and Omega with 130 cars and 10 computers. Both are better off than they would be if they did not trade.

This is true even though Alpha has an absolute advantage in making both computers and cars. The reason is that each country has a different comparative advantage. Alpha's edge is greater in computers than in cars. Omega, although a costlier producer in both industries, is a less expensive maker of cars. If each country specialises in products in which it has a comparative advantage, both will gain from trade.

In essence, the theory of comparative advantage says that it pays countries to trade because they are different. It is impossible for a country to have no comparative advantage in anything. It may be the least efficient at everything, but it will still have a comparative advantage in the industry in which it is relatively least bad.

There is no reason to assume that a country's comparative advantage will be static. If a country does what it has a comparative advantage in and sees its INCOME grow as a result, it can afford better education and INFRASTRUCTURE. These, in turn, may give it a comparative advantage in other economic activities in future.

Competition

The more competition there is, the more likely are FIRMS to be efficient and PRICES to be low. Economists have identified several different sorts of competition. PERFECT COMPETITION is the most competitive market imaginable in which products are identical and everybody is a price taker. Firms earn only normal PROFITS, the bare minimum necessary to keep them in business. If firms earn more than this (excess profits), other firms will enter the market and drive the price level down until there are only normal profits to be made.

Most markets exhibit some form of imperfect or MONOPOLISTIC COMPETITION. There are fewer firms than in a perfectly competitive market and each can to some degree create BARRIERS TO ENTRY. So firms can earn some excess profits without a new entrant being able to compete to bring prices down.

The least competitive market is a MONOPOLY, dominated by a single firm that can earn substantial excess profits by controlling either the amount of OUTPUT in the market or the price (but not both). In this sense it is a price setter. When there are few firms in a market (OLIGOPOLY), they have the opportunity to behave as a monopolist through some form of collusion (see CARTEL). A market dominated by a single firm does not necessarily have monopoly power if it is a CONTESTABLE MARKET. In such a market, a single firm can dominate only if it produces as efficiently as possible and does not earn excess profits. If it becomes inefficient or earns excess profits, another more efficient or less profitable firm will enter the market and dominate it instead.

Competitive advantage

Something that gives a firm (or a person or a country) an edge over its rivals.

Competitiveness

"Real economists don't talk about competitiveness," said Paul Krugman, the 2008 winner of the NOBEL PRIZE IN ECONOMICS. Real businessmen and real politicians talk about it all the time, however. Many FIRMS have undergone savage downsizing to remain competitive, and GOVERNMENTS have set up numerous committees to examine how to sharpen their countries' economic performance.

Krugman's objection was not to the use of the term competitiveness by companies, which often do have competitors that they must beat, but to applying it to countries. At best, it is a meaningless word when applied to national economies; at worst, it encourages PROTECTIONISM. Countries, he claimed, do not compete in the same way as companies. When two companies compete, one's gain is the other's loss, whereas international trade, Krugman argued, is not a ZERO-SUM GAME: when two countries compete through trade they both win.

Yet measures of national competitiveness are not complete nonsense. A country's future prosperity depends on its ability to increase its PRODUCTIVITY, which government policies can influence. Countries do compete in that they choose policies to promote higher living standards. Even so, conceptual and measurement difficulties mean that the growing number of indices purporting to compare the competitiveness of different countries should probably be taken with a large pinch of salt.

Complementary goods

When you buy a computer, you will also need to buy software. Computer hardware and software are therefore complementary goods: two products, for which an increase (or fall) in DEMAND for one leads to an increase (fall) in demand for the other. Complements are the opposite of SUBSTITUTE GOODS. For instance,

Microsoft Windows-based personal computers and Apple Macs are substitutes.

Compound interest

If a deposit account of $100 earns an INTEREST RATE of 10% a year, at the end of the year the account will contain $110. If all of that money is left in the account, the 10% interest will be paid on the $110, so at the end of the second year $11 of interest will be added, making $121 in all. This is known as compound interest. By contrast, SIMPLE INTEREST pays the 10% only on the original sum in the account.

Concentration

The tendency of a market to be dominated by a few big FIRMS. A high degree of concentration may be evidence of ANTITRUST problems, if it reflects a lack of COMPETITION. Traditionally, economists examined whether there was too much concentration using the HERFINDAHL-HIRSCHMAN INDEX, which is determined by adding the squares of the market shares of all firms involved. A low Herfindahl indicated many competitors and thus great difficulty in exercising MARKET POWER; a high Herfindahl, however, suggested a concentrated market in which PRICE rises are easier to sustain. More recently, antitrust authorities have placed less emphasis on concentration. One reason is that it is hard to define the market in which concentration should be measured. Instead, antitrust authorities have turned their attention to finding examples of firms earning excessive profits or holding back INNOVATION, although this too raises tricky conceptual and practical questions.

Conditionality

When there are strings attached – for example, to INTERNATIONAL AID or loans from the IMF or WORLD BANK. Delivery of the MONEY may be made subject to the GOVERNMENT of the country implementing economic or political reforms desired by the donor or lender.

Consumer confidence

How good consumers feel about their economic prospects. Measures of AVERAGE consumer confidence can be a useful, though not infallible, indicator of how much consumers are likely to spend. Combined with measures such as BUSINESS CONFIDENCE, it can shed light on overall levels of economic activity.

Consumer prices

What people are usually thinking of when they worry about INFLATION. The PRICES paid by whoever finally consumes goods or SERVICES, as opposed to prices paid by FIRMS at various stages of the production process (see, for example, FACTORY PRICES). Usually changes in consumer prices are reported in the form of a consumer price index. Typically, this comes in two forms: one that includes all changes in consumer prices and one that smooths out one-off changes to track "core" consumer-price inflation.

Consumer surplus

The difference between what a consumer would be willing to pay for a good or service and what that consumer actually has to pay. Added to PRODUCER SURPLUS, it provides a measure of the total economic benefit of a sale.

Consumption

What consumers do. Within an economy, this can be broken down into private and public consumption (see PUBLIC SPENDING). The more resources a society consumes, the less it has to save or invest, although, paradoxically, higher consumption may encourage higher INVESTMENT. The LIFE-CYCLE HYPOTHESIS suggests that at certain stages of life individuals are more likely to be saving than consuming, and at other stages they are more likely to be heavy consumers. Some economists argue that consumption taxes are a more efficient form of TAXATION than taxes on wealth, CAPITAL, property or INCOME.

Contagion

The domino effect, such as when economic problems in one country spread to another.

Contestable market

A market in which an inefficient firm, or one earning excess PROFITS, is likely to be driven out by a more efficient or less profitable rival. A market can be contestable even if it is dominated by a single firm, which appears to enjoy a MONOPOLY with MARKET POWER, and the new entrant exists only as potential COMPETITION (see ANTITRUST).

Convergence

See CATCH-UP EFFECT and DEVELOPING COUNTRIES.

Corruption

Being corrupt is not just bad for the soul, it also harms the economy. Research has found that in countries with a lot of corruption, less of their GDP goes into INVESTMENT and they have lower GROWTH rates. Corrupt countries invest less in education, a sector of the economy that pays big economic dividends but small bribes, than do clean countries, thereby reducing their HUMAN CAPITAL. They also attract less FOREIGN DIRECT INVESTMENT.

There is no such thing as good corruption, but some sorts of corruption are less bad than others. Some economists point to similarities between bribery and paying taxes or buying a licence to operate. Where it is predictable – where the briber knows what to pay and can be sure of getting what it pays for – corruption harms the economy far less than where it is capricious.

The absence of corruption has huge economic benefits, however, by allowing the development of institutions that enable a market economy to function efficiently. In many of the world's more corrupt countries, the distinction between private interest and public duty is still unfamiliar. Countries that have made graft the exception rather than the rule in the conduct of public affairs have been helped to grow by the emergence of institutions such as an independent judiciary, a free press, a well-paid civil service and, perhaps crucially, an economy in which FIRMS have to compete for customers and CAPITAL.

Cost-benefit analysis

A method of reaching economic decisions by comparing the costs of doing something with its benefits. It sounds simple and common-sensical, but, in practice, it can easily become complicated and is much abused. With careful selection of the assumptions used in cost-benefit analysis it can be made to support, or oppose, almost anything. This is particularly so when the decision being contemplated involves some cost or benefit for which there is no market PRICE or which, because of an EXTERNALITY, is not fully reflected in the market price. Typical examples would be a project to build a hydroelectric dam in an area of outstanding natural beauty or a law to require factories to limit emissions of gases that may cause ill-health. (See SHADOW PRICE.)

Cost of capital

The amount a firm must pay the owners of CAPITAL for the privilege of using it. This includes INTEREST payments on corporate DEBT, as well as the DIVIDENDS generated for shareholders. In deciding whether to proceed with a project, FIRMS should calculate whether the project is likely to generate sufficient revenue to cover all the costs incurred, including the cost of capital. Calculating the cost of EQUITY can be tricky (see CAPITAL ASSET PRICING MODEL and BETA).

Creative capitalism

See PHILANTHROCAPITALISM.

Creative destruction

See SCHUMPETER.

Credit

A loan extended or (sometimes) taken by, for example, delayed payment of an invoice.

Credit creation

Making loans. Often the amount of credit creation is subject to REGULATION. Lenders may have limits on the amount of loans they can make relative to the ASSETS they have, so that they run little RISK of BANKRUPTCY (see BASEL 1 AND 2 and CAPITAL ADE-QUACY RATIO). A CENTRAL BANK tries to keep the amount of credit creation below the level at which it would increase the MONEY SUPPLY so much that INFLATION accelerates. This was never easy to get right even when most lending was by BANKS, but it has become much harder since the 1980s with the growth of lending by institutions other than regulated banks.

Credit crunch

When BANKS and other suppliers of CREDIT suddenly stop lending. The most serious credit crunch at least since the 1930s began in 2007, when LIQUIDITY in the BOND market suddenly evaporated. Economists disagreed over whether this was a result of lenders becoming more RISK AVERSE, less able to lend because of declining CAPITAL ADEQUACY RATIOS following big invest-ment losses, or rising UNCERTAINTY about the economic outlook. Once a credit crunch begins it can be hard to uncrunch it, not least because of what KEYNES called the PARADOX OF THRIFT. There is much debate among economists about whether a bank-based credit crunch is easier or harder to solve, or requires different sorts of solutions, than one more centred in the FINANCIAL MARKETS, such as that which began in 2007.

Credit default swap

A financial contract that pays out if a specified company defaults on its DEBT. In recent years, the credit default swap (CDS) market has boomed as investors bought them as a form of INSURANCE against companies they invest in going bust. See DERIVATIVES.

Creditor

A lender, whether by making a loan, buying a BOND or allowing MONEY owed now to be paid in the future.

Crony capitalism

An approach to business based on looking after yourself by looking out for your own. At least until the crisis of the late 1990s, some Asian FIRMS, and even GOVERNMENTS, were notable for awarding contracts only to family and friends. This was often a form of CORRUPTION, resulting in economic inefficiency.

Crowding out

When the state does something it may discourage, or crowd out, private-sector attempts to do the same thing. At times, excessive GOVERNMENT borrowing has been blamed for low private-sector borrowing and, consequently, low INVESTMENT and (because the economic RETURNS on public borrowing are typically lower than those on private DEBT, especially corporate debt) slower economic GROWTH. This became less of a concern as government indebtedness in many countries declined during the 1980s and 1990s and, because of GLOBALISATION, FIRMS and governments (including that of the United States, as its public debt burden soared in the first decade of this century) found it easier to raise CAPITAL outside their home country. Crowding out may also come from state spending on things that might be provided more efficiently by private for-profit FIRMS or even by charitable PHILANTHROCAPITALISM.

Crowds

In 1906, Francis Galton, a Victorian polymath, visited a livestock fair at which villagers were invited to guess the weight of an ox after it was slaughtered and dressed. Not one of the 800 who guessed hit the exact mark: 1,198 pounds. However, the median (see AVERAGE) of the 800 guesses was very close indeed, at 1,197 pounds. This finding, with its implication that the insights of the many can surpass the wisdom of any one individual, has been the subject of growing attention in recent years. The soaring volume of mass data and the opportunities for interaction provided by the internet, together with today's more sophisticated analytical technologies, has inspired numerous efforts to tap the "wisdom of crowds". Some FIRMS now engage in "crowd-sourcing" to generate both incremental product-improvements and breakthrough ideas. The trick is to know the difference between when a crowd is being insightful and when, as BEHAVIOURAL ECONOMICS has shown, INFORMATION flows and psychological biases within the crowd can lead to irrational outcomes, such as BUBBLES.

Currency board

A means by which some countries try to defend their currency from speculative attack. A country that introduces a currency board commits itself to converting its domestic currency on demand at a fixed EXCHANGE RATE. To make this commitment credible, the currency board holds RESERVES of foreign currency (or GOLD or some other liquid ASSET) equal at the fixed rate of exchange to at least 100% of the value of the domestic currency that is issued.

Unlike a conventional CENTRAL BANK, which can print MONEY at will, a currency board can issue domestic notes and coins only when there are enough foreign exchange reserves to back it. Under a strict currency board regime, INTEREST RATES adjust automatically. If investors want to switch out of domestic currency into, say, US dollars, the SUPPLY of domestic currency will automatically shrink. This will cause domestic interest rates to rise, until eventually it becomes attractive for investors to hold local currency again.

Like any fixed exchange rate system, a currency board offers the prospect of a stable exchange rate and its strict discipline also brings benefits that ordinary exchange rate pegs lack. Profligate GOVERNMENTS, for instance, cannot use the central bank's printing presses to fund large DEFICITS. Hence currency boards are more credible than fixed exchange rates. The downside is that, like other fixed exchange rate systems, currency boards prevent governments from setting their own interest rates.

If local INFLATION remains higher than that of the country to which the currency is pegged, because of loose FISCAL POLICY, say, the currencies of countries with currency boards can become overvalued and uncompetitive. Governments cannot use the exchange rate to help the economy adjust to an outside SHOCK, such as a fall in export PRICES or sharp shifts in capital flows. Instead, domestic WAGES and prices must adjust, which may not happen for many years, if ever.

A currency board can also put pressure on banks and other financial institutions if interest rates rise sharply as investors dump local currency. For emerging markets with fragile banking systems, this can be a dangerous drawback. Furthermore, a classic currency board, unlike a central bank, cannot act as a LENDER OF LAST RESORT. A conventional central bank can stem a potential banking panic by lending money freely to banks that are feeling the pinch. A classic currency board cannot, although in practice some currency boards have more freedom than the classic description implies. The danger is that if they use this freedom, governments may cause currency speculators and others to doubt the government's commitment to living within the strict disciplines imposed by the currency board.

Argentina's decision to devalue the peso amid economic and political crisis in January 2002, a decade after it adopted a currency board, showed that adopting a currency board is neither a panacea nor a guarantee that an exchange rate backed by one will remain fixed come what may.

Currency peg

When a GOVERNMENT announces that the EXCHANGE RATE of its currency is fixed against another currency or currencies. (See also CURRENCY BOARD.)

Currency swap

See DERIVATIVES.

Current account

See BALANCE OF PAYMENTS.

Cyclical unemployment

See UNEMPLOYMENT.

Deadweight cost/loss

The extent to which the value and impact of TAXATION, tax relief or SUBSIDY is reduced because of its side-effects. For instance, increasing the amount of tax levied on workers' pay will lead some workers to stop working or work less, so reducing the amount of extra tax to be collected. However, creating a tax relief or subsidy to encourage people to buy life insurance would have a deadweight cost because people who would have bought insurance anyway would benefit.

Debt

"Neither a borrower nor a lender be," wrote Shakespeare in *Hamlet*. Actually, the availability of debt, and the willingness to take it on, is a crucial ingredient of economic GROWTH, because it allows individuals, FIRMS and GOVERNMENTS to make investments they would not otherwise be able to afford. The PRICE of debt is INTEREST. Until recently, lending was an activity dominated by BANKS (although mortgages for individuals buying their homes have long been available from special housing SAVINGS institutions). Starting in the 1960s, debt became increasingly available from other sources. Companies have sold trillions of dollars-worth of BONDS to investors in the FINANCIAL MARKETS. Individuals have been able to borrow with credit cards, and for those who have nowhere else to turn there are pawn shops and loan sharks, which charge very high rates of interest.

In most countries, by far the biggest single borrower is the state, through the NATIONAL DEBT. Total private-sector debt in

2007 was 216% of GDP in the United States, compared with less than 100% in 1928. Starting in the late 1990s, some economists expressed concern about the rising levels of consumer debt, in particular, and about the loosening of lending standards for individuals, firms, HEDGE FUNDS and PRIVATE EQUITY investors borrowing in the financial markets. The CREDIT CRUNCH that started in 2007 seemed to prove that much of this borrowing was unsustainable and imprudent, having exposed the global economy to excessive RISK.

Debt forgiveness

Cancelling or rescheduling a borrower's debts to lessen the pain of the DEBT burden. Many economists regard debt forgiveness as the best way to relieve the financial problems facing poorer countries. Some countries have had to pay so much in INTEREST each year to foreign lenders that little MONEY remained to spend on the long-term solutions to their POVERTY, such as educating their workers and building a modern INFRASTRUCTURE. In 1998, when the debt crisis in DEVELOPING COUNTRIES was arguably at its worst, the WORLD BANK calculated that around 40 of the world's poorest countries had an "unsustainably high" debt burden: the present value of their total debts was more than 220% of their EXPORTS.

Debt forgiveness has potential drawbacks. For instance, there is a risk of MORAL HAZARD. If countries that borrow too much are let off their financial obligations, poor countries may feel they have nothing to lose by borrowing as much as they can. The money goes straight into the hands of the poor country's GOVERNMENT, which may deliver little benefit to the people in greatest need, if the government is rife with CORRUPTION, which is often the case in such countries. This is why policymakers often argue that debt forgiveness should come with a CONDITIONALITY clause, for instance, a requirement that countries have a track record of implementing economic reforms designed to prevent a repeat of the errors that first created the need for debt forgiveness. This is the approach taken by the World Bank's HPIC (highly indebted poor country) initiative, launched in 1996 and expanded in 1999. However, by early 2009, only 24 of the 38 poor countries eligible under the programme had made enough progress in reform to have some debt forgiven.

Debt-equity ratio

See CAPITAL STRUCTURE.

Decoupling

The theory, hatched during the emerging market boom in the first decade of the 21st century, that internal DEMAND growth in some DEVELOPING COUNTRIES, especially the BRICS, was now strong enough that it would continue to push up their GDP regardless of whether or not rich economies, especially the United States, grew. Previously, it was believed that developing economies were so reliant on EXPORTS to rich countries that if, say, the United States sneezed (economically speaking), they would catch a cold. As the economic crisis went global during 2008, hitting many emerging markets especially hard, talk of decoupling ceased abruptly.

Default

Failure to fulfil the terms of a loan agreement. For example, a borrower is in default if he or she does not make scheduled INTEREST payments on a loan or fails to pay off the loan at the agreed time. Judging the likelihood of default is a crucial part of pricing a loan. INTEREST RATES are set so that, on average, a portfolio of loans will be profitable to the CREDITOR, even if some individual loans are loss-making as a result of borrowers defaulting.

Deficit

In the red – when more MONEY goes out than comes in. A BUDGET deficit occurs when PUBLIC SPENDING exceeds GOVERNMENT revenue. A current-account deficit occurs when EXPORTS and inflows from private and official TRANSFERS are worth less than IMPORTS and transfer outflows (see BALANCE OF PAYMENTS).

Deflation

Since 1930 it has been the norm in most developed countries for AVERAGE PRICES to rise year after year. However, before 1930 deflation (falling prices) was as likely as INFLATION. On the eve of the first world war, for example, prices in the UK, overall, were almost exactly the same as they had been at the time of the great fire of London in 1666. Even in the modern economy, inflation is not inevitable. Deflation occurred in Japan during the 1990s, and the CREDIT CRUNCH that began in 2007, and the global economic crisis that followed it, prompted some economists to predict deflation in the United States and some other big economies.

Deflation is a persistent fall in the general price level of goods and SERVICES. It is not to be confused with a decline in prices in one economic sector or with a fall in the inflation rate (which is known as DISINFLATION).

Sometimes deflation can be harmless, perhaps even a good thing, if lower prices lift real INCOME and hence spending power. In the last 30 years of the 19th century, for example, consumer prices fell by almost half in the United States, as the expansion of railways and advances in industrial technology brought cheaper ways to make everything. Yet annual real GDP growth over the period averaged more than 4%.

Deflation is dangerous, however – more so even than inflation – when it reflects a sharp slump in DEMAND, excess CAPACITY and a shrinking MONEY SUPPLY, as in the Great DEPRESSION of the 1930s. In the four years to 1933, American consumer prices fell by 25% and real GDP by 30%. Runaway deflation of this sort can be much more damaging than runaway inflation, because it creates a vicious spiral that is hard to escape. The expectation that prices will be lower tomorrow may encourage consumers to delay purchases, depressing demand and forcing FIRMS to cut prices by even more. Falling prices also inflate the real burden of DEBT (that is, increase real INTEREST RATES) causing BANKRUPTCY and BANK failure. This makes deflation particularly dangerous for economies that have large amounts of corporate debt. Most serious of all, deflation can make MONETARY POLICY ineffective: nominal interest rates cannot be negative, so real rates can get stuck too high.

Demand

One of the two words economists use most; the other is SUPPLY. These are the twin driving forces of the market economy. Demand is not just about measuring what people want; for economists, it refers to the amount of a good or service that people are both willing and able to buy. The DEMAND CURVE measures the relationship between the PRICE of a good and the amount of it demanded. Usually, as the price rises, fewer people are willing and able to buy it; in other words, demand falls (but see GIFFEN GOODS, NORMAL GOODS and INFERIOR GOODS). When demand changes, economists explain this in one of two ways. A movement along the demand curve occurs when a price change alters the quantity demanded; but if the price were to go back to where it was before, so would the amount demanded. A shift in the demand curve occurs when the amount demanded would be different from what it was previously at any chosen price, for example if there is no change in the market price, but demand rises or falls. The slope of the demand curve indicates the ELASTICITY of demand. For approaches to modelling demand see REVEALED PREFERENCE.

Policymakers seek to manipulate aggregate demand to keep the economy growing as fast as is possible without pushing up INFLATION. Keynesians try to manage demand through FISCAL POLICY; monetarists prefer to use the MONEY SUPPLY. Neither approach has been especially successful in practice, particularly when attempting to manage short-term demand through FINE TUNING.

Demand curve

A graph showing the relationship between the price of a good and the amount of DEMAND for it at different PRICES. (See also SUPPLY CURVE.)

Demographics

People, and the statistical study of them. In the 200 years since Thomas Malthus forecast that POPULATION GROWTH would result in mass starvation, dire predictions based on demographic trends have come to be taken with a pinch of salt. Even so, demography does matter. In developed countries, economists have studied the impact of the post-war "baby-boomer" population bulge as it has grown older. In the 1980s, as the bulge dominated the workforce, it may have contributed to a sharp, if temporary, rise in UNEMPLOYMENT in many countries. Boomers starting to save for retirement may have increased DEMAND for SHARES, so fuelling the BULL stockmarket of the 1990s; as they now retire and sell their shares for spending MONEY, they may cause a long BEAR market. Furthermore, as they become elderly and retire, health-care spending and retirement pensions are likely to eat up a growing share of GDP. To the extent that these are provided by the state, this will mean increased PUBLIC SPENDING and higher taxes. But whether they are provided by the state or by the private sector, the ageing of baby-boomers will impose a growing financial burden on the younger workers that have to support them (see REPLACEMENT RATE). Economists have tried to measure the extent of this burden using GENERATIONAL ACCOUNTING, which looks at the amount of wealth transferred from one generation to another over the lifetimes of the members of each generation.

Economists have also developed many different theories to explain why populations grow and why the fertility rate slowed sharply, to below the replacement rate, in many developed countries during the 1990s. One explanation is based on the notion that people have children so that there is somebody to look after them in old age. Fertility rates fell because the state increasingly looked after retired people, and infant mortality rates were lower so fewer births were required to ensure that there were some children around in the parental dotage. Also, with a lower PROBABILITY of a child dying, it paid the parents to have fewer children and to channel their energy and resources into maximising the HUMAN CAPITAL of the few. Alternatively, it may have had something to do with an important INNOVATION: the cheap and easy availability of reliable contraception.

Deposit insurance

Protection for your SAVINGS, in case your BANK goes bust. Arrangements vary around the world, but in most countries deposit insurance is required by the GOVERNMENT and paid for by banks (and ultimately their customers), which contribute a small slice of their ASSETS to a central, usually government-run, insurance fund. If a bank defaults, this fund guarantees its custom-ers' deposits, at least up to a certain amount. By reassuring banks' customers that their cash is protected, deposit insurance aims to prevent them from panicking and causing a bank run, and thereby reduces SYSTEMIC RISK. The United States introduced it in 1933, after a massive bank panic led to widespread BANKRUPTCY, deep-ening its DEPRESSION. As fear of bank failure grew during the global economic crisis that began in 2007, governments in many countries, including the United States, significantly expanded the coverage of deposit insurance.

The downside of deposit insurance is that it creates a MORAL HAZARD. By insulating depositors from defaults, deposit insur-ance reduces their incentive to monitor banks closely. Also banks can take greater risks, safe in the knowledge that there is a state-financed safety net to catch them if they fall.

There are no easy solutions to this moral hazard. One approach is to monitor what banks do very closely. This is easier said than done, not least because of the high cost. Another is to ensure capital adequacy by requiring banks to set aside, just in case, specified amounts of CAPITAL when they take on different amounts of RISK.

Alternatively, the state safety net could be shrunk, by splitting banks into two types: super-safe, government-insured "narrow banks", which stick to traditional business and invest only in secure assets; and uninsured institutions, "broad banks", which could range more widely under a much lighter regulatory system. Savers who invested in a broad bank would probably earn much higher RETURNS because it could invest in riskier assets; but they would also lose their shirts if it went bust.

Yet another possible answer is to require every bank to finance a small proportion of its assets by selling subordinated DEBT to other institutions, with the stipulation that the YIELD on this debt must not be more than so many (say 50) basis points higher than the rate on a corresponding risk-free instrument. Subordinated debt (uninsured certificates of deposit) is simply junior debt. Its holders are at the back of the queue for their MONEY if the bank gets into trouble and they have no safety net. Investors will buy subordinated debt at a yield quite close to the risk-free INTEREST RATE only if they are sure the bank is low risk. To sell its debt, the bank will have to persuade informed investors of this. If it cannot convince them, it cannot operate. This exploits the fact that bankers know more about banking than do their supervisors. It asks banks not to be good citizens but to look only to their profits. Unlike the present regime, it exploits all the available INFORMATION and properly aligns everybody's incentives. This ingenious idea was first tried in Argentina, where it became a victim of the country's economic, banking and political crisis of 2001–02 before it really had a chance to prove itself.

Depreciation

A fall in the value of an ASSET or a currency; the opposite of APPRECIATION.

Depression

A bad, depressingly prolonged RECESSION in economic activity. According to an old joke, when your neighbour loses his job, it's a recession; when you lose your job it's a depression. The textbook definition of a recession is two consecutive quarters of declining OUTPUT. A slump is where output falls by at least 10%. A depression is an even deeper and more prolonged slump.

The most famous example is the Great Depression of the 1930s. After growing strongly during the "roaring 20s", the American economy (among others) went into prolonged recession. Output fell by 30%. UNEMPLOYMENT soared and stayed high: in 1939 the jobless rate was still 17% of the workforce. Roughly half of the 25,000 BANKS in the United States failed. An attempt to stimulate growth, the New Deal, was the most far-reaching example of active FISCAL POLICY then seen and greatly extended the role of the state in the American economy. However, the depression only ended with the onset of preparations to enter the second world war.

Why did the Great Depression happen? It is not entirely clear, but forget the popular explanation: that it all went wrong with the Wall Street stockmarket crash of October 1929; that the slump persisted because policymakers just sat there; and that it took the New Deal to put things right. As early as 1928 the FEDERAL RESERVE, worried about financial SPECULATION and inflated stock prices, began raising INTEREST RATES. In the spring of 1929, industrial production started to slow; the recession started in the summer, well before the stockmarket lost half of its value between October 24th and mid-November. Coming on top of a recession that had already begun, the crash set the scene for a severe contraction but not for the decade-long slump that ensued.

So why did a bad downturn keep getting worse, year after year, not just in the United States but also around the globe? In 1929 most of the world was on the GOLD STANDARD, which should have helped stabilise the American economy. As DEMAND in the United States slowed its IMPORTS fell, its BALANCE OF PAYMENTS moved further into surplus and GOLD should have flowed into the country, expanding the MONEY SUPPLY and boosting the economy. But the Fed, which was still worried about easy CREDIT and speculation, dampened the impact of this adjustment mechanism, and instead the money supply got tighter. This was accompanied by a rise in PROTECTIONISM. GOVERNMENTS everywhere, hit by falling demand, tried to reduce imports through TARIFFS, causing international trade to collapse. Then American banks started to fail, and the Fed let them. As the crisis of confidence spread more banks failed, and as people rushed to turn bank deposits into cash the money supply collapsed.

Bad MONETARY POLICY was abetted by bad fiscal policy.

Taxes were raised in 1932 to help balance the BUDGET and restore confidence. The New Deal brought DEPOSIT INSURANCE and boosted government, but it also piled taxes on business and sought to prevent "excessive" COMPETITION. Price controls were brought in, along with other anti-business regulations. None of this stopped – and indeed may well have contributed to – the economy falling into recession again in 1937–38, after a brief recovery starting in 1935.

Deregulation

Cutting red tape. The process of removing legal or quasi-legal restrictions on the amount of COMPETITION, the sorts of business done, or the PRICES charged within a particular industry. During the last two decades of the 20th century, many GOVERNMENTS committed to the free market pursued policies of LIBERALISATION based on substantial amounts of deregulation hand-in-hand with the PRIVATISATION of industries owned by the state. The aim was to decrease the role of government in the economy and to increase competition. Even so, red tape remained alive and well. In the United States, with some 60 federal agencies issuing more than 1,800 rules a year, in 1998 the Code of Federal Regulations was more than 130,000 pages thick. That was not all bad. According to estimates by the American Office of Management and Budget, the annual cost of these rules was $289 billion, but the annual benefits were $298 billion.

The extent of deregulation even during the gung-ho liberalising era of Reaganism and Thatcherism was over-hyped. No modern economy could function effectively without plenty of REGULATION. The real debate, beneath the hype, is over how to design regulation that improves the functioning of the economy, and especially of markets, rather than making matters worse. Many commentators blamed deregulation for the global economic crisis that began in 2007. However, there is plenty of evidence that badly designed or executed regulation – so-called REGULATORY FAILURE – played a significant role in the crisis.

Derivatives

Financial ASSETS that "derive" their value from other assets. For example, an option to buy a SHARE is derived from the share. Even before the economic crisis that began in 2007, which many commentators linked to the rapid rise of derivatives use, some politicians and others responsible for financial REGULATION blamed the growing use of derivatives for increasing VOLATILITY in asset prices, and for being a source of danger to their users. Warren Buffett, a famed American investor, described them as "financial weapons of mass destruction".

Until the economic crisis, economists mostly regarded derivatives as a good thing, allowing more precise pricing of financial risk and better RISK MANAGEMENT. Even then, however, they conceded that when derivatives were misused the LEVERAGE that is often an integral part of them could have devastating consequences. So they came with an economists' health warning: if you don't understand it, don't use it. Now, at least temporarily, many economists are taking a view of the usefulness of derivatives that is closer to Buffett's, as are many erstwhile users of these FINANCIAL INSTRUMENTS.

The world of derivatives is riddled with jargon. Here are translations of the most important bits:

- A forward contract commits the user to buying or selling an asset at a specific price on a specific date in the future.

- A future is a forward contract that is traded on an exchange.

- A swap is a contract by which two parties exchange the cash flow linked to a liability or an asset. For example, two companies, one with a loan on a fixed INTEREST RATE over ten years and the other with a similar loan on a floating interest rate over the same period, may agree to take over each other's obligations, so that the first pays the floating rate and the second the fixed rate. A currency swap involves an agreement between, say, a borrower in dollars and another borrower in pounds to take over each other's interest and principal payments, in the currency in which the borrowing took place.

- An option is a contract that gives the buyer the right, but not the obligation, to sell or buy a particular asset at a particular price, on or before a specified date.

- An over-the-counter is a derivative that is not traded on an exchange but is purchased from, say, an investment BANK.

- Exotics are derivatives that are complex or are available in emerging economies.

- Plain-vanilla derivatives, in contrast to exotics, are typically exchange-traded, relate to developed economies and are comparatively uncomplicated.

Many derivatives are the result of SECURITISATION, in which investors buy a contract the value of which is linked to a bundle of assets created by a bank or company. These include collateralised debt obligations such as SUB-PRIME mortgage-backed SECURITIES, the sharp fall in the value of which helped to trigger the economic crisis that began in 2007.

De Soto, Hernando

A Peruvian economist who advocates establishing formal property rights for the poor to help them rapidly escape from POVERTY. In books such as The Other Path and The Mystery of Capital, he argued that, in DEVELOPING COUNTRIES, CAPITALISM will thrive in the LONG RUN only if legal systems change so that most of the people feel that the law is on their side. One of the best ways to achieve this is to give full legal protection to the de facto PROP-ERTY RIGHTS that are observed informally by the poor, such as when a community recognises that a certain family is entitled to occupy a particular piece of land.

According to his research, carried out in several countries with his think-tank, the Institute for Liberty and Democracy, such informal property rights cover ASSETS (notably land and housing) worth many billions of dollars. Informal systems of property rights usually make such assets "dead CAPITAL", meaning that it is hard to use them as COLLATERAL for a loan, which might be used to start a business, for example. He argues that an efficient, inclusive legal system preceded rapid development in every rich country and that bringing these rights into the formal legal system of poor, developing countries will unleash this hitherto dead capital and spur growth.

His ideas are controversial among economists, some of whom argue that he oversimplifies the debate about economic develop-ment by offering property rights as a "magic bullet". In 2008, the UN offered support for his ideas by publishing a report on the legal empowerment of the poor written by a high-level commis-sion led by de Soto and Madeleine Albright, a former American secretary of state.

Devaluation

A sudden fall in the value of a currency against other currencies. Strictly, devaluation refers only to sharp falls in a currency within a fixed EXCHANGE RATE system. Also it usually refers to a deliber-ate act of GOVERNMENT policy, although in recent years reluctant devaluers have blamed financial SPECULATION. Most studies of devaluation suggest that its beneficial effects on

COMPETITIVENESS are only temporary; over time they are eroded by higher PRICES (see J-CURVE).

Developing countries

A euphemism for the world's poor countries, also known, often optimistically, as emerging economies. Some four-fifths of the world's 6 billion people already live in developing countries, many of them in abject POVERTY. Developing countries account for less than one-fifth of total world GDP.

Economists disagree about how likely – and how fast – developing countries are to become developed. NEO-CLASSICAL ECONOMICS predicts that poor countries will grow faster than richer ones. The reason is DIMINISHING RETURNS on CAPITAL. Since poor countries start with less capital, they should reap higher RETURNS than a richer country with more capital from each slice of new INVESTMENT. But this CATCH-UP EFFECT (or convergence) is not supported by the data. For one thing, there is no such thing as a typical developing country. The official developing world includes the (sometimes) fast-growing BRIC economies and the poorest nations in Africa. Studies of the relationship between GROWTH and GDP per head in rich and poor countries found no evidence that poorer countries grew faster. Indeed, if anything, poorer countries have grown more slowly.

DEVELOPMENT ECONOMICS has argued that this is because poor countries have unique problems that require different policy solutions from those offered by conventional developed-world economics. But new ENDOGENOUS growth theory instead argues that there is conditional convergence. Hold constant such factors as a country's fertility rate, its HUMAN CAPITAL and its GOVERNMENT policies (proxied by the share of current government spending in GDP), and poorer countries generally grow faster than richer ones. Since, in reality, other factors are not constant (not all countries have the same level of human capital or the same government policies), absolute convergence does not happen.

Government policies seem to be crucial. Countries with broadly free-market policies – in particular, FREE TRADE and the maintenance of secure PROPERTY RIGHTS – have raised their growth rates. Open economies have grown much faster on average than closed economies, including, in the first decade of the 21st century, formerly slow-growing parts of Africa (thanks especially to their openness to trade with China). Higher PUBLIC SPENDING relative to GDP is usually associated with slower growth. Furthermore, high INFLATION is bad for growth and so is political instability. The poorest countries can indeed catch up. Their chances of doing so are maximised by policies that give a greater role to COMPETITION and incentives, at home and abroad.

Despite starting with a big disadvantage, there is evidence that some developing countries do not help themselves because they squander the resources they have. Institutions that produce effective governance of an economy are crucial. Those countries that use their resources well can grow quickly. Indeed, the world's fastest-growing economies over the past decade or so have been a small subgroup of exceptional performers among the poor countries. Many developing economies suffered as the economic crisis spread from the United States to the rest of the world in 2008, confounding fashionable DECOUPLING theories.

Development economics

Spawned by the end of the colonial era in the 1950s and 1960s, a whole branch of economic theory grew up around the question of how to promote economic development in poor countries. The proposition on which development economics was built was that poor countries were intrinsically different from rich ones and so needed their own set of economic models. Some development economists argued, for instance, that the self-interested, rational individual (*homo economicus*) did not exist in traditional tribal societies. They claimed that because many poor countries had large agricultural populations and were often dependent on a few COMMODITY EXPORTS for foreign exchange earnings, economic policies that suited rich countries would not work for them.

With hindsight, much of this was misguided, and policies based on it had disastrous effects. Development economists believed that the state had to play a big role in fostering modernisation. Instead, the result was huge, inefficient bureaucracies riddled with CORRUPTION, massive BUDGET DEFICITS and rampant INFLATION. During the 1990s, most GOVERNMENTS of DEVELOPING COUNTRIES started to reverse these policies and undo the damage they had done by introducing policies based on similar economic models to those that had worked in rich countries. However, the SEQUENCING of these new policies seemed to make a big difference to how well they worked. Doing the right things in the right order is crucial.

Diminishing returns

The more you have, the smaller is the extra benefit you get from having even more; also known as diseconomies of scale (see ECONOMIES OF SCALE). For instance, when workers have a lot of CAPITAL, giving them a little more may not increase their PRODUCTIVITY anywhere near as much as would giving the same amount to workers who currently have little or no capital. This underpins the CATCH-UP EFFECT, whereby there is (supposedly) convergence between the rates of GROWTH of DEVELOPING COUNTRIES and developed ones. In the NEW ECONOMY of the 21st century, some economists argue, capital may not suffer from diminishing returns, or at least the amount of diminishing will be much smaller. There may even be ever increasing returns.

Direct taxation

Taxes levied on the INCOME or wealth of an individual or company. Contrast with INDIRECT TAXATION. In much of the world, direct tax rates fell during the 1980s and 1990s, partly because some economists argued that high rates of tax on income discouraged people from working, and that high rates of tax on PROFIT encouraged companies to move to countries with lower rates. Furthermore, high rates of INCOME TAX were viewed as politically unpopular. Even so, although rates were cut, because both personal income and corporate profits grew steadily throughout this period the total amount collected via direct taxation continued to rise. Economists often disagree about which of direct taxes or indirect taxes are the least inefficient method of taxation. The sharp increase in PUBLIC SPENDING in response to the economic crisis that started in 2007 prompted renewed consideration of the case for higher taxes, especially on the rich.

Discounted cash flow

How much less is a sum of MONEY due in the future worth today? The answer is found by discounting the future cash flow, using an INTEREST RATE that reflects the fact that money in future is worth less than money now, because money now could be invested and earn INTEREST, whereas future money cannot. FIRMS use discounted cash flow to judge whether an INVESTMENT project is worthwhile. The interest rate is a means of reflecting the OPPORTUNITY COST of tying up money in the investment project. To test whether an investment makes economic sense, the INCOME must be discounted so that it can be measured against the costs. If the present value of the benefits exceeds the costs, the investment is a good one.

Discount rate

The rate of INTEREST charged by a CENTRAL BANK when lending to other financial institutions. It also refers to a rate of interest used when calculating DISCOUNTED CASH FLOW.

Diseconomies of scale

See ECONOMIES OF SCALE.

Disequilibrium

When SUPPLY and DEMAND in a market are not in balance. Contrast with EQUILIBRIUM.

Disinflation

A fall in the rate of INFLATION. This means a slower increase in PRICES but not a fall in prices, which is known as DEFLATION.

Disintermediation

Cutting out the middleman. Disintermediation has become a buzz word in financial services in particular, as competitive and technological changes have reduced the need for established intermediaries. At least until the economic crisis that began in 2007, BANKS were seeing much of their business slip away, such as lending to companies that found they could tap CAPITAL MARKETS directly. At the end of the 1990s, NEW ECONOMY theorists argued that many retailers would be disintermediated as the internet enabled customers to transact directly with producers without needing to visit a shop. But this happened only partially, because many established retailers created internet distribution in tandem with their offline stores as part of a "bricks-and-clicks" strategy.

Diversification

Not putting all your eggs in one basket. Investors are encouraged to do this by MODERN PORTFOLIO THEORY, as holding many different SHARES and other ASSETS helps to reduce RISK. At the sharp end of business, however, diversification is somewhat out of fashion. Economic studies of diversifying corporate MERGERS have found that these often hurt the shareholders of the acquiring firm; by contrast, diversified FIRMS that have sold off non-core businesses have typically made their shareholders much better off.

Dividend

The part of a company's PROFIT distributed to shareholders. Unlike INTEREST on DEBT, the payment of a dividend is not automatic. It is decided by the company's managers, subject to the approval of the company's owners (shareholders). However, when a company cuts its dividend, this usually triggers a sharp fall in its SHARE PRICE by more than would be appear to be justified by the reduced dividend. Economists theorise that this is because a dividend cut signals to shareholders that the company is in a bad way, with more bad news to follow. The tax treatment of dividends can influence how FIRMS return money to their shareholders; often, a more TAX EFFICIENT method than paying dividends is for the firm to repurchase some of its own shares in the stockmarket.

Division of labour

People are better off specialising than trying to be jacks of all trades and ending up masters of none. The logic of dividing the workforce into different crafts and professions is the same as that underpinning the case for FREE TRADE: everybody benefits from doing those things in which they have a COMPARATIVE ADVANTAGE and using INCOME from doing so to meet their other needs.

Dollarisation

When a country's own MONEY is replaced as its citizens' preferred currency by the US dollar. This can be a deliberate GOVERNMENT policy or the result of many private choices by buyers and sellers (for instance, at the first sign of trouble, investors across Latin America generally flee into dollars). When it is government policy, dollarisation is, in essence, a beefed up CURRENCY BOARD.

The appeal of dollarisation is that the value of the dollar is more stable than the distrusted local currency, which may well have a history of suddenly falling in value. By eliminating all possible RISK of DEVALUATION against the dollar, the cost of local companies' and the government's borrowing in international markets is reduced, as the currency risk is removed. A big downside is that the country hands over control of MONETARY POLICY to the FEDERAL RESERVE, and the right INTEREST RATE for the United States may not be appropriate for the dollarised country, if that country and the United States do not constitute an OPTIMAL CURRENCY AREA. This is one reason that in some countries the local currency has been displaced by another stable currency, such as, in some central European economies, the EURO (and before that the D-mark).

Dominant firm

A firm with the ability to set PRICES in its market (see MONOPOLY, OLIGOPOLY and ANTITRUST).

Dumping

Selling something for less than the cost of producing it. This may be used by a DOMINANT FIRM to attack rivals, a strategy known to ANTITRUST authorities as PREDATORY PRICING. Participants in international trade are often accused of dumping by domestic FIRMS charging more than rival IMPORTS. Countries can slap duties on cheap imports that they judge are being dumped in their markets. Often this amounts to thinly disguised PROTECTIONISM against more efficient foreign firms.

In practice, genuine predatory pricing is rare – certainly much rarer than anti-dumping actions – because it relies on the unlikely ability of a single producer to dominate a world market. In any case, consumers gain from lower PRICES; so do companies that can buy their supplies more cheaply abroad.

Disputes about dumping, or anti-dumping policies imposed on imports, can be referred for adjudication to the WORLD TRADE ORGANISATION.

Econometrics

Mathematics and sophisticated computing applied to ECONOM-ICS. Econometricians crunch data in search of economic relationships that have STATISTICAL SIGNIFICANCE. Sometimes this is done to test a theory; at other times the computers churn the numbers until they come up with an interesting result. Some economists are fierce critics of theory-free econometrics, which they dismiss as "data mining".

Economic and monetary union

In January 1999, 11 of the 15 countries in the EUROPEAN UNION merged their national currencies into a single European currency, the EURO. This decision was motivated partly by politics and partly by hoped-for economic benefits from the creation of a single, integrated European economy. These benefits included currency stability and low INFLATION, underwritten by an independent EUROPEAN CENTRAL BANK (a particular boon for countries with poor inflation records, such as Italy and Spain, but less so for traditionally low-inflation Germany). Furthermore, European businesses and individuals stood to save from handling one currency rather than many. Comparing PRICES and WAGES across the EURO ZONE became easier, increasing COMPETITION by making it easier for companies to sell throughout the euro zone and for consumers to shop around.

Forming the single currency also involved big risks, however. Euro members gave up both the right to set their own INTEREST RATES and the option of moving EXCHANGE RATES against each other. They also agreed to limit their BUDGET DEFICITS under a STABILITY AND GROWTH PACT. Some economists argued that this loss of flexibility could prove costly if their economies did not behave as one and could not easily adjust in other ways. How well the euro zone functions will depend on how closely it resembles what economists call an OPTIMAL CURRENCY AREA. When the euro economies are not growing in unison, a common MONETARY POLICY risks being too loose for some and too tight for others. If so, there may need to be large transfers of funds from regions doing well to those doing badly. But if the effects of shocks persist, fiscal transfers would merely delay the day of reckoning; ultimately, wages or people (or both) would have to shift.

In its first few years, the euro fell sharply against the dollar, though it recovered during late 2002. Sluggish growth in some European economies led to intense pressure for interest rate cuts, and to the stability and growth pact being breached, though not scrapped. Even so, by 2009 16 of the 27 member countries of the European Union had adopted the euro, and the currency was informally used by five other countries. Despite some speculation that Italy might try to withdraw from the euro (how it could do so was not clear) because of its difficulties during the global economic crisis that started in 2007, in 2008 the exchange rate of the euro against the dollar reached a record high and remained strong into 2009.

Economic indicator

A statistic used for judging the health of an economy, such as GDP per head, the rate of UNEMPLOYMENT or the rate of INFLATION. Such statistics are often subject to huge revisions in the months and years after they are first published, thus causing difficulties and embarrassment for the economic policymakers who rely on them.

Economic man

At the heart of economic theory is *homo economicus*, the economist's model of human behaviour. In traditional CLASSICAL ECONOMICS and in NEO-CLASSICAL ECONOMICS it was assumed that people acted in their own self-interest. Adam SMITH argued that society was made better off by everybody pursuing their selfish interests through the workings of the INVISIBLE HAND. However, in recent years, mainstream economists have tried to include a broader range of human motivations in their models. There have been attempts to model ALTRUISM and CHARITY. Recently, BEHAVIOURAL ECONOMICS and NEUROECONOMICS have drawn on studies of human psychology and the brain to explain economic phenomena.

Economic rent

See RENT.

Economics

The "dismal science", according to Thomas Carlyle, a 19th-century Scottish writer. It has been described in many ways, few of them flattering. The most concise, non-abusive, definition is the study of how society uses its scarce resources.

Economic sanctions

A way of punishing errant countries, which is currently more acceptable than bombing or invading them. One or more restrictions are imposed on international trade with the targeted country in order to persuade the target's GOVERNMENT to change a policy. Possible sanctions include limiting export or import trade with the target; constraining INVESTMENT in the target; and preventing transfers of money involving citizens or the government of the target. Sanctions can be multilateral, with many countries acting together, perhaps under the auspices of the UN, or unilateral, when one country takes action on its own.

How effective sanctions are is debatable. According to one study, between 1914 and 1990 there were 116 occasions on which various countries imposed economic sanctions. Two-thirds of these failed to achieve their stated goals. The cost to the country imposing sanctions can be large, particularly when it is acting unilaterally. It is estimated that in 1995 imposing sanctions on other countries cost the American economy over $15 billion in lost exports and 200,000 in lost jobs in export industries.

Widely considered a notable success was the use of economic sanctions against the apartheid regime in South Africa, although some economists question how big a part the sanctions actually played. Clearly important was the fact that the sanctions were imposed multilaterally by the international community, so there were comparatively few breaches of the restrictions. But, arguably, the most crucial factor in persuading the government in Pretoria to cave in was that foreign companies, fearing that their SHARE PRICE would fall because their investments in South Africa would attract bad publicity, voluntarily chose for commercial reasons to disinvest.

The failure of economic sanctions to deliver regime change in Iraq was used as one justification for the American-led invasion of the country in 2003.

Economies of scale

Bigger is better. In many industries, as OUTPUT increases, the AVERAGE cost of each unit produced falls. One reason is that overheads and other FIXED COSTS can be spread over more units of output. However, getting bigger can also increase average costs (diseconomies of scale) because it is more difficult to manage a big operation, for instance.

Effective exchange rate

See TRADE-WEIGHTED EXCHANGE RATE.

Efficiency

Getting the most out of the resources used. For a particular sort of efficiency often favoured by economists, see PARETO EFFICIENT.

Efficiency wages

WAGES that are set at above the market clearing rate so as to encourage workers to increase their PRODUCTIVITY.

Efficient market hypothesis

You can't beat the market. The efficient market hypothesis says that the PRICE of a financial ASSET reflects all the INFORMATION available and responds only to unexpected news. Thus prices can be regarded as optimal estimates of true INVESTMENT value at all times. It is impossible for investors to predict whether the price will move up or down (future price movements are likely to follow a RANDOM WALK), so on average an investor is unlikely to beat the market. This belief underpins ARBITRAGE PRICING THEORY, the CAPITAL ASSET PRICING MODEL and concepts such as BETA.

The hypothesis had few critics among financial economists during the 1960s and 1970s, but it has come under increasing attack since then and intensified during the global economic crisis that began in 2007. The fact that financial prices were far more volatile than appeared to be justified by new information, and that financial BUBBLES sometimes formed, led economists to question the theory. BEHAVIOURAL ECONOMICS has challenged one of the main sources of market EFFICIENCY, the idea that all investors are fully rational *homo economicus*. Some economists have noted the fact that information gathering is a costly process, so it is unlikely that all available information will be reflected in prices. Others have pointed to the fact that ARBITRAGE can become more costly, and thus less likely, the further away from fundamentals prices move. The efficient market hypothesis is now one of the most controversial and well-studied propositions in ECONOMICS, although no consensus has been reached on which markets, if any, are efficient. However, even if the ideal does not exist, the efficient market hypothesis is useful in judging the relative efficiency of one market compared with another.

Elasticity

A measure of the responsiveness of one variable to changes in another. Economists have identified four main types:

- PRICE ELASTICITY measures how much the quantity of SUPPLY of a good, or DEMAND for it, changes if its PRICE changes. If the percentage change in quantity is more than the percentage change in price, the good is price elastic; if it is less, the good is price INELASTIC.

- INCOME elasticity of demand measures how the quantity demanded changes when income increases.

- Cross-elasticity shows how the demand for one good (say, coffee) changes when the price of another good (say, tea) changes. If they are SUBSTITUTE GOODS (tea and coffee), the cross-elasticity will be positive: an increase in the price of tea will increase demand for coffee. If they are COMPLEMENTARY GOODS, (tea and teapots) the cross-elasticity will be negative. If they are unrelated (tea and OIL), the cross-elasticity will be zero.

▪ Elasticity of substitution describes how easily one input in the production process, such as LABOUR, can be substituted for another, such as machinery.

Emerging markets

See DEVELOPING COUNTRIES.

Emissions trading

See ENVIRONMENTAL ECONOMICS.

Endogenous

Inside the economic model; the opposite of EXOGENOUS (see also GROWTH).

Engel's law

People generally spend a smaller share of their BUDGET on food as their INCOME rises. Ernst Engel, a Russian statistician, first made this observation in 1857. The reason is that food is a necessity, which poor people have to buy. As people get richer they can afford better-quality food, so their food spending may increase, but they can also afford LUXURIES beyond the budgets of poor people. Hence the share of food in total spending falls as incomes grow.

Enron

In a word, all that was wrong with American CAPITALISM at the start of the 21st century. Until late 2001, Enron, an energy company turned financial powerhouse based in Houston, Texas, had been one of the most admired firms in the United States and the world. It was praised for everything from pioneering energy trading via the internet to its innovative corporate culture and its system of employment evaluation by peer review, which resulted in those that were not rated by their peers being fired. However, revelations of accounting fraud by the firm led to its BANKRUPTCY, prompting what was widely described as a crisis of confidence in American capitalism.

This, as well as further scandals involving accounting fraud (WorldCom) and other dubious practices (many by Wall Street firms), resulted in efforts to reform corporate governance, the legal liability of company bosses, accounting, Wall Street research and REGULATION. Much of this regulation was introduced by the controversial Sarbanes-Oxley Act, which critics said added greatly to the cost of doing business without significantly reducing the risk of fraud and other criminal behaviour by executives.

Enterprise

One of the factors of production, along with LAND, LABOUR and CAPITAL. The creative juices of CAPITALISM; the ANIMAL SPIRITS of the ENTREPRENEUR.

Entrepreneur

The life and soul of the capitalist party. Somebody who has the idea and ENTERPRISE to mix together the other FACTORS OF PRODUCTION to produce something valuable. An entrepreneur must be willing to take a RISK in pursuit of a PROFIT.

Environmental economics

Some people think CAPITALISM is wholly bad for the environment as it is based on consuming scarce resources. They want less CONSUMPTION and greater reliance on renewable resources. They oppose FREE TRADE because they favour self-sufficiency (AUTARKY), or at least so-called FAIR TRADE, and because they believe it encourages poorer countries to destroy their natural resources in order to get rich quick. Although few professional economists would share these views, in recent years many attempts have been made to incorporate environmental concerns within mainstream economics.

The traditional measure of GDP incorporates only those things that are paid for; this may include things that reduce the overall quality of life, including harming the environment. For instance, cleaning up an OIL spill will increase GDP if people are paid for the clean-up. Attempts have been made to devise an alternative environmentally friendly measure of NATIONAL INCOME, but so far progress has been limited. At the very least, traditional economists increasingly agree that maximising GDP growth does not necessarily equal maximising social WELFARE.

Much of the damage done to the environment may be a result of externalities. An EXTERNALITY can arise when people engaged in economic activity do not have to take into account the full costs of what they are doing. For instance, car drivers do not have to bear the full cost of making their contribution to global warming, even though their actions may one day impose a huge financial burden on society.

One way to reduce externalities is to tax them, say, through a fuel tax. Another is prohibition, say, limiting car drivers to one gallon of fuel per week. This could result in black markets, however. Allowing trade in pollution rights may encourage "efficient pollution", with the pollution permits ending up in the hands of those for which pollution has the greatest economic upside. As this still allows some environmental destruction, it is unpopular with extreme greens. Trading in carbon emissions was introduced within the EUROPEAN UNION in 2005 to help meet targets agreed in the Kyoto Protocol on climate change. After initial problems, the trading regime was strengthened in 2008. Other carbon emissions trading schemes, mostly local and voluntary, have been launched elsewhere, including in the United States. Although many economists argue that a tax is more efficient at curbing carbon emissions than a trading system, the practical difficulties of creating a global carbon tax mean that carbon emissions trading is expected to be a key part of the expected successor to the Kyoto treaty.

There may be a case for international eco markets. For instance, people in rich countries might pay people in poor countries to stop doing activities that cause environmental damage outside the poor countries, or that rich people disapprove of, such as chopping down the rain forests. Choices on environmental policy, notably on measures to reduce the threat of global warming, involve costs today with benefits delayed until the distant future.

How are these choices to be made? Traditional COST-BENEFIT ANALYSIS does not help much. In measuring costs and benefits in the far distant future, two main things seem to intervene and spoil the conventional calculations. One is UNCERTAINTY. We know nothing about what the state of the world will be in 2200. The other is how much people today are willing to pay in order to raise the welfare of others who are so remote that they can barely be imagined, yet who seem likely to be much better off materially than people today. Some economists take the view that the welfare of each future generation should be given the same weight in the analysis as the welfare of today's generation. This implies that a much lower DISCOUNT RATE should be used than the one appropriate for short-term projects. Another option is to use a high discount rate for costs and benefits arising during the first 30 or so years, then a lower rate or rates for more distant periods. Many studies by economists and psychologists have found that people do in fact discount the distant future at lower rates than they apply to the near future.

Equilibrium

When SUPPLY and DEMAND are in balance. At the equilibrium price, the quantity that buyers are willing to buy exactly matches the quantity that sellers are willing to sell. So everybody is satisfied, unlike when there is DISEQUILIBRIUM. In CLASSICAL ECONOMICS, it is assumed that markets always tend towards equilibrium and return to it in the event that something causes a temporary disequilibrium. GENERAL EQUILIBRIUM is when supply and demand are balanced simultaneously in all the markets in an economy. KEYNES questioned whether the economy always moved to equilibrium, for instance to ensure FULL EMPLOYMENT.

Equities

See SHARES.

Equity

There are two definitions in ECONOMICS:

- The CAPITAL of a firm, after deducting any liabilities to outsiders other than shareholders, who are typically the legal owners of the firm's EQUITY. This ownership right is the reason SHARES are also known as equities.

- Fairness. Dividing up the economic pie. Economists have been particularly interested in this with regard to how systems of TAXATION work. They have examined whether taxes treat fairly people with the same ability to pay (HORIZONTAL EQUITY) and people with different abilities to pay (VERTICAL EQUITY).

The fairness of other aspects of how the gains from economic activity are distributed through society has also been debated by economists, especially those interested in WELFARE ECONOMICS. Some economists start with the presumption that the free-market outcome is inherently inequitable, and that equity (sharing out the pie) must be traded off against EFFICIENCY (maximising the size of the pie). Others argue that it is inequitable to take money away from someone who has created economic value to give to people who have been less skilled or industrious.

Equity risk premium

The extra reward investors get for buying a SHARE over what they get for holding a less risky ASSET, such as a GOVERNMENT BOND. Modern financial theory assumes that the premium will be just big enough on average to compensate the investor for the extra RISK. However, studies have found that the AVERAGE equity premium over many years has been much larger than appears to be justified by the average riskiness of shares. To solve this so-called equity premium puzzle, some economists have suggested that investors may have greater risk aversion towards shares than traditional theory assumes. Some claim that the past equity premium was mismeasured, or reflected an unrepresentative sample of share PRICES. Others suggest that the high premium is evidence that the EFFICIENT MARKET HYPOTHESIS does not apply to the stockmarket. Some economists think that the premium fell to more easily explained levels during the 1990s. Nobody really knows which, if any, of these interpretations is right.

Ethical consumerism

Shopping with a conscience. In recent years, pressure from consumers and NGOs has led to a growing number of products being labelled according to their ethical as well as their physical ingredients. These standards were initially set by NGOs, although increasingly they are taking the form of an agreed "compact" between NGOs and industry groups. For instance, "FAIR TRADE" coffee has been produced according to agreed standards on WAGES and sustainability. Some paper products have been made in accordance with standards on the protection of rain forests. Some fish is identified as being caught in accordance with sustainable fishing standards. Initially, ethically branded products cost more than similar products not produced according to the agreed standards; however, as ethical consumerism becomes increasingly mainstream, that price differential is starting to narrow thanks, in part, to ECONOMIES OF SCALE.

Euro

The main currency of the EUROPEAN UNION, launched in January 1999 and in general circulation since 2002 (see ECONOMIC AND MONETARY UNION).

Eurodollar

A deposit in dollars held in a BANK outside the United States. Such deposits are often set up to avoid taxes and currency exchange costs. They are frequently lent out and have become an important method of CREDIT CREATION.

European Central Bank

The CENTRAL BANK of the EUROPEAN UNION, responsible since January 1999 for setting the official short-term INTEREST RATE in countries using the euro as their domestic currency. In this role, the European Central Bank (ECB) replaced national central banks such as Germany's Bundesbank, which became local branches of the ECB.

European Union

A club of European countries. Initially a six-country TRADE AREA established by the 1957 Treaty of Rome and known as the European Economic Community, it has become an increasingly political union. In 1999 a single currency, the EURO, was launched in 11 of the then 15 member countries. Viewed as a single entity, the EU has a bigger economy than the United States. In 2002, a further ten countries were invited to join the EU in 2004 and another two in 2007, increasing its membership to 27 countries, with more countries likely to follow later.

Euro zone

The economy comprising all the countries that have adopted the EURO. There is much debate among economists about whether the euro zone is in fact an OPTIMAL CURRENCY AREA.

Evolutionary economics

See INSTITUTIONAL ECONOMICS.

Excess returns

Getting more money from an economic INVESTMENT than you needed to justify investing. In PERFECT COMPETITION, the FACTORS OF PRODUCTION earn only normal returns, that is, the minimum amount of WAGES, PROFIT, INTEREST or RENT needed to secure their use in the economic activity in question, rather than in an alternative. Excess returns can be earned for more than a short period only when there is MARKET FAILURE, especially MONOPOLY, because otherwise the existence of excess returns would quickly attract COMPETITION, which would drive down returns until they were normal.

Exchange controls

Limits on the amount of foreign currency that can be taken into a country, or of domestic currency that can be taken abroad.

Exchange rate

The price at which one currency can be converted into another. Over the years, economists and politicians have often changed their minds about whether it is a good idea to try to hold a country's exchange rate steady, rather than let it be decided by MARKET FORCES. For two decades after the second world war, many of the major currencies were fixed under the BRETTON WOODS agreement. During the following two decades the number of currencies allowed to float increased, although in the late 1990s a number of European currencies were permanently fixed under ECONOMIC AND MONETARY UNION and some other countries established CURRENCY BOARDS.

When CAPITAL can flow easily around the world, countries cannot fix their exchange rate and at the same time maintain an independent MONETARY POLICY. They must choose between the confidence and stability provided by a fixed exchange rate and the control over INTEREST RATE policy offered by a floating exchange rate. On the face of it, in a world of capital MOBILITY a more flexible exchange rate seems the best bet. A floating currency will force firms and investors to HEDGE against fluctuations, not lull them into a false sense of stability. It should make foreign banks more circumspect about lending. At the same time it gives policy-makers the option of devising their own monetary policy. But floating exchange rates have a big drawback: when moving from one EQUILIBRIUM to another currencies can overshoot and become highly unstable, especially if large amounts of capital flow in or out of a country, perhaps because of SPECULATION by investors. This instability has real economic costs.

To get the best of both worlds, many emerging economies have tried a hybrid approach, loosely tying their exchange rate either to a single foreign currency, such as the dollar, or to a basket of currencies. But the currency crises of the late 1990s, and the failure of Argentina's currency board, led many economists to conclude that, if not a currency union such as the EURO, the best policy may be to have a freely floating exchange rate.

Exogenous

Outside the model. For instance, in traditional NEO-CLASSICAL ECONOMICS models of GROWTH rely on an exogenous factor. To keep growing, an economy needs continual infusions of technological progress. Yet this is a force that the neo-classical model makes no attempt to explain. The rate of technological progress comes from outside the model; it is simply assumed by the economic modellers. In other words, it is exogenous. New growth theory tries to calculate the rate of technological progress inside the economic model by mapping its relationship to factors such as HUMAN CAPITAL, free markets, COMPETITION and GOVERNMENT expenditure. Thus, in these models, growth is ENDOGENOUS.

Expectations

What people assume about the future, especially when they make decisions. Economists debate whether people have irrational or RATIONAL EXPECTATIONS, or ADAPTIVE EXPECTATIONS that change to reflect learning from past mistakes. How people form their expectations has important implications for policymaking.

Expected returns

The CAPITAL GAIN plus INCOME that investors think they will earn by making an INVESTMENT, at the time they invest.

Expenditure tax

A tax on what people spend, rather than what they earn or their wealth. Economists often regard it as more efficient than other taxes because it may discourage productive economic activity less; it is not the creating of INCOME and wealth that is taxed, but the spending of it. It can be a form of INDIRECT TAXATION, added to the PRICE of a good or service when it is sold, or direct taxation, levied on people's income minus their SAVINGS over a year.

Export credit

Loans to boost EXPORTS. In many countries these are subsidised by a GOVERNMENT keen to encourage exports. Typically, the CREDIT comes in two forms: loans to foreign buyers of domestic produce; and guarantees on loans made by BANKS to domestic companies so they can produce the exports that should pay off the loan. This effectively insures producers against non-payment. When governments compete aggressively with export credits to win business for domestic FIRMS the sums involved can become large. The economic benefit of export credits is unclear at the best of times. This may be because they are largely motivated by political goals.

Exports

Sales abroad. Exports grew steadily as a share of world OUTPUT during the second half of the 20th century. Yet by some measures this share was no higher than it was at the end of the 19th century, before FREE TRADE fell victim to a political backlash.

Externality

An economic side-effect. Externalities are costs or benefits arising from an economic activity that affect somebody other than the people engaged in the economic activity and are not reflected fully in prices. For instance, smoke pumped out by a factory may impose clean-up costs on nearby residents; bees kept to produce honey may pollinate plants belonging to a nearby farmer, thus boosting his crop. Because these costs and benefits do not form part of the calculations of the people deciding whether to go ahead with the economic activity they are a form of MARKET FAILURE, since the amount of the activity carried out if left to the free market will be an inefficient use of resources. If the externality is beneficial, the market will provide too little; if it is a cost, the market will supply too much.

One potential solution is REGULATION: a ban, say. Another, when the externality is negative, is a tax on the activity or, if the externality is positive, a SUBSIDY. Another approach is to issue limited rights to do an activity that may be traded, such as has been attempted with carbon emissions trading under the Kyoto Protocol to deal with the externality of climate change.

For economists, for a solution to externalities to be efficient, ideally it should require them to be included in the costings of those engaged in the economic activity, so there is self-regulation. For instance, the externality of pollution can be addressed by creating PROPERTY RIGHTS over clean air, entitling their owner to a fee if they are infringed by a factory pumping out smoke. According to the Coase theorem (named after a Nobel Prize-winning economist, Ronald Coase), it does not matter who has ownership, so long as property rights are fully allocated and completely FREE TRADE of all property rights is possible. Some economists think that using tax as a means to include the cost of externalities in economic decision-making is more efficient than the property rights approach. (See ENVIRONMENTAL ECONOMICS.)

Factor cost

A measure of OUTPUT reflecting the costs of the FACTORS OF PRODUCTION used, rather than market PRICES, which may differ because of INDIRECT TAX and SUBSIDY (see GDP).

Factors of production

The ingredients of economic activity: LAND, LABOUR, CAPITAL and ENTERPRISE.

Factory prices

The PRICES charged by producers to wholesalers and retailers. Because these prices are eventually passed on to the end customer, changes in factory prices, also known as producer prices, can be a LEADING INDICATOR of consumer price INFLATION.

Fair trade

Many politicians and NGOS argue that FREE TRADE is not enough; it should also be fair. On the face of it, fairness is self-evidently a good thing. However, fairness, in trade as in beauty, lies in the eye of the beholder. Frédéric Bastiat, a 19th-century French satirist, once observed that the sun offered unfair COMPETITION to candlemakers. If windows could be boarded up during the day, he argued, more jobs could be created making candles. American trade UNIONS complain that Mexicans' lower WAGES, say, give them an unfair advantage. Mexicans say they cannot compete fairly against more productive American counterparts. Both sides are wrong. Mexicans are paid less than Americans largely because they are, in general, less productive. There is nothing unfair about that; indeed, it helps to make trade mutually beneficial. The mutual benefits of trade also disprove the fair traders' other complaint, that free trade harms poor countries. (See COMPARATIVE ADVANTAGE.)

One meaning of fair trade which can have a beneficial effect is "fair trade" labelling of products, such as coffee, which are produced in ways that meet acceptable standards on wages and sustainability. Although there is debate about what exactly these standards should be, this form of label is an important component of ETHICAL CONSUMERISM, and does not involve the sort of regulatory costs that can arise from trying to impose fair trade through GOVERNMENT policy.

FDI

See FOREIGN DIRECT INVESTMENT.

Federal Reserve System

America's CENTRAL BANK. Set up in 1913, and popularly known as the Fed, the system divides the United States into 12 Federal Reserve districts, each with its own regional Federal Reserve bank. These are overseen by the Federal Reserve Board, consisting of seven governors based in Washington, DC. MONETARY POLICY is decided by its Federal Open Market Committee.

Financial centre

A place in which an above-average amount of financial business takes place. The big ones are New York, London, Tokyo and Frankfurt. Small ones such as Dubai, Dublin, Bermuda, Luxembourg and the Cayman Islands also play an important part in the global FINANCIAL SYSTEM. GLOBALISATION and the increase in electronic trading have raised concerns about whether there will be as much need for financial centres in the 21st century as there was in the 19th and 20th centuries. So far, the evidence suggests that the biggest, at least, will remain important – if somewhat smaller, thanks to the global economic crisis that began in 2007.

Financial instrument

Certificate of ownership of a financial ASSET, such as a BOND or a SHARE.

Financial intermediary

A middleman. An individual or institution that brings together investors (the source of funds) and users of funds (such as borrowers). May be increasingly at risk of DISINTERMEDIATION.

Financial literacy

Remarkably few people have even a basic understanding of finance or ECONOMICS, which may be why the sorts of widespread bad decisions were taken that helped create the global economic crisis that began in 2007. Research into why so many SUB-PRIME mortgages went into default, triggering the crisis, found that many borrowers did not understand the RISKS involved when they took out their mortgage, including such basics as the fact that their monthly payments would rise if the INTEREST RATE went up. The bankers who invested in BONDS backed by subprime mortgages did not seem to have a significantly better grasp of the risks.

A survey in 2004 by Cambridge University and Prudential, a big insurer, found that some 9m Britons are "financially phobic", meaning that "they shy away from anything to do with financial information, from bank statements to savings accounts to life assurance". Research by the Financial Services Authority, a British regulator, found that one-quarter of adults did not realise that their pensions were invested in the stockmarket.

Perhaps financial illiteracy is a key reason for the widespread irrational behaviour identified by BEHAVIOURAL ECONOMICS. That is why economists increasingly argue that financial literacy should be a core component of the education curriculum, perhaps for children aged five, or even younger. When it comes to learning about how MONEY makes the world go round, you cannot start too early.

Financial markets

See CAPITAL MARKETS and MONEY MARKETS.

Financial system

The FIRMS and institutions that together make it possible for MONEY to make the world go round. This includes financial markets, securities exchanges, BANKS, pension funds, mutual funds, insurers, national regulators, such as the Securities and Exchange Commission (SEC) in the United States, CENTRAL BANKS, GOVERNMENTS and multinational institutions, such as the IMF and WORLD BANK.

Fine tuning

A favourite GOVERNMENT policy in the KEYNESIAN-dominated 1950s and 1960s, involving frequent adjustments to FISCAL POLICY and/or MONETARY POLICY to alter the level of DEMAND to keep the economy growing at a steady rate. The trouble was and is, partly because of the inadequacies of economic FORECASTING, that these frequent adjustments were and are often mistaken, making the economy's GROWTH path more, rather than less, erratic. In the 1990s, fine tuning was increasingly shunned by CENTRAL BANKS and governments, which stopped trying to manage short-term demand and instead aimed to pursue long-term macroeconomic goals, which required fewer adjustments to policy. Or so they claimed. In practice, there continued to be some attempted fine tuning.

Firms

For many years, economists had little interest in what happened inside firms, preferring instead to examine the workings of the different sorts of industries in which firms operate, ranging from PERFECT COMPETITION to MONOPOLY. Since the 1960s, however, sophisticated economic theories of how firms work have been developed. These have examined why firms grow at different rates and tried to model the normal life cycle of a company, from fast-growing start-up to lumbering mature business. The aim is to explain when it pays to conduct an activity within a firm and when it pays to externalise it through short- or long-term arrangements with outsiders, be they individuals, exchanges or other companies. The theories also look at the economic consequences of the different incentives influencing individuals working within companies, tackling issues such as pay, AGENCY COSTS and corporate governance structures.

First-mover advantage

The early bird gets the worm. GAME THEORY shows that being the first to enter a market or to introduce an INNOVATION can be a huge advantage, not just because the first firm in can erect BARRIERS TO ENTRY, but also because potential rivals may be discouraged from committing the resources necessary to compete successfully. However, this advantage may sometimes be cancelled out by the benefits enjoyed by followers, such as the chance to avoid – and learn from – the mistakes made by the first mover. (See INCUMBENT ADVANTAGE.)

Fiscal drag

A nice little earner for the state. Fiscal drag is the tendency of revenue from TAXATION to rise as a share of GDP in a growing economy. Tax allowances, progressive tax rates and the threshold above which a particular rate of tax applies usually remain constant or are changed only gradually. By contrast, when the economy grows, INCOME, spending and corporate PROFIT rise. So the tax-take increases too, without any need for GOVERNMENT action. This helps slow the rate of increase in DEMAND, reducing the pace of GROWTH, making it less likely to result in higher INFLATION. Thus fiscal drag is an automatic stabiliser, as it acts naturally to keep demand stable.

Fiscal neutrality

When the net effect of TAXATION and PUBLIC SPENDING is neutral, neither stimulating nor dampening DEMAND. The term can be used to describe the overall stance of FISCAL POLICY: a balanced BUDGET is neutral, as total tax revenue equals total public spending. It can also refer more narrowly to the combined impact of new measures introduced in an annual budget: the budget can be fiscally neutral if any new taxes equal any new spending, even if the overall stance of the budget either boosts or slows demand.

Fiscal policy

One of the two instruments of MACROECONOMIC POLICY; MONETARY POLICY's side-kick. It comprises PUBLIC SPENDING and TAXATION, and any other GOVERNMENT income or assistance to the private sector (such as tax breaks). It can be used to influence the level of DEMAND in the economy, usually with the twin goals of getting UNEMPLOYMENT as low as possible without triggering excessive INFLATION. At times it has been deployed to manage short-term demand through FINE TUNING, although since the end of the KEYNESIAN era it has more often been targeted at long-term goals, with monetary policy more often used for shorter-term adjustments.

For a government, there are two main issues in setting fiscal policy: what should be the overall stance of policy, and what form should its individual parts take?

Some economists and policymakers argue for a BALANCED BUDGET. Others say that a persistent DEFICIT (public spending exceeding revenue) is acceptable provided, in accordance with the GOLDEN RULE, the deficit is used for INVESTMENT (in INFRA-STRUCTURE, say) rather than consumption. However, there may be a danger that public-sector investment will result in the CROWDING OUT of more productive private investment. Whatever the overall stance on average over an economic cycle, most economists agree that fiscal policy should be counter-cyclical, aiming to automatically stabilise demand by increasing public spending relative to revenue when the economy is struggling and increasing taxes relative to spending towards the top of the cycle.

For instance, social (WELFARE) handouts from the state usually increase during tough times, and FISCAL DRAG boosts government revenue when the economy is growing.

As for the bits and pieces making up fiscal policy, one debate is about how high public spending should be relative to GDP. In the United States and many Asian countries, public spending is less than 30% of GDP; in European countries, such as Germany and Sweden, it has been as high as 40–50%. Some economic studies suggest that lower public spending relative to GDP results in higher rates of growth, though this conclusion is controversial. Certainly, over the years, much public spending has been highly inefficient.

Another issue is the form that taxation should take, especially the split between DIRECT TAXATION and INDIRECT TAXATION and between CAPITAL, INCOME and EXPENDITURE TAX.

The global economic crisis that began in 2007 revived the debate about the relative merits of monetary policy and fiscal policy in reviving an economy during a RECESSION or DEPRESSION. Despite many economists continuing to argue that monetary policy offered the best way to boost the economy fast, by cutting INTEREST RATES, governments around the world also implemented massive programmes of fiscal stimulus.

Fixed costs

Production costs that do not change when the quantity of OUTPUT produced changes, for instance, the cost of renting an office or factory space. Contrast with VARIABLE COSTS.

Flotation

Going public. When SHARES in a company are sold to the public for the first time through an initial public offering. The number of shares sold by the original private investors is called the "float". Also, when a BOND issue is sold in the FINANCIAL MARKETS.

Forecasting

Best guesses about the future. Despite complex economic theories and cutting-edge ECONOMETRICS, the forecasts economists make are often badly wrong. Indeed, following economic forecasts has been likened to driving a car blindfolded, following directions given by a person who is looking out of the back window. Some of the inaccuracies in forecasts reflect badly designed models; often, the problem is that the future actually is unpredictable. Maybe it would be better to take the advice of Sam Goldwyn, a movie mogul: "Never prophesy, especially about the future."

Foreign direct investment

Investing directly in production in another country, either by buying a company there or by establishing new operations of an existing business. This is done mostly by companies as opposed to financial institutions, which prefer indirect INVESTMENT abroad such as buying small parcels of a country's supply of SHARES or BONDS. Foreign direct investment (FDI) grew rapidly, starting in the 1990s, before slowing along with the global economy during the crisis that began in 2007. Most of this investment went from one OECD country to another, but the share going to DEVELOPING COUNTRIES, especially in Asia, increased steadily.

There was a time when economists considered FDI as a substitute for trade. Building factories in foreign countries was one way of jumping TARIFF barriers. Now economists typically regard FDI and trade as complementary. For example, a firm can use a factory in one country to supply neighbouring markets. Some investments, especially in SERVICES industries, are essential prerequisites for selling to foreigners. Who would buy a Big Mac in London if it had to be sent from New York?

GOVERNMENTS used to be highly suspicious of FDI, often regarding it as corporate imperialism. Nowadays they are more likely to court it. They hope that investors will create jobs, and bring expertise and technology that will be passed on to local FIRMS and workers, helping to sharpen up their whole economy. Furthermore, unlike financial investors, multinationals generally invest directly in plant and equipment. Since it is hard to uproot a chemicals factory, these investments, once made, are far more enduring than the flows of HOT MONEY that whisk in and out of emerging markets.

MERGERS AND ACQUISITIONS are a significant form of FDI. For instance, in 2007, 92% of the $277 billion of FDI into the United States took the form of mergers rather than of setting up new subsidiaries and opening factories.

Forward contracts

See DERIVATIVES.

Free lunch

There's no such thing. See OPPORTUNITY COST.

Free riding

Getting the benefit of a good or service without paying for it, not necessarily illegally. This may be possible because certain types of goods and SERVICES are actually hard to charge for – a firework display, for instance. Another way to look at this may be that the good or service has a positive EXTERNALITY. However, there can sometimes be a free-rider problem, if the number of people willing to pay for the good or service is not enough to cover the cost of providing it. In this case, the good or service might not be produced, even though it would be beneficial for the economy as a whole to have it. PUBLIC GOODS are often at risk of free riding; in their case, the problem can be overcome by financing the good by imposing a tax on the entire POPULATION.

Free trade

The ability of people to undertake economic transactions with people in other countries free from any restraints imposed by GOVERNMENT or other regulators. Measured by the volume of IMPORTS and EXPORTS, world trade has become increasingly free in the years since the second world war. A fall in barriers to trade, as a result of the GENERAL AGREEMENT ON TARIFFS AND TRADE and its successor, the WORLD TRADE ORGANISATION, has helped stimulate this GROWTH. The volume of world merchandise trade at the start of the 21st century was about 17 times what it was in 1950, and the world's total OUTPUT was not even six times as big. The ratio of world exports to GDP had more than doubled since 1950. Of this, trade in manufactured goods was worth three times the value of trade in SERVICES, although the share of services trade was growing fast.

For economists, the benefits of free trade are explained by the theory of COMPARATIVE ADVANTAGE, with each country doing those things in which it is comparatively more efficient. As long as each country specialises in products in which it has a comparative advantage, trade will be mutually beneficial. Some critics of free trade argue that trade with DEVELOPING COUNTRIES, where WAGES are usually lower and working hours longer than in developed countries, is unfair and will wipe out jobs in high-wage countries. They want AUTARKY or fair trade.

Real-world trade patterns sometimes seem to challenge the theory of comparative advantage (see NEW TRADE THEORY).

Most trade occurs between countries that do not have huge cost differences. The biggest trading partner of the United States, for instance, is Canada. Well over half the exports from France, Germany and Italy go to other EUROPEAN UNION countries. Moreover, these countries sell similar things to each other: cars made in France are exported to Germany, and German cars go to France. The main reason seems to be cross-border differences in consumer tastes. But the agricultural exports of Australia, say, or Saudi Arabia's reliance on OIL, do clearly stem from their particular stock of natural resources. Also poorer countries often have more unskilled labour, so they export simple manufactures such as clothing.

Frictional unemployment

That part of the jobless total caused by people simply changing jobs and taking their time about it, because they are spending time on JOB SEARCH or are taking a break before starting with a new employer. There is likely to be some frictional unemployment even when there is technically FULL EMPLOYMENT, because most people change jobs from time to time.

Friedman, Milton

Loved and loathed; perhaps the most influential economist of his generation. He won the NOBEL PRIZE IN ECONOMICS in 1976, one of many CHICAGO SCHOOL economists to receive that honour. Friedman, who died in 2006 aged 94, was recognised for his achievements in the study of CONSUMPTION, monetary history and theory, and for demonstrating how complex policies aimed at economic STABILISATION can be.

A fierce advocate of free markets, Friedman argued for MON-ETARISM at a time when KEYNESIAN policies were dominant.

Unusually, his work is readily accessible to the layman. He argued that the problems of INFLATION and short-run UNEMPLOYMENT would be solved if the FEDERAL RESERVE had to increase the MONEY SUPPLY at a constant rate.

Like Adam SMITH and Friedrich HAYEK, who inspired him, Friedman praised the free market not just for its economic EFFICIENCY but also for its moral strength. He saw freedom – economic, political and civil – as an end in itself, not a means to an end. It is what makes life worthwhile. He said he would prefer to live in a free country, even if it did not provide a higher standard of living, than a country run by an alternative regime. However, the likelihood of a free country being poorer than an unfree one struck him as implausible; the economic as well as the moral superiority of free markets is, he declared, "now proven".

An adviser to Richard Nixon, he was disappointed when the president went against the spirit of monetarism in 1971 by asking him to urge the chairman of the Federal Reserve to increase the money supply more rapidly. The 1980s economic policies of Margaret Thatcher and General Pinochet were inspired – and defended – by Friedman. However, in 2003, he admitted that one of those policies, the targeting of the money supply, had "not been a success" and that he doubted he would "as of today push it as hard as I once did".

Full employment

Jobs for all that want them. This does not mean zero unemployment because at any point in time some people do not want to work. Also, because some people are always between jobs, there will usually be some FRICTIONAL UNEMPLOYMENT. Full employment means that everyone who wants work and is willing to work at the market wage is in work. Most GOVERNMENTS aim to achieve full employment, although nowadays they rarely try to lower UNEMPLOYMENT below the NAIRU: the lowest jobless rate consistent with stable, low INFLATION.

Fungible

You can't tell them apart. Something is fungible when any one single specimen is indistinguishable from any other. Somebody who is owed $1 does not care which particular dollar he gets. Anything that people want to use as MONEY must be fungible, whether it be GOLD bars, beads or shells.

Futures

See DERIVATIVES.

Gg

G7, G8, G10, G20, G21, G22, G33

"I don't want to belong to any club that will accept me as a member," quipped Groucho Marx. But the world's politicians are desperate to join the economic clubs that are the Group of Seven (G7), G8, G10 and so on. Being a member shows that, economically speaking, your country matters. Alas, beyond making politicians feel good, there has not been much evidence in recent years that they do anything useful, apart from letting GOVERNMENT officials and journalists talk to each other about economics and politics, usually in beautiful locations with lots of fine food and drink on hand.

In 1975, six countries, the world's leading capitalist countries, ranked by GDP, were represented in France at the first annual summit meeting: the United States, the UK, Germany, Japan and Italy, as well as the host country. The following year they were joined by Canada and, in 1977, by representatives of the EURO-PEAN UNION, although the group continued to be known as the G7. At the 1989 summit, 15 developing countries were also represented, although this did not give birth to the G22, which was not set up until 1997 and swiftly grew into the G33. At the 1991 G7 summit, a meeting was held with the Soviet Union, a practice that continued (with Russia) in later years. In 1998, although it was not one of the world's eight richest countries, Russia became a full member of the G8. Meetings of the IMF are attended by the G10, which includes 11 countries – the original members of the G7 as well as representatives of Switzerland, Belgium, Sweden and the Netherlands. In 2003, 21 developing countries, representing half of the world's POPULATION and two-thirds of its farmers, formed the G21 to lobby for more FREE TRADE in AGRICULTURE.

With the growing importance in the global economy of countries other than the traditional rich industrialised nations, the importance of the G8 has declined, but at the same time there has been a rise in the significance of discussions at the G20. Formed in 1999, the G20 brings together 19 countries and the European Union, which together account for 90% of global GDP, 80% of world trade and two-thirds of the people on earth, and thus is much more representative of the global economy than all the other Gs.

Game theory

How to win at Twister? No, but maybe at Monopoly. Game theory is a technique for analysing how people, FIRMS and GOVERNMENTS should behave in strategic situations (in which they must interact with each other), and in deciding what to do must take into account what others are likely to do and how others might respond to what they do. For instance, COMPETITION between two firms can be analysed as a game in which firms play to achieve a long-term COMPETITIVE ADVANTAGE (perhaps even a MONOPOLY). The theory helps each firm to develop its optimal strategy for, say, pricing its products and deciding how much to produce; it can help the firm to anticipate in advance what its competitor will do and shows how best to respond if the competitor does something unexpected. It is particularly useful for understanding behaviour in MONOPOLISTIC COMPETITION.

In game theory, which can be used to describe anything from wage negotiations to arms races, a dominant strategy is one that will deliver the best results for the player, regardless of what anybody else does. One finding of game theory is that there may be a large FIRST-MOVER ADVANTAGE for companies that beat their rivals into a new market or come up with an INNOVATION. One special case identified by the theory is the ZERO-SUM GAME, where players see that the total winnings are fixed; for some to do well, others must lose. Far better is the positive-sum game, in which competitive interaction has the potential to make all the players richer. Another problem analysed by game theorists is the PRISONERS' DILEMMA. (See also NASH EQUILIBRIUM.)

GATT

See GENERAL AGREEMENT ON TARIFFS AND TRADE and WORLD TRADE ORGANISATION.

GDP

Gross domestic product, a measure of economic activity in a country. It is calculated by adding the total value of a country's annual OUTPUT of goods and SERVICES. GDP = private CONSUMPTION + INVESTMENT + PUBLIC SPENDING + the change in inventories + (EXPORTS − IMPORTS). It is usually valued at market PRICES; by subtracting indirect tax and adding any GOVERNMENT SUBSIDY, however, GDP can be calculated at FACTOR COST. This measure more accurately reveals the INCOME paid to FACTORS OF PRODUCTION. Adding income earned by domestic residents from their investments abroad, and subtracting income paid from the country to investors abroad, gives the country's gross national product (GNP).

The effect of INFLATION can be eliminated by measuring GDP GROWTH in constant real prices. However, some economists argue that hitting a nominal GDP target should be the main goal of MACROECONOMIC POLICY. This is because it would remind policymakers to take into account the effect of their decisions on inflation, as well as on growth.

GDP can be calculated in three ways. The income method adds the income of residents (individuals and FIRMS) derived from the production of goods and services. The output method adds the value of output from the different sectors of the economy. The expenditure method totals spending on goods and services produced by residents, before allowing for DEPRECIATION and CAPITAL consumption. As one person's output is another person's income, which in turn becomes expenditure, these three measures ought to be identical. They rarely are because of statistical imperfections. Furthermore, the output and income measures exclude unreported economic activity that takes place in the BLACK ECONOMY but that may be captured by the expenditure measure.

GDP is disliked as an objective of economic policy by some because it is not a perfect measure of WELFARE. It does not include aspects of the good life such as some leisure activities. Nor does it include economically valuable activities that are not paid for, such as parents teaching their children to read. But it does include some things that lower the quality of life, such as activities that damage the environment. One alternative that has been proposed, albeit without much detail, is to try to measure gross national happiness.

Gearing

A company's DEBT expressed as a percentage of its EQUITY; also known as leverage. (See also CAPITAL STRUCTURE and LEVERAGED BUY-OUT.)

General Agreement on Tariffs and Trade

Or GATT, the vehicle for promoting international FREE TRADE, through a series of rounds of negotiations between the GOVERNMENTS of trading countries. The first GATT round began in 1945.

The last led to the establishment of the WORLD TRADE ORGAN-
ISATION in 1995.

General equilibrium

Economic perfection. This is when DEMAND and SUPPLY are in
balance (the market is in EQUILIBRIUM) for each and every good
and service in the economy. Nobody thinks that real-world economies can ever be that perfect; at best there is "partial equilibrium". But most economists think that general equilibrium is
something worth aspiring to.

Generational accounting

A relatively new way of analysing FISCAL POLICY by identifying
the financial costs and benefits of GOVERNMENT policies to
people of different ages, now living or yet to be born. Fiscal policy
can distribute resources between different generations, sometimes
deliberately and often inadvertently. At any moment in time, one
generation may be in work and paying taxes that support other
generations (those at school or retired) that are not working. Over
its lifetime, one generation's mix of taxes paid and benefits
received may differ sharply from that of another generation. Politicians are often tempted to ignore the needs of future generations
(who, clearly, cannot vote at the time) in order to win the support
of current generations, for instance by borrowing heavily to fund
current spending. More fundamentally, because it incorporates all
the tax and spending, current and future, to which a government
is committed, generational accounting is a much better guide to
whether fiscal policy is sustainable than measures such as the
BUDGET DEFICIT, which looks only at taxes and spending in the
current year.

Giffen goods

Named after Robert Giffen (1837–1910), a good for which DEMAND increases as its PRICE rises. But such goods may not exist in the real world.

Gilts

Shorthand for gilt-edged SECURITIES, meaning a safe bet, at least as far as receiving INTEREST and avoiding default goes. The PRICE of gilts can vary considerably over time, however, creating a degree of RISK for investors. Usually the term is applied only to GOVERNMENT BONDS.

Gini coefficient

An INEQUALITY indicator. The Gini coefficient measures the inequality of INCOME distribution within a country. It varies from zero, which indicates perfect equality, with every household earning exactly the same, to one, which implies absolute inequality, with a single household earning a country's entire income. Latin America is the world's most unequal region, with a Gini coefficient of around 0.5; in rich countries the figure is closer to 0.3.

Globalisation

The trend for people, FIRMS and GOVERNMENTS around the world to become increasingly dependent on and integrated with each other. This can be a source of tremendous opportunity, as new markets, workers, business partners, goods and SERVICES and jobs become available, but also of competitive threat, which may undermine economic activities that were viable before globalisation.

The term first surfaced during the 1980s to characterise huge changes that were taking place in the international economy, notably the GROWTH in international trade and in flows of CAPITAL around the world. Globalisation has also been used to describe growing INCOME INEQUALITY between the world's rich and poor; the growing power of multinational companies relative to national government; and the spread of CAPITALISM into former communist countries. Usually, the term is synonymous with international integration, the spread of free markets and policies of LIBERALISATION and FREE TRADE. The process is not the result simply of economic forces. The decisions of policymakers have also played an important part, although not all governments have embraced the change warmly.

The driving force of globalisation has been multinational companies, which since the 1970s have constantly, and often successfully, lobbied governments to make it easier for them to put their skills and capital to work in previously protected national markets. Firms enjoying some national protection, and their (often unionised) workers, have been some of the main opponents of globalisation, along with advocates of FAIR TRADE. In recent years, critics of globalisation have focused increasingly on firms OUTSOURCING (or, more accurately, offshoring) jobs to cheaper workers abroad.

Despite all the talk of globalisation during the 1990s, in some respects the world economy was more integrated in the late 19th century. The LABOUR market was certainly more global. For example, the flow of people out of Europe, 300,000 people a year in the mid-19th century, reached 1m a year after 1900. Now governments are much fussier about immigration, and people are no longer free to migrate as they wish. As for CAPITAL MARKETS, only in the 1990s did international capital flows, relative to the size of the world economy, recover to the levels of the few decades before the first world war.

This early globalised economy did not last for long, however.

Between the two world wars, the flows of trade, capital and people collapsed to a trickle. Even before the first world war, governments started to put up the shutters against migrants and IMPORTS. Could such a backlash against globalisation happen again?

Global public goods

PUBLIC GOODS that cannot be provided by one country acting alone but only by the joint efforts of many (strictly, all) countries. Some economists, along with global institutions such as the UN, reckon that such goods include international law and law enforcement, a stable global FINANCIAL SYSTEM, an open trading system, health, peace and environmental sustainability, especially a stable climate.

GNI

Short for gross national INCOME, a term now used instead of GNP in national accounts.

GNP

Short for gross national product, another measure of a country's economic performance. It is calculated by adding to GDP the INCOME earned by residents from investments abroad, less the corresponding income sent home by foreigners who are living in the country.

Gold

For much of human history gold has been an important ingredient of economic activity. But its importance declined during the

20th century and may continue to shrink in future. The GOLD STANDARD, which fixed EXCHANGE RATES to the value of gold during the 19th and early 20th centuries, has been long abandoned. CENTRAL BANKS, which in 2000 still owned 30,000 tonnes, over one-quarter of all the gold ever mined, no longer feel a need to have large RESERVES of the metal to support the value of their currency. It does not pay them any INTEREST, though they may earn a little by lending it to bullion dealers. So they have started to sell.

GOVERNMENTS and investors have traditionally held gold as a HEDGE against INFLATION and to provide security at times of international crisis. But its role as a store of value has been tarnished. During the 1980s and 1990s, the value of gold generally failed to keep pace with inflation. The LIQUIDITY of gold is also less than that of a foreign currency so it cannot as easily be used for foreign exchange intervention in defence of a currency under attack. In short, gold is no longer a monetary ASSET. It has become just another commodity, although so-called gold-bugs still believe that it remains the thing to have at times of soaring inflation or financial turmoil and uncertainty – which is why its priced soared during the global economic crisis that began in 2007.

Gold standard

A monetary system in which a country backs its currency with a reserve of GOLD, and allows currency holders to exchange their notes and coins for gold. For many years up to 1914, most of the world's leading currencies had their EXCHANGE RATE determined by the gold standard. The economic disruption resulting from the first world war led the combatants to abandon the link to gold. The UK (with others) returned to the gold standard in 1925, before quitting it for good in 1931. The widespread use of the gold standard ended during 1930–33 as a result of global depression and large cuts in international lending. The United States left the gold standard in 1933 and partially returned to it in 1934. After the second world war, a limited form of gold standard continued but only directly applied to the dollar; other major currencies had their exchange rate fixed to the dollar under the BRETTON WOODS arrangements. The dollar was finally cut loose from the gold standard in 1971.

Golden rule

Over the economic cycle, a GOVERNMENT should borrow only to invest and not to finance current spending. This controversial rule is certainly a prudent approach to FISCAL POLICY, provided that governments are honest in describing spending as INVESTMENT, that they invest in appropriate things and do so efficiently, and that they are careful to avoid CROWDING OUT superior private investment. But there are other fiscal policy options that may make as much sense. See, for example, BALANCED BUDGET.

Government

There are few more hotly debated topics in ECONOMICS than what role the state should play in the economy. Plenty of economists provided intellectual support for state intervention during the era of big government, particularly from the 1930s to the 1980s. KEYNESIANS argued that the state should manage the amount of DEMAND in the economy to maintain FULL EMPLOYMENT. Others advocated a COMMAND ECONOMY, in which the government would decide PRICE levels, oversee the allocation of scarce resources and run the most important parts of the economy (the "commanding heights") or, in communist countries, the entire economy. The role of the state increased at the expense of MARKET FORCES. Economists provided plenty of examples of MARKET FAILURE that seemed to justify this.

From the 1950s onwards there was growing evidence that government intervention could also be flawed, and often imposed even greater costs on an economy than market failure. One reason is that when a government acts, it usually does so as a MONOPOLY, with all the attendant economic inefficiencies this implies.

In practice, policies of Keynesian demand management often resulted in INFLATION, and thus lost much of their credibility. There was growing concern that public INVESTMENT was CROWDING OUT superior private investment, and that other PUBLIC SPENDING on things such as health care, education and pensions was similarly discouraging private provision. Government management of commercial enterprises was often seen to be inefficient and, starting in the 1980s, NATIONALISATION gave way to PRIVATISATION. Even when the state was not directly responsible for economic activity, but instead set the rules governing private behaviour, there was evidence of REGULATORY FAILURE. High rates of taxation started to discourage people and companies from undertaking economic activities that would, without the tax, have been profitable; wealth creation suffered.

Most economists agree that there is a need for some government role in the economy. A market economy can function only if there is an adequate legal system, and, in particular, clearly defined, enforceable PROPERTY RIGHTS. The legal system is probably an example of what economists call a PUBLIC GOOD (although the existence in many countries and industries of some self-regulation shows it is not always so).

Although politicians in many countries spent most of the period since 1980 talking about the need to reduce the role of the state in the economy, and in many cases introduced policies of privatisation, DEREGULATION and LIBERALISATION to help this happen, public spending continued to increase as a share of GDP. Within the OECD, public spending accounted for a larger slice of GDP in 2008 than in 1990, which was in turn higher than in 1980. Indeed, it has risen during every decade since the start of the 20th century. One reason was that governments had to honour spending commitments on pensions and health care made by previous generations of politicians.

The global economic crisis that began in 2007 ushered in a new era of activist government. Vast sums of MONEY were pumped into the FINANCIAL SYSTEM to shore it up, and some governments even moved towards the nationalisation of some BANKS by buying SHARES in them. Government spending soared as fiscal stimulus packages sought to prevent sharp declines in economic activity. In large part, this expansion of government was the result of necessity. Yet it also reflected a change in the intellectual climate, as faith declined sharply in the abilities of business leaders, especially those working in the FINANCIAL MARKETS, and the public turned for solutions to politicians. The multitrillion-dollar question was whether these politicians had learnt anything from past government failures so that government would not only become bigger but also better.

Government bonds

See BONDS and GILTS.

Government debt

See FISCAL POLICY and NATIONAL DEBT.

Government expenditure

Spending by national and local GOVERNMENT and some government-backed institutions. See FISCAL POLICY, GOLDEN RULE and BUDGET.

Government revenue

See TAXATION.

Government-sponsored enterprise

Giant mortgage-lenders Fannie Mae and Freddie Mac were the two most prominent American government-sponsored enterprises (GSEs) until they were rescued by the GOVERNMENT in 2008 amid feverish speculation that the economic crisis that began a year earlier would cause them to fail, with catastrophic consequences. Fannie (the nickname of the Federal National Mortgage Association) and Freddie (the Federal Home Loan Mortgage Corporation) were both created by the government to support the development of home ownership among those who could not previously afford their own place. Fannie was founded during the Great DEPRESSION of the 1930s and Freddie in 1970. Although both were public companies, not owned by the government, the perception that the government, which "sponsored" their creation, would bail them out if they got into difficulties created a classic MORAL HAZARD. They were able to grow rapidly because investors stumped up vast amounts of MONEY to buy the SECURITIES they issued, assuming that they were in reality protected from losses by the government – an assumption that turned out to be correct. For years before they were rescued, their rapid GROWTH had alarmed critics. Early in 2005, ALAN GREENSPAN told Congress that by letting these two GSEs grow unchecked, "we are placing the total FINANCIAL SYSTEM of the future at a substantial RISK". He was right.

Great moderation

For about two decades starting in the mid-1980s there was a sharp decline in macroeconomic VOLATILITY, particularly in the United States. During that period, the variability of quarterly GROWTH in real OUTPUT declined by half, and the variability of quarterly INFLATION declined by about two-thirds. James Stock, a Harvard economist, coined the phrase "great moderation" in 2002 to describe this flattening of the BUSINESS CYCLE, and two years later it was popularised in a speech by Ben Bernanke, who was to succeed ALAN GREENSPAN as chairman of the FEDERAL RESERVE in 2006. Alas, just as everyone was getting used to the great moderation, in 2007 the global economy fell into crisis, and instead economists started worrying about another Great DEPRESSION.

Greenspan, Alan

The most famous of all CENTRAL BANK bosses, so far. A former jazz musician turned economist, he became chairman of the board of governors of America's FEDERAL RESERVE in 1987, shortly before Wall Street crashed. He held the post until 2006, shortly before Wall Street crashed again. He won admirers for delivering MONETARY POLICY that helped to bring down INFLATION and create the conditions for strong economic GROWTH. Some people considered him the nearest thing CAPITALISM had to God. In 1996, he famously wondered aloud whether rising SHARE PRICES were the result of "irrational exuberance". However, many economists have pinned on him much of the blame for the global economic crisis that began in 2007, because he did not prevent the growth of a huge BUBBLE in America's economy, the bursting of which helped to trigger the crisis.

Gresham's law

Bad MONEY drives out good. One of the oldest laws in economics, named after Sir Thomas Gresham, an adviser to Queen Elizabeth I of England. He observed that when a currency has been debased and a new one is introduced to replace it, the new one will be hoarded and effectively taken out of circulation, while the old one will continue to be used for transactions, to be got rid of as fast as possible.

Gross domestic product

See GDP.

Gross national product

See GNP.

Growth

What economic activity is all about, but how can it be made to happen? Economists have plenty of theories, but none of them has all the answers.

Adam SMITH attributed growth to the INVISIBLE HAND, a view shared by most followers of CLASSICAL ECONOMICS. NEO-CLASSICAL ECONOMICS had a different theory of growth, devised by Robert Solow during the 1950s. This argued that a sustained increase in INVESTMENT increases an economy's growth rate only temporarily: the ratio of CAPITAL to LABOUR goes up, the MAR-GINAL product of capital declines and the economy moves back to a long-term growth path. OUTPUT will then increase at the same rate as the growth in the workforce (quality-adjusted, in later ver-sions) plus a factor to reflect improvements in PRODUCTIVITY.

This theory predicts specific relationships among some basic economic statistics. Yet some of these predictions fail to fit the facts. For example, income disparities among countries are greater than the differences in their SAVINGS rates would suggest. Moreover, although the model says that economic growth ultimately depends on the rate of technological change, it fails to explain exactly what determines this rate. Technological change is treated as EXOGENOUS.

Some economists argued that doing this ignored the main engine of growth. They developed a new growth theory, in which improvements in productivity were ENDOGENOUS, meaning that they were the result of things taking place within the economic model being used and not merely assumed to happen, as in the neo-classical models. Endogenous growth was due, in particular, to technological INNOVATION and investments in HUMAN CAPITAL. In looking for explanations for differences in rates of growth, including between rich and DEVELOPING COUNTRIES, the new growth theory concentrates on what the incentives are in an economy to create additional human capital and to invent new products.

Factors determining these incentives include GOVERNMENT policies. Countries with broadly free-market policies, in particular FREE TRADE and the maintenance of secure PROPERTY RIGHTS, typically have higher growth rates. Open economies have grown much faster on average than closed economies. Higher PUBLIC SPENDING relative to GDP is generally associated with slower growth. Also bad for growth are high INFLATION and political instability.

As countries grew richer during the 20th century, annual growth rates declined as a result of DIMINISHING RETURNS on capital. By 1990, most developed countries reckoned to have long-term trend growth rates of 2–2.5% a year. However, during the 1990s, growth rates started to rise, especially in the United States. Some economists said this was the result of the birth of a NEW

ECONOMY based on a revolution in productivity, largely because of rapid technological innovation but also (perhaps directly stemming from the spread of new technology) to increases in the value of human capital.

> *Ask five economists and you'll get five different answers – six if one went to Harvard.*
> Edgar Fiedler, economist

GSE

See GOVERNMENT-SPONSORED ENTERPRISE.

Hard currency

MONEY you can TRUST. A hard currency is expected to retain its value, or even benefit from APPRECIATION, against softer currencies. This makes it a popular choice for people involved in international transactions. The dollar, D-mark, sterling and the Swiss franc each became a hard currency, if only some of the time, during the 20th century.

Hawala

An ancient system of moving MONEY based on TRUST. It predates western BANK practices. Although it is now more associated with the Middle East, a version of *hawala* existed in China in the second half of the Tang dynasty (618–907), known as *fei qian*, or flying money. In *hawala*, no money moves physically between locations; nowadays it is transferred by means of a telephone call, fax or e-mail between dealers in different countries. No legal contracts are involved, and recipients are given only a code number or simple token, such as a low-value banknote torn in half, to prove that money is due. Over time, transactions in opposite directions cancel each other out, so physical movement is minimised. Trust is the only CAPITAL that the dealers have. With it, the users of *hawala* have a worldwide money-transmission service that is cheap, fast and free of bureaucracy.

From a GOVERNMENT'S point of view, however, informal money networks are threatening, since they lie outside official channels that are regulated and taxed. They fear they are used by criminals, including terrorists. Although this is probably true, by far the main users of *hawala* networks are overseas workers, who do not trust official money transfer methods or cannot afford them, remitting earnings to their families.

Hayek, Friedrich

An influential economist of the Austrian school, who won the NOBEL PRIZE IN ECONOMICS in 1974 for his theory of the BUSINESS CYCLE many years after this body of work seemed to have been disproved by KEYNES. Born in 1899, Hayek attended his home-town University of Vienna after the first world war. He was attracted to SOCIALISM until he read a pioneering Austrian economist, Ludwig von Mises, on the subject, after which, he said, "the world was never the same again".

Hayek argued that the business cycle originated from expanded CREDIT CREATION by BANKS, which was followed by FIRMS and people making mistaken CAPITAL INVESTMENTS in producing things for which the market turns out to be smaller (or larger) than expected. But after an initially enthusiastic reception, the Austrian business-cycle theory lost out in policy debates to Keynes's General Theory. After the second world war, Hayek was a leading member of the CHICAGO SCHOOL along with Milton FRIEDMAN, among others.

Hayek was a noted proponent of the free-market system and a critic of state planning. His 1944 book, *The Road to Serfdom*, anticipated the demise of COMMAND ECONOMIES that sought to suppress PRICE signals. This prediction came from his belief in the limits of human reason and his faith in the superior ability of CAPITALISM to make efficient use of limited INFORMATION and to learn by trial and error. His views, which echo Adam SMITH's INVISIBLE HAND, are said to have inspired the free-market economic reforms undertaken in the 1980s by Margaret Thatcher and Ronald Reagan. He died in 1992.

Hedge

Reducing your RISKS. Hedging involves deliberately taking on a new risk that offsets an existing one, such as your exposure to an adverse change in an EXCHANGE RATE, INTEREST RATE or COMMODITY PRICE. Imagine, for example, that you are British and you are to be paid $1m in three months' time. You are worried that the dollar may have fallen in value by then, thus reducing the number of pounds you will be able to convert the $1m into. You can hedge away that currency risk by buying $1m worth of pounds at the current exchange rate (in effect) in the futures market. Hedging is most often done by commodity producers and traders, financial institutions and, increasingly, by non-financial FIRMS.

It used to be fashionable for firms to hedge by following a policy of DIVERSIFICATION. More recently, firms have hedged using FINANCIAL INSTRUMENTS and DERIVATIVES. Another popular strategy is to use "natural" hedges wherever possible. For example, if a company is setting up a factory in a particular country, it might finance it by borrowing in the currency of that country. An extension of this idea is operational hedging – for example, relocating production facilities to get a better match of costs in a given currency to revenue.

Hedging sounds prudent, but some economists reckon that firms should not do it because it reduces their value to shareholders. In the 1950s, two economists, Merton Miller (1923–2000) and Franco Modigliani, argued that firms make money only if they make good INVESTMENTS, the kind that increase their operating cash flow. Whether these investments are financed through DEBT, EQUITY or retained earnings is irrelevant. Different methods of financing simply determine how a firm's value is divided between its various sorts of investors (for example, shareholders or bondholders), not the value itself. This surprising insight helped win each of them a NOBEL PRIZE FOR ECONOMICS. If they are right, there are big implications for hedging. If methods of financing and the character of financial risks do not matter, managing them is pointless. It cannot add to the firm's value; on the contrary, as hedging does not come free, doing it might actually lower that value. Moreover, argued Miller and Modigliani, if investors want to avoid the financial risks attached to holding shares in a firm, they can diversify their portfolio of shareholdings. Firms need not manage their financial risks; investors can do it for themselves. Few managers agree.

Hedge funds

These bogey-men of the FINANCIAL MARKETS are often blamed, usually unfairly, when things go wrong – most recently for helping to turn the CREDIT CRUNCH of 2007 into a full-blown global economic crisis by SHORTING (and naked shorting) BANK shares. There is no simple definition of a hedge fund (few of them actually HEDGE). But they all aim to maximise their absolute RETURNS rather than relative ones; that is, they concentrate on making as much MONEY as possible, not (like many mutual funds) simply on outperforming an index. Although they are often accused of disrupting financial markets by their SPECULATION, their willingness to bet against the herd of other investors may push security PRICES closer to their true fundamental values, not away. The amount of money invested in hedge funds grew rapidly from the early 1990s until 2008, when many funds went out of business as investors took their money back to avoid further losses.

Herfindahl-Hirschman index

A warning signal of possible MONOPOLY. ANTITRUST economists often gauge the competitiveness of an industry by measuring the extent to which its OUTPUT is concentrated among a few FIRMS. One such measure is a Herfindahl-Hirschman index. To calculate it, take the market share of each firm in the industry, square it, then add them all up. If there are 100 equal-sized firms (a market with close to PERFECT COMPETITION), the index is 100. If there are four equal-sized firms (possible OLIGOPOLY), it will be 2,500. The higher the Herfindahl number, the more concentrated is market power.

The main virtue of the Herfindahl is its simplicity. But it has two unfortunate shortcomings. It relies on defining correctly the industry or market for which the degree of competitiveness is open to question. This is rarely simple and can be a matter of fierce debate. Even when the scope of the market is clear, the relation between the Herfindahl and market power is not. When there is a CONTESTABLE MARKET, even a firm with a Herfindahl of 10,000 (the classic definition of a monopoly) may behave as if it was in a perfectly competitive market.

Homo economicus

See ECONOMIC MAN.

Horizontal equity

One way to keep TAXATION fair. Horizontal equity means that people with a similar ability to pay taxes should pay the same amount. (See EQUITY and VERTICAL EQUITY.)

Horizontal integration

Merging with another firm just like yours; for example, two biscuitmakers becoming one. Contrast with VERTICAL INTEGRATION, which is merging with a firm at a different stage in the SUPPLY chain. Horizontal integration often raises ANTITRUST concerns, as the combined firm will have a larger market share than either firm did before merging.

Hot money

MONEY that is held in one currency but is liable to switch to another currency at a moment's notice in search of the highest available RETURNS, thereby causing the first currency's EXCHANGE RATE to plummet. It is often used to describe the money invested in currency markets by speculators.

House prices

When they go through the roof it is usually a warning sign that an economy is overheating. House prices often rise after INTEREST RATE reductions, which lower mortgage payments and thus give buyers the ability to fund a larger amount of borrowing and so offer a higher price for their new home. Strangely, people often regard house-price INFLATION as good news, even though it creates as many losers as gainers. They argue that rising house prices help to boost consumer confidence and are part of the WEALTH EFFECT: as house prices rise, people feel wealthier and so spend more. However, against this must be set a negative wealth effect. An increase in house prices makes many people worse off, such as first-time buyers and anyone planning to trade up to a better property. A fall in house prices, such as the one that followed the bursting of the housing BUBBLE in the United States in 2006–07, can have severe economic consequences – for consumers, for investors who fund mortgages and also for ENTREPRENEURS, who often use their homes as COLLATERAL for loans they take out to fund new businesses.

As long as people think that their house is a vehicle for SPECULATION, rather than merely accommodation, it seems inevitable that prices will be volatile, prone to a boom-bust cycle. As house prices rise, profits are made, tempting more speculative buyers into the market; eventually, they start to pay too much, interest rates rise, DEMAND falls and prices plunge. People have also invested in housing as a HEDGE against INFLATION: house prices generally rise when other prices rise, whereas the real value of mortgage debt is eroded by inflation. However, when mortgage interest rates are variable (as they generally are in the UK) rather than fixed (as in the United States), they may rise painfully during times of high inflation as a result of MACROECONOMIC POLICY efforts to slow the pace of economic GROWTH.

One of the reasons the United States has long-term fixed mortgage rates is the financing provided by GOVERNMENT-SPONSORED ENTERPRISES such as the Federal National Mortgage Association and the Federal Home Loan Mortgage Corporation, nicknamed, respectively, Fannie Mae and Freddie Mac. Economists increasingly debate their role, especially as they have grown into some of the world's largest lenders. Supporters claim that, as well as reducing macroeconomic VOLATILITY, they make housing more affordable, particularly for poorer people, and that other governments should play a similar role in the mortgage market. Critics argued that Fannie and Freddie had become a huge potential risk in the global FINANCIAL SYSTEM even before they were bailed out by the government in 2008.

Human capital

The stuff that enables people to earn a living. Human capital can be increased by investing in education, training and health care. Economists increasingly argue that the accumulation of human as well as physical CAPITAL (plant and machinery) is a crucial ingredient of economic GROWTH, particularly in the NEW ECONOMY. Even so, this conclusion is largely a matter of theory and faith, rather than the result of detailed empirical analysis. Economists have made little progress in solving the tricky problem of how to measure human capital, even within the same country over time, let alone for comparisons between countries. Levels of spending on, say, education are not necessarily a good indicator of how much human capital an education system is creating; indeed, some economists argue that higher education spending may be a consequence of a country becoming wealthy rather than a cause. Nevertheless, even modest estimates of the stock of human capital in most countries suggests that it would pay to greatly increase INVESTMENT in medical technologies that would extend the working lives of most people. The non-economic benefits would be worth having, too.

Human Development Index

The "good life" guide. Calculated since 1990 by the United Nations Development Programme, the Human Development Index quantifies a country's development in terms of such things as education, length of life and clean water, as well as INCOME. Since the mid-1970s, the quality of life for humans throughout the world has improved enormously overall. America's human development index rose by around one-tenth between 1975 and 2001, for example. More spectacularly, during the same period, China's rose by around 40% and Indonesia's by nearly 50%. Even so, in 2001 some 54 countries were poorer than they were in 1990, and in 34, mostly in Africa and the former Soviet Union, life expectancy had fallen, reversing an impressive long-term trend, largely because of the HIV/AIDS epidemic and crime. Some 21 countries had a lower overall human development index in 2003 than in 1990.

Hyperinflation

Very, very bad. Although people debate when, precisely, rapid INFLATION turns into hyperinflation (a 100% or more increase in prices a year, perhaps?) nobody questions that it wreaks huge economic damage. After the first world war, German prices at one point were rising at a rate of 23,000% a year before the country's economic system collapsed, creating a political opportunity grasped by the Nazis. In former Yugoslavia in 1993, prices rose by around 20% a day. In July 2008, Zimbabwe's official inflation rate reached an astonishing 231,000,000%. Typically, hyperinflation quickly leads to a complete loss of confidence in a country's currency, and causes people to search for other forms of MONEY that are a better store of value. These may include physical ASSETS, GOLD and foreign currency. Hyperinflation might be easier to live with if it was stable, as people could plan on the basis that PRICES would rise at a fast but predictable rate. However, there are no examples of stable hyperinflation, precisely because it occurs only when there is a crisis of confidence across the economy, with all the behavioural unpredictability this implies.

Hypothecation

Earmarking taxes for a specific purpose. It may be a clever way to get around public hostility to paying more in TAXATION. If people are told that a specific share of their INCOME TAX will go to some popular cause, say education or health, they may be more willing to cough up. At the very least they may be forced to make more informed decisions about the trade-offs between taxes and public SERVICES. There is a downside, however. Hypothecated taxes may tie the hands of a GOVERNMENT at times when the hypothecated revenue could be spent to better effect elsewhere in the public sector. Conversely, and perhaps more likely, hypothecated taxes may prove to be less hypothecated than the public is led to believe. Civil servants, doubtless under pressure from their political bosses, can usually find ways to fudge the definition of the specific purpose for which a tax is hypothecated, letting government regain control over how the money is spent.

Hysteresis

Lagging; slow to respond. Traditionally, economists believed that high UNEMPLOYMENT was a cyclical phenomenon. Eventually, unemployment would cause people to lower their wage demands, and so new job opportunities would arise and unemployment would fall. More recently, however, economists have suggested that some unemployed people, especially the long-term jobless, can display hysteresis. They find it hard, perhaps impossible, to return to work, even when jobs become available. For instance, unemployed workers may gradually lose the motivation, self-confidence or the self-discipline needed to get to the workplace and fulfil job requirements. Or their skills may become outdated and redundant. State benefits for the jobless may contribute to this hysteresis by making it easier from them to stay out of work.

ILO

Short for International Labour Organisation, founded in 1919 as part of the Treaty of Versailles, which created the League of Nations. In 1946, it became the first specialised agency of the UN. Based in Geneva, it formulates international LABOUR standards, setting out desired minimum rights for workers: freedom of association; the right to organise and engage in collective bargaining; equality of opportunity and treatment; and the abolition of forced labour. It also compiles international labour statistics. One reason for its formation was the hope that international labour standards would stop countries using lower standards to gain a COMPETITIVE ADVANTAGE. From the 1980s onwards, the ILO approach came under attack as attention turned to the costs of high labour standards, notably slower economic GROWTH. Universal minimum labour standards might also work against FREE TRADE. Imposing rich-country labour standards on poorer countries might help keep the rich rich and the poor poor.

IMF

Short for International Monetary Fund, referee and, when the need arises, rescuer of the world's FINANCIAL SYSTEM. The IMF was set up in 1944 at BRETTON WOODS, along with the WORLD BANK, to supervise the newly established fixed EXCHANGE RATE system. After this fell apart in 1971-73, the IMF became more involved with its member countries' economic policies, doling out advice on FISCAL POLICY and MONETARY POLICY as well as microeconomic changes such as PRIVATISATION, of which it became a forceful advocate. In the 1980s, it played a leading part in sorting out the problems of DEVELOPING COUNTRIES' mounting DEBT. More recently, it has several times co-ordinated and helped to finance assistance to countries with a currency crisis.

The Fund has been criticised for the CONDITIONALITY of its support, which is usually given only if the recipient country promises to implement IMF-approved economic reforms. Unfortunately, the IMF has often approved "one size fits all" policies that, not much later, turned out to be inappropriate. However, it cannot force a country to do anything, unless the country decides to accept its MONEY. The IMF has also been accused of creating MORAL HAZARD, in effect encouraging GOVERNMENTS (and FIRMS, BANKS and other investors) to behave recklessly by giving them reason to expect that if things go badly the Fund will organise a bail-out. Indeed, some financiers have described an INVESTMENT in a financially shaky country as a "moral-hazard play" because they were so confident that the Fund would ensure the safety of their money, one way or another. Following the economic crisis in Asia during the late 1990s, and again after the crisis in Argentina in the early 2000s, some policymakers argued (to no avail) for the IMF to be abolished, as the absence of its safety net would encourage more prudent behaviour all round. More sympathetic folk argued that the IMF should evolve into a global LENDER OF LAST RESORT. The global economic crisis that began in 2007 prompted further debate on what role the IMF should play in future.

Imperfect competition

See MONOPOLISTIC COMPETITION and OLIGOPOLY.

Imports

Purchases of foreign goods and SERVICES; the opposite of EXPORTS.

Income

The flow of MONEY to the FACTORS OF PRODUCTION: WAGES to LABOUR; profit to ENTERPRISE and CAPITAL; INTEREST also to capital; RENT to LAND. Wages left for spending after paying taxes is known as disposable income. For countries, see NATIONAL INCOME.

Income effect

A change in the DEMAND for a good or service caused by a change in the INCOME of consumers rather than, say, a change in consumer tastes. Contrast with SUBSTITUTION EFFECT.

Income tax

A much-loathed method of TAXATION based on earnings. It was first collected in 1797 by the Dutch Batavian Republic. In the UK it was introduced in 1799 as a "temporary" measure to finance a war against Napoleon, abolished in 1816 and reintroduced, forever, in 1842. In most countries, people do not pay it until their INCOME exceeds a minimum threshold, and richer people pay a higher rate of income tax than poorer people. Since the 1980s, the unpopularity with voters of high rates of income tax and concern that high rates discourage valuable economic activity have led many GOVERNMENTS to reduce income-tax rates. However, this has not necessarily reduced the amount of total revenue collected in income tax (see LAFFER CURVE). Nor do governments that have reduced income tax rates always cut other sorts of taxes; on the contrary, they have often increased them sharply to make up for any revenue lost as a result of lower rates of income tax.

Incumbent advantage

The importance of being there already. FIRMS that are in a market can have a significant COMPETITIVE ADVANTAGE over aspiring entrants to that market, for instance, through having the opportunity to erect BARRIERS TO ENTRY. (See FIRST-MOVER ADVANTAGE.)

Indexation

Keeping pace with INFLATION. In many countries, WAGES, pensions, UNEMPLOYMENT benefits and some other sorts of INCOME are automatically raised according to recent movements in the consumer PRICE index. This allows these different sorts of income to retain their value in REAL TERMS.

Index numbers

Economists love to compile indices aggregating lots of individual data, so they can analyse broad trends in the behaviour of an economy. INFLATION is measured by an index of consumer (retail) PRICES. There are indices of all sorts of things that are bought and sold of which perhaps the best known are SHARE price indices like the Dow Jones Industrial Average or FTSE 100. The main challenges in compiling an index are what, exactly, to include in it and what weight to give the different things that are included. A particularly tricky question is how to change an index over time. Measures of inflation are based on the price of a basket of things bought by a typical consumer. As the quality and choice of products in the basket change over time, the inflation index ought to take this into account. How, exactly, is much debated.

Indifference curve

A curve that joins together different combinations of goods and SERVICES that would each give the consumer the same amount of satisfaction (UTILITY). In other words, consumers are indifferent to which of the combinations they get.

Indirect taxation

Taxes that do not come straight out of a person's pay packet or ASSETS, or out of company PROFIT. For example, a CONSUMPTION tax, such as VALUE-ADDED tax (see EXPENDITURE TAX). Contrast with DIRECT TAXATION, such as INCOME TAX. Indirect taxation has become increasingly popular with politicians because it may be less noticeable to people paying it than income tax and is harder to avoid paying.

Inelastic

When the SUPPLY or DEMAND for something is insensitive to changes in another variable, such as PRICE. (See ELASTICITY.)

Inequality

Does economic GROWTH create more or less equality? Do unequal societies grow more or less slowly than equal ones? Economists have debated these questions for as long as anyone can remember. One problem is to agree which sort of inequality matters: equality of outcome (that is, INCOME) or of opportunity? Another is how then to measure it. Equality of opportunity, which, in theory, should make a difference to growth, because it is about giving people the chance to make the most of their HUMAN CAPITAL, is probably beyond the ability of statisticians to analyse rigorously. The most often used measure of income inequality is the GINI COEFFICIENT.

The evidence suggests that extreme POVERTY is more likely to slow growth than income inequality itself. This is because very poor people cannot buy the education they need to enable them to become richer and their children may be forced to forgo schooling in order to work for money.

Economic growth has generally reduced inequality within a country. This has been partly as a result of redistributive tax and benefits systems, which have become so significant that they may now be causing slower growth in some countries. The availability of WELFARE benefits may have discouraged unemployed people from seeking out a better job; and the high taxes needed to pay for the benefits may have discouraged some wealthy people from working as hard as they would have done under a friendlier tax regime. However, from the mid-1990s, inequality in rich countries began to widen significantly because of an increasingly winner-takes-all distribution of financial rewards. This growing inequality became a matter of growing political debate, particularly with regard to the soaring pay of corporate bosses. It remains to be seen if the global economic crisis that began in 2007 will end the trend for growing rich-country inequality, or instead perhaps accelerate it.

Infant industry

A favourite argument of protectionists is that new industries should be spared the rigours of international trade and foreign competitors for a few years, until the domestic firms in the industry are strong enough to compete with foreign rivals. Free traders counter that unrestrained COMPETITION helps make infant industries strong.

Inferior goods

Products that are less in demand as consumers get richer. For NORMAL GOODS, DEMAND increases as consumers have more to spend.

Inflation

Rising PRICES, across the board. Inflation means less bang for your buck, as it erodes the purchasing power of a unit of currency. Inflation usually refers to CONSUMER PRICES, but it can also be applied to other prices (wholesale goods, WAGES, ASSETS, and so on). It is usually expressed as an annual percentage rate of change on an INDEX NUMBER. For much of human history inflation has not been an important part of economic life. Before 1930, prices were as likely to fall as rise during any given year, and in the LONG RUN these ups and downs usually cancelled each other out. By contrast, by the end of the 20th century, 60-year-old Americans had seen prices rise by over 1,000% during their lifetime. The most spectacular period of inflation in industrialised countries took place during the 1970s, partly as a result of sharp increases in OIL prices implemented by the OPEC CARTEL. Although these countries have mostly regained control over inflation since the 1980s, it continued to be a source of serious problems in many developing countries.

Inflation would not do much damage if it were predictable, as everybody could build into their decision-making the prospect of higher prices in future. In practice, it is unpredictable, which means that people are often surprised by price increases. This reduces economic EFFICIENCY, not least because people take fewer risks to minimise the chances of suffering too severely from a PRICE SHOCK. The faster the rate of inflation, the harder it is to predict future inflation. Indeed, this uncertainty can cause people to lose confidence in a currency as a store of value. This is why HYPERINFLATION is so damaging.

Most economists agree that an economy is most likely to function efficiently if inflation is low. Ideally, MACROECONOMIC POLICY should aim for stable prices. Some economists argue that a low level of inflation can be a good thing, however, if it is a result of INNOVATION. New products are launched at high prices, which quickly come down through COMPETITION. Most economists reckon that DEFLATION (falling AVERAGE prices) is best avoided.

To keep inflation low you need to know what causes it. Economists have plenty of theories but no absolutely cast-iron conclusions. Inflation, Milton FRIEDMAN once said, "is always and everywhere a monetary phenomenon". Monetarists reckon that to stabilise prices the rate of GROWTH of the MONEY SUPPLY needs to be carefully controlled. However, implementing this has proven difficult, as the relationship between measures of the money supply identified by monetarists and the rate of inflation has typically broken down as soon as policymakers have tried to target it. KEYNESIAN economists believe that inflation can occur independently of monetary conditions. Other economists focus on the importance of institutional factors, such as whether the INTEREST RATE is set by politicians or (preferably) by an independent CENTRAL BANK, and whether that central bank is set an INFLATION TARGET.

Is there a relationship between inflation and the level of unemployment? In the 1950s, the PHILLIPS CURVE seemed to indicate that policymakers could trade off higher inflation for lower UNEMPLOYMENT. Later experience suggested that although inflating the economy could lower unemployment in the short run, in the long run you ended up with unemployment at least as high as before and rising inflation as well. Economists then came up with the idea of the NAIRU (non-accelerating inflation rate of unemployment), the rate of unemployment below which inflation would start to accelerate. However, in the late 1990s, in both the United States and the UK, the unemployment rate fell well below what most economists thought was the NAIRU yet inflation did not pick up. This caused some economists to argue that technological and other changes wrought by the NEW ECONOMY meant that inflation was dead. Others argued that sound MONETARY POLICY, including low inflation targets, had led the public to lower their inflation expectations, which in turn helped to lower inflation as people no longer automatically demanded much higher wages or set much higher prices as they had done when they expected high inflation. Traditionalists said it was merely resting.

Inflation target

The goal of MONETARY POLICY in many countries is to ensure that INFLATION is neither to high nor too low. It became fashionable during the 1990s to set a country's CENTRAL BANK an explicit rate of inflation to target. By 1998, some 54 central banks had an inflation target, compared with just eight at the end of 1990, the year in which New Zealand's Reserve Bank became the first to be set a target. In most industrialised countries, the target, or, typically, the mid-point of a target range, for consumer-price inflation is between 1% and 2.5%. The reasons it is not zero are that official price indices overstate inflation and that these countries would prefer a little inflation to any DEFLATION.

Monetary policy takes time to have an impact. So central banks usually base their policy changes on a forecast of inflation, not its current rate. If forecast inflation in two years' time, say, is above the target, INTEREST RATES are raised. If it is below target, rates are cut.

Why have an inflation target? Setting an inflation target usually goes hand-in-hand with allowing a central bank considerable discretion in setting policy, so TRANSPARENCY in its decision-making is vital and is therefore usually increased as part of the process of adopting a target. More fundamentally, by making it easier to judge whether policy is on track, an inflation target makes it easier to hold a central bank to account for its performance. The pay of central bankers can be designed to reward them for achieving the target. But some central bankers argue that an inflation target restricts their policy flexibility too much, which is one reason the world's most powerful central bank, America's FEDERAL RESERVE, has argued (so far successfully) against having one.

Although for most of the past two decades, consumer prices have performed broadly in line with the target in countries that have them, some economists argue that targeting consumer prices distracted central bankers from the broader problem of controlling asset prices, a failure which ultimately led to a BUBBLE and, in turn, starting in 2007, to a global economic crisis.

Information

The oil that keeps the economy working smoothly. Economic EFFICIENCY is likely to be greatest when information is comprehensive, accurate and cheaply available. Many of the problems facing economies arise from people making decisions without all the information they need. One reason for the failure of the COMMAND ECONOMY is that GOVERNMENT planners were not good at gathering and processing information. Adam SMITH's metaphor of the INVISIBLE HAND is all about how, in many cases, free markets are much more efficient at processing information on the needs of all the participants in an economy than is the visible, and often dead, hand of state planners. ASYMMETRIC INFORMATION, when one party to a deal knows more than the other party, can be a serious source of inefficiency and MARKET FAILURE. Uncertainty can also impose large economic costs. The internet, by greatly increasing the availability and lowering the price of information, is helping to boost economic efficiency. But there are inefficiencies the internet will not be able to solve. Uncertainty will remain a huge source of economic inefficiency. Alas, potentially the most useful information, about what will happen in the future, is never available until it is too late.

Infrastructure

The economic arteries and veins. Roads, ports, railways, airports, power lines, pipes and wires that enable people, goods, commodities, water, energy and INFORMATION to move about efficiently. Increasingly, infrastructure is regarded as a crucial source of economic COMPETITIVENESS. INVESTMENT in infrastructure can yield unusually high RETURNS because it increases people's choices: of where to live and work, what to consume, what sort of economic activities to carry out, and of other people to communicate with. Some parts of a country's infrastructure may be a natural MONOPOLY, such as water pipes. Others, such as traffic lights, may be PUBLIC GOODS. Some may have a NETWORK EFFECT, such as telephone cables. Each of these factors has encouraged GOVERNMENT provision of infrastructure, often with the familiar downsides of state intervention: bad planning, inefficient delivery and CORRUPTION. Investing in infrastructure was a central plank of many fiscal stimulus programmes launched by governments around the world in response to the economic crisis that started in 2007.

Innovation

A vital contributor to economic growth. The big challenge for FIRMS and GOVERNMENTS is to make it happen more often. Although nobody is entirely sure why innovation takes place, new theories of ENDOGENOUS GROWTH try to model the innovation process, rather than just assume it happens for unexplained, EXOGENOUS reasons. The role of incentives seems to be particularly important. Although some innovations are the result of scientists and others engaging in the noble pursuit of knowledge, most, especially their commercial applications, are the result of ENTREPRENEURS seeking PROFIT. Joseph SCHUMPETER described this as a process of "creative destruction". A firm innovates successfully and is rewarded with unusually high profits, which in turn encourages rivals to come up with a superior innovation.

To encourage innovation, innovators must be allowed to make a decent profit, otherwise they will not incur the RISK and expense of trying to come up with useful innovations. Most countries have PATENTS and other laws protecting INTELLECTUAL PROPERTY, which allow innovators to enjoy a (usually temporary) MONOPOLY over their innovation. Economists disagree over how long that protection should last, given the inefficiencies that result from any monopoly.

For most of the second half of the 20th century, governments played a crucial role in funding and directing pure research and early-stage development. In the 1980s, however, legal changes in the United States started to reduce this role. One change aimed to move technological development out of the country's state-financed national laboratories. Another allowed universities, not-for-profit research institutes and small businesses doing research under government contract to keep the technologies they had developed and to apply for patents in their own names. This appears to have contributed to a surge in innovation in the United States, as government researchers and university professors teamed up with outside firms, or started their own. Hoping for similar results, many other countries have followed suit.

Is innovation all it is cracked up to be, or is it just change for change's sake? A few years ago, Robert Solow, a Nobel Prize-winning economist, observed that "you can see the computer age everywhere these days except in the PRODUCTIVITY statistics". Although new computer technology clearly had affected people and firms in visible and obvious ways, the slowdown in productivity growth that had afflicted the American economy since the 1970s did not appear to have been reversed. Believers in the NEW ECONOMY argued that the "Solow Paradox" no longer held true; in the late 1990s, the computer revolution started to deliver the productivity growth long promised. Even so, this shows that innovation can take a long time to deliver the goods.

Insider trading

A practice that was made illegal in the United States in 1934 and in the UK in 1980, and is now banned (for SHARES, at least) in most countries. Insider trading involves using INFORMATION that is not in the public domain but that will move the PRICE of a share, BOND or currency when it is made public. An insider trade takes place when someone with privileged, confidential access to that information trades to take advantage of the fact that prices will move when the news gets out. This is frowned on because investors may lose confidence in FINANCIAL MARKETS if they see insiders taking advantage of advantageous ASYMMETRIC INFORMATION to enrich themselves at the expense of outsiders. But some economists reckon that insider trading leads to more efficient markets: by transmitting the inside information to the market, it makes the price of, say, a company's shares more accurate. This may be true, but most financial regulators are willing to sacrifice a degree of accuracy in pricing to ensure that outsiders (the great majority of investors) feel they are being treated fairly.

Institutional economics

A Darwinian version of the dismal science, also known as evolutionary ECONOMICS. At one time the dominant school of economics in the United States, it views the economy as an evolving system and places a strong emphasis on dynamics, changing structures (including technologies, institutions, beliefs and behaviour) and DISEQUILIBRIUM processes (such as INNOVATION, selection and imitation). Early giants of institutional economics include Thorstein Veblen, author of *The Theory of the Leisure Class*, and Adolphe Berle, co-author with Gardiner Means of *The Modern Corporation and Private Property*, an influential early theory of the modern FIRM which highlighted the AGENCY COSTS arising from the separation of ownership and management.

In recent years, there has been a revival of interest in the role that institutions play in the economy. This "new institutional economics" argued that institutions should be integrated into NEOCLASSICAL ECONOMICS as a solution to some of the problems caused by dispersed and ASYMMETRIC INFORMATION. This approach initially argued that institutions were rational solutions to these problems, but increasingly insights into the irrationality of some institutions have been added from BEHAVIOURAL ECONOMICS. In 1993, the leading practitioner of new institutional economics, Douglass North, was awarded a Nobel Prize.

Institutional investors

The big hitters of the FINANCIAL MARKETS: pension funds, fund-management companies, INSURANCE companies, investment BANKS, HEDGE FUNDS, charitable endowment trusts. In the United States, around half of publicly traded shares are owned by institutions and half by individual investors. In the UK, institutions own over two-thirds of listed SHARES. This gives them considerable clout, including the ability to move the PRICES in financial markets and to call company bosses to account. But because institutions mostly invest other people's MONEY, they are themselves prone to AGENCY COSTS, sometimes acting against the best long-term interests of the people who trust them with their SAVINGS.

Insurance

In economic terms, anything used to reduce the downside of RISK. In its most familiar form, insurance is provided through a policy purchased from an insurance company. But a fuller definition would also include, say, a financial security (or anything else) used to HEDGE, as well as assistance available in the event of disaster. It could even be provided by the GOVERNMENT, in various ways, including WELFARE payments to sick or poor people and legal protection from CREDITORS in the event of BANKRUPTCY.

Conventional insurance works by pooling the risks of many people (or FIRMS, and so on), all of whom might claim but in practice only a few actually do. The cost of providing assistance to those that claim is spread over all the potential claimants, thus making the insurance affordable to all.

Despite the enormous attraction of insurance, private markets in insurance often work badly, or not at all. Economists have identified three main reasons for this:

- Private firms are unwilling to provide insurance if they are uncertain about the likely cost of providing sufficient cover, especially if it is potentially unlimited.

- MORAL HAZARD means that people with insurance may take greater risks because they know they are protected, so the insurer may get a bigger bill than it bargained for.

- Insurers are at risk of ADVERSE SELECTION. The people who are most likely to claim buy insurance, and those who are least likely to claim do not buy it. In this situation, setting a price for insurance that will generate enough premiums to cover all claims is tricky, if not impossible.

Insurers have found ways of reducing the impact of these problems. For example, to counter adverse selection, they set higher health-insurance rates for people who smoke. To limit moral hazard, they offer reduced premiums to people who agree to pay the first so-many dollars or pounds of any claim.

An efficient system of insurance, in its broadest sense, can contribute to economic growth by encouraging entrepreneurial risk-taking and by enabling people to choose which risks they take and which they protect themselves against.

Intangible assets

Valuable things, even though you cannot drop them on your foot – an idea, say, especially one protected by a patent; an effective corporate culture; human capital; a popular BRAND. Contrast with TANGIBLE ASSETS.

Intellectual capital

The part of a country's or a FIRM'S CAPITAL or an individual's HUMAN CAPITAL that consists of ideas rather than something more physical. It can often be protected through PATENTS or other INTELLECTUAL PROPERTY laws.

Intellectual property

Ownership of a stake in the economic value of an idea, such as trade marks or PATENTS. INNOVATION is encouraged by strong intellectual property laws, as they provide innovators with a means to earn MONEY on their innovations by allowing a temporary MONOPOLY. Attempts to ensure that intellectual property rights granted in one country are honoured in others has been a controversial element in the construction of the WORLD TRADE ORGANISATION, with some DEVELOPING COUNTRIES objecting that intellectual property rights simply allow companies from rich countries to impose their higher costs on poor countries. Generally, however, these arguments have not stopped the spread of intellectual property laws throughout the world – though getting the laws properly enforced in some countries is another matter.

Interest

The cost of borrowing, which compensates lenders for the RISK they take in making their MONEY available to borrowers. Without interest there would be little lending and thus a lot less economic activity. The charging of interest is contrary to Sharia (Islamic) law, being considered USURY. Some American states also have usury laws, imposing tough conditions on the terms set by lenders, although not actually prohibiting interest. Yet, as the recent rise of a substantial banking industry in Islamic Middle Eastern countries shows, when economic GROWTH is a priority, ways can usually be found to pay lenders to lend.

Interest rate

INTEREST is usually expressed at an annual rate: the amount of interest that would be paid during a year divided by the amount of MONEY loaned. Developed economies offer many different interest rates, reflecting the length of the loan and the riskiness and wealth of the borrower. People often use the term "interest rate" when they mean the short-term interest rate charged to BANKS. For instance, when a CENTRAL BANK raises or cuts interest rates, it changes only the price it charges to banks borrowing money overnight, expressed as an annual rate. BOND yields are a better measure of the interest rate on loans that do not have to be repaid for many years. Unlike short-term interest rates, bond yields are determined not by central bankers but by the SUPPLY of and DEMAND for money, which is heavily influenced by the expected rate of INFLATION.

International aid

A helping hand for poor countries from rich countries. This, at least, is the intention. In practice, in many cases aid has done little good for its intended recipients (improved health care is a notable exception) and has sometimes made matters worse. Poor countries that receive lots of aid grow no faster, on average, than those that receive very little. By contrast, perhaps the most successful aid programme ever – the MARSHALL PLAN for rebuilding Europe after the second world war – involved rich countries giving to other hitherto rich countries.

During the second half of the 20th century rich countries gave over $1 trillion in aid to poor ones. During the 1990s, however, flows of official aid stagnated. In 2001, official aid was a little over $50 billion, roughly one-quarter of the GDP of donor countries. On top of this were private-sector donations from NGOs worth an estimated $6 billion. Increasingly, such sums were exceeded by private FOREIGN DIRECT INVESTMENT and REMITTANCES. In an attempt to reinvigorate international aid, in 2000 the UN committed itself to eight ambitious Millennium Development Goals for reducing global POVERTY by 2015. At the G8 summit in 2005, the world's richest countries committed themselves to a sharp increase in aid to the poorest nations, along with DEBT FORGIVENESS and further trade LIBERALISATION.

Why has aid achieved so little? Donations have often ended

up in the offshore bank accounts of corrupt politicians and officials in poor countries. MONEY has often been given with strings attached, so that much of this "tied" aid is spent on companies and corrupt politicians and officials in the donor country. War has ravaged many potentially beneficial aid projects. Moreover, some aid has been motivated by political goals – for example, shoring up anti-communist governments – rather than economic ones.

The lesson of history is that aid will often be wasted, or cause harm, unless it is carefully aimed at countries with a genuine commitment to sound economic management. Analysis by the WORLD BANK sorted 56 aid-receiving countries by the quality of their economic management. Those with good policies (low INFLATION, a BUDGET surplus and openness to trade) and good institutions (little CORRUPTION, strong rule of law, effective bureaucracy) benefited from the aid they received. Those with poor policies and institutions did not. This accounts for the growing popularity of CONDITIONALITY in aid.

International Labour Organisation

See ILO.

International Monetary Fund

See IMF.

International trade

See FREE TRADE.

Intervention

When CENTRAL BANKS try to influence an EXCHANGE RATE by buying the currency they want to appreciate and selling the one they want to weaken. The evidence seems to suggest that it is at best a short-term measure. In the longer term, GOVERNMENTS probably do not have the resources to beat MARKET FORCES.

Investment

Putting MONEY to work, in the hope of making even more money. Investment takes two main forms: direct spending on buildings, machinery and so forth, and indirect spending on financial SECURITIES, such as BONDS and SHARES.

Traditionally, economic theory says that a country's total investment must equal its total SAVINGS. But this has never been true in the short run and, as a result of GLOBALISATION, may never be even in the LONG RUN, as countries with low savings can attract investment from overseas and foreign savers lacking opportunities at home can invest abroad (see FOREIGN DIRECT INVESTMENT).

The more of its GDP a country invests, the faster its economy should grow. This is why GOVERNMENTS try so hard to increase total investment, for instance, using tax breaks and SUBSIDY, or direct PUBLIC SPENDING on INFRASTRUCTURE. However, recent evidence suggests that the best way to encourage private-sector investment is to pursue a stable MACROECONOMIC POLICY, with low INFLATION, low INTEREST RATES and low rates of TAXATION. Curiously, economic studies have not found evidence that higher levels of investment lead to higher rates of GDP GROWTH. One explanation for this is that the circumstances and manner in which money is invested count at least as much as the total sums invested. It ain't how much you do, it's the way that you do it.

Invisible hand

Adam SMITH's shorthand for the ability of the free market to allocate FACTORS OF PRODUCTION, goods and SERVICES to their most valuable use. If everybody acts from self-interest, spurred on by the PROFIT motive, the economy will work more efficiently, and more productively, than it would do were economic activity directed instead by some sort of central planner. It is, wrote Smith, as if an "invisible hand" guides the actions of individuals to combine for the common good. Smith recognised that the invisible hand was not infallible, however, and that some GOVERNMENT action might be needed, such as to impose ANTITRUST laws, enforce PROPERTY RIGHTS, and to provide policing and national defence.

Invisible trade

EXPORTS and IMPORTS of things you cannot touch or see: SERVICES such as banking or ADVERTISING, and other intangibles such as copyrights. Invisible trade accounts for a growing slice of the value of world trade.

Inward investment

Investment from abroad; the opposite of outward investment (see FOREIGN DIRECT INVESTMENT).

Irrational exuberance

ALAN GREENSPAN's famous description in 1996 of the American public's enthusiasm for buying overpriced SHARES. Every BUBBLE is the product of some form of irrational exuberance.

J-curve

The shape of the trend of a country's trade balance following a DEVALUATION. A lower EXCHANGE RATE initially means cheaper EXPORTS and more expensive IMPORTS, making the current account worse (a bigger DEFICIT or smaller surplus). After a while, though, the volume of exports will start to rise because of their lower PRICE to foreign buyers, and domestic consumers will buy fewer of the costlier imports. Eventually, the trade balance will improve on what it was before the devaluation. If there is a currency APPRECIATION there may be an inverted J-curve.

Job search

The time taken to find a new job. Because some people will devote all their time to this search, there will always be some FRICTIONAL UNEMPLOYMENT, even when there is otherwise FULL EMPLOYMENT.

Joint supply

Some products or production processes have more than one use. For instance, cows can both provide milk and be eaten. If farmers increase the number of cows they own in response to an increase in DEMAND for milk, they are also likely to increase, a little later, the SUPPLY of meat, causing beef prices to fall.

Keynes, John Maynard

A much quoted, great British economist, not famous for holding the same opinion for long. Born in 1883, he studied at Cambridge but came to reject much of the CLASSICAL ECONOMICS and NEO-CLASSICAL ECONOMICS associated with that university. Keynes helped set up the BRETTON WOODS framework, but he is best known for his *General Theory of Employment, Interest and Money*, published in 1936 in the depths of the Great DEPRESSION. This invented modern MACROECONOMICS. It argued that economies could sometimes be stable (in EQUILIBRIUM) even when they did not have FULL EMPLOYMENT, but that a GOVERNMENT could remedy this under-employment problem by increasing PUBLIC SPENDING and/or reducing TAXATION, thereby increasing the level of aggregate DEMAND in the economy. Many politicians picked up on these ideas. As President Richard Nixon observed in 1971, "We are all Keynesians now." However, it is much debated whether Keynes would have supported the way many of them put his thoughts into practice.

Keynes identified the economic importance of ANIMAL SPIRITS. Making and losing fortunes in the FINANCIAL MARKETS led him to refer to the "casino CAPITALISM" of the stockmarket. He also noted that "there is nothing so dangerous as the pursuit of a rational INVESTMENT policy in an irrational world". He had an amusingly accurate view of the impact and transmission of economic ideas: "Practical men, who believe themselves to be quite exempt from any intellectual influences, are usually the slaves of some defunct economist." As for the frequency with which his opinions would evolve: "When the facts change, I change my mind – what do you do, sir?" "In the LONG RUN we are all dead," he said. For him, the long run arrived in 1946.

Keynesian

A branch of ECONOMICS, based, often loosely, on the ideas of KEYNES, characterised by a belief in active GOVERNMENT and suspicion of market outcomes. It was dominant in the 30 years following the second world war, and especially during the 1960s, when FISCAL POLICY became bigger-spending and looser in most developed countries as policymakers tried to kill off the BUSINESS CYCLE. During the 1970s, widely blamed for the rise in INFLATION, Keynesian policies gradually gave way to MONETARISM and microeconomic policies that owed much to the NEO-CLASSICAL ECONOMICS that Keynes had at times opposed. Even so, the idea that PUBLIC SPENDING and TAXATION have a crucial role to play in managing DEMAND, in order to move towards FULL EMPLOYMENT, remained at the heart of MACROECONOMIC POLICY in most countries, even after the monetarist and supply-side revolution of the 1980s and 1990s.

Recently, a school of new, more pro-market Keynesian economists has emerged, believing that most markets work, but sometimes only slowly. In reaction to the global economic crisis that began in 2007, there was a revival of enthusiasm for Keynesian ideas, as governments sharply increased public spending in an effort to prevent economic disaster.

Kleptocracy

Corrupt, thieving GOVERNMENT, in which the politicians and bureaucrats in charge use the powers of the state to feather their own nests. Russia in the years immediately after the fall of COMMUNISM was a clear-cut example, with Mafia-friendly government members allocating themselves valuable shares during the PRIVATISATION of state-owned companies, accepting bribes from foreign businesses, not collecting taxes from "helpful" companies and siphoning off INTERNATIONAL AID into their personal OFFSHORE BANK accounts.

Kondratieff wave

A 50-year-long BUSINESS CYCLE, named after Nikolai Kondratieff, a Russian economist. He claimed to have identified cycles of economic activity lasting half a century or more in his 1925 book, *The Long Waves in Economic Life*. Because this implied that CAPITALISM was, ultimately, a stable system, in contrast to the Marxist view that it was self-destructively unstable, he ended up in one of Stalin's prisons, where he died. Alas, there is little hard evidence to support Kondratieff's conclusion.

Labour

One of the factors of production, with LAND, CAPITAL and ENTER-PRISE. Among the things that determine the SUPPLY of labour are the number of able people in the POPULATION, their willingness to work, labour laws and regulations, and the health of the economy and FIRMS. DEMAND for labour is also affected by the health of the economy and firms, labour laws and regulations, as well as the PRICE and supply of other factors of production.

In a perfect market, WAGES (the price of labour) would be determined by supply and demand. But the labour market is often far from perfect. Wages can be less flexible than other prices; in particular, they rarely fall even when demand for labour declines or supply increases. This wage rigidity can be a cause of UNEMPLOYMENT.

Labour intensive

A production process that involves large amounts of LABOUR; the opposite of CAPITAL INTENSIVE.

Labour market flexibility

A flexible LABOUR market is one in which it is easy and inexpensive for FIRMS to vary the amount of labour they use, including by changing the hours worked by each employee and the number of employees. This often means minimal REGULATION of the terms of employment (no MINIMUM WAGE, say) and weak (or no) trade UNIONS. Such flexibility is characterised by its opponents as giving firms all the power, allowing them to fire employees at a moment's notice and leaving workers feeling insecure.

Opponents of labour market flexibility claim that labour laws that make workers feel more secure encourage employees to invest in acquiring skills that enable them to do their current job better but that could not be taken with them to another firm if they were let go. Supporters claim that it improves economic EFFI-CIENCY by leaving it to MARKET FORCES to decide the terms of employment. Broadly speaking, the evidence is that greater flexibility is associated with lower rates of UNEMPLOYMENT and higher GDP per head.

Labour theory of value

The notion that the value of any good or service depends on how much LABOUR it uses up. First suggested by Adam SMITH, it took a central place in the philosophy of Karl MARX. Some neo-classical economists disagreed with this theory, arguing that the PRICE of something was independent of how much labour went into producing it and was instead determined solely by SUPPLY and DEMAND.

Laffer curve

Legend has it that in November 1974 Arthur Laffer, a young economist, drew a curve on a napkin in a Washington bar, linking AVERAGE tax rates to total tax revenue. Initially, higher tax rates would increase revenue, but at some point further increases in tax rates would cause revenue to fall, for instance by discouraging people from working. The curve became an icon of supply-side ECONOMICS. Some economists said that it proved that most GOV-ERNMENTS could raise more revenue by cutting tax rates, an argument that was often cited in the 1980s by the tax-cutting governments of Ronald Reagan and Margaret Thatcher. Other economists reckoned that most countries were still at a point on the curve at which raising tax rates would increase revenue. The lack of empirical evidence meant that nobody could really be sure where the United States and other countries were on the Laffer curve. However, after the Reagan administration cut tax rates revenue fell at first. American tax rates were already low compared with some countries, especially in continental Europe, and it remains possible that these countries are at a point on the Laffer curve where cutting tax rates would pay.

Lagging indicators

Old news. Some economic statistics move weeks or months after changes in the BUSINESS CYCLE or INFLATION. They may not be a reliable guide to the current state of an economy or its future path. Contrast with LEADING INDICATORS.

Laissez-faire

Let-it-be ECONOMICS: the belief that an economy functions best when there is no interference by GOVERNMENT. It can be traced to the 18th-century French physiocrats, who believed in government according to the natural order and opposed MERCANTILISM. Adam SMITH and others turned it into a central tenet of CLASSICAL ECONOMICS, as it allowed the INVISIBLE HAND to operate efficiently. (But even they saw a need for some limited government role in the economy.) In the 19th century, it inspired the British political movement that secured the repeal of the Corn Laws and promoted FREE TRADE, and gave birth to *The Economist* in 1843. In the 20th century, laissez-faire was often seen as synonymous with supporting MONOPOLY and allowing the BUSINESS

CYCLE to boom and bust, and it came off second best against KEYNESIAN policies of interventionist government. However, mounting evidence of the inefficiency of state intervention inspired the free market policies of Ronald Reagan and Margaret Thatcher in the 1980s, both of whom stressed the importance of laissez-faire.

After nearly three decades of intellectual ascendancy, however, the validity of this approach to economics was called into question by the global economic crisis that began in 2007. In 2008, the French president, Nicolas Sarkozy, declared: "Laissez-faire, c'est fini."

Land

One of the factors of production, along with LABOUR, CAPITAL and ENTERPRISE. Pending colonisation of the moon, it is in fairly fixed SUPPLY. Marginal increases are possible by reclaiming land from the sea and cutting down forests (which may impose large economic costs by damaging the environment), but the expansion of deserts may slightly reduce the amount of usable land. Owners earn MONEY from land by charging RENT.

Land tax

Henry George, a 19th-century American economist, believed that taxes should be levied only on the value of LAND, not on LABOUR or CAPITAL. This "single tax", he asserted in his book, *Progress and Poverty*, would end UNEMPLOYMENT, POVERTY, INFLATION and INEQUALITY. Many countries levy some tax on land or property values, although George's single tax has never been fully implemented. This is mainly because of fears that it would drive down land prices too much or discourage efforts to improve the quality (that is, the economic value) of land. George addressed this concern by arguing that the tax should be levied only against the value of "unimproved" land. Certainly, a land tax has obvious advantages: it is simple and cheap to levy; evasion is all but impossible; and it penalises owners who do not put their land to work.

Law and economics

Laws can be an important source of economic EFFICIENCY – or inefficiency. Early economists such as Adam SMITH often wrote about the economic impact of legal matters. But economics subsequently focused more narrowly on things monetary and commercial. It was only in the 1940s and 1950s, at the University of Chicago Law School, that the discipline of law and economics was born. It is now a substantial branch of ECONOMICS and has had an impact beyond the ivory towers.

Until recently, the "economics" of law and economics was firmly in the LIBERAL ECONOMICS camp, favouring free markets and arguing that REGULATION often does more harm than good. Its growth went hand-in-hand with the revival of the LAISSEZ-FAIRE thinking that was championed by Ronald Reagan and Margaret Thatcher. It stressed the economic value of having clear, enforceable PROPERTY RIGHTS, and of ensuring that these can be bought and sold. It encouraged many ANTITRUST policymakers to focus on maximising consumer WELFARE, rather than, say, protecting small FIRMS or opposing big ones just because they are big. It also ventured into broader sociological issues, such as analysing the economic causes of criminality and how to structure legal incentives to reduce crime. (See also INSTITUTIONAL ECONOMICS.)

More recently, academic practitioners of law and economics have approached the subject more broadly, not always staying true to the liberal economics of the pioneers of the subject.

LBO

See LEVERAGED BUY-OUT.

Leading indicators

Economic crystal balls. Also known as cyclical indicators, these are groups of statistics that point to the future direction of the economy and the BUSINESS CYCLE. Certain economic variables, fairly consistently, precede changes in GDP and certain others precede changes in INFLATION. In some countries, statisticians combine the various different leading indicators into an overall leading index of economic GROWTH or inflation. However, there is not necessarily any causal relationship between the leading indicators and what they are predicting, which is why, like other crystal balls, they are fallible. Contrast with LAGGING INDICATORS.

Lender of last resort

One of the main functions of a CENTRAL BANK. When financially troubled BANKS need cash and nobody else will lend to them, a central bank may do so, perhaps with strings attached, or even by taking control of the troubled bank, closing it or finding it a new owner. This role of the central bank makes CREDIT CREATION easier by increasing confidence in the banking system and minimising the RISK of a bank run by reassuring depositors that their MONEY is safe. However, it also creates a potential MORAL HAZARD: that banks will lend more recklessly because they know they will be bailed out if things go wrong.

Leverage

See GEARING.

Leveraged buy-out

Buying a company using borrowed MONEY to pay most of the purchase PRICE. The DEBT is secured against the ASSETS of the company being acquired. The INTEREST will be paid out of the company's future cash flow. Leveraged buy-outs (LBOS) became popular in the United States during the 1980s, as public debt markets grew rapidly and opened up to borrowers that would not previously have been able to raise loans worth millions of dollars to pursue what was often an unwilling target. They were popular again during the easy-credit years in the mid-2000s, by then rebranded as PRIVATE EQUITY. Although some LBOS end up with the borrower going bust, in most cases the need to meet demanding interest bills drives the new managers to run the firm more efficiently than their predecessors. For this reason, some economists see LBOS as a way of tackling AGENCY COSTS associated with corporate governance.

Liberal economics

LAISSEZ-FAIRE CAPITALISM by another name.

Liberalisation

A policy of promoting LIBERAL ECONOMICS by limiting the role of GOVERNMENT to the things it can do to help the market economy work efficiently. This can include PRIVATISATION and DEREGULATION.

LIBOR

Short for London interbank offered rate, the rate of INTEREST that top-quality BANKS charge each other for loans. As a result, it is often used by banks as a base for calculating the INTEREST RATE they charge on other loans. LIBOR is a floating rate, changing all the time.

Life

Human life is priceless. But this has not stopped economists trying to put a financial value on it. One reason is to help FIRMS and policymakers to make better decisions on how much to spend on costly safety measures designed to reduce the loss of life. Another is to help insurers and courts judge how much compensation to pay in the event of, say, a fatal accident.

One way to value a life is to calculate a person's HUMAN CAPITAL by working out how much he or she would earn were they to survive to a ripe old age. This could result in very different sums being paid to victims of the same accident. After an air crash, probably more MONEY would go to the family of a first-class passenger than to that of someone flying economy. This may not seem fair. Nor would using this method to decide what to spend on safety measures, as it would mean much higher expenditure on avoiding the death of, say, an investment banker than on saving the life of a teacher or coal miner. It would also imply spending more on safety measures for young people and being positively reckless with the lives of retired people.

Another approach is to analyse the RISKS that people are voluntarily willing to take, and how much they require to be paid for taking them. Taking into account differences in WAGES for high death-risk and low death-risk jobs, and allowing for differences in education, experience, and so on, it is possible to calculate roughly what value people put on their own lives. In industrialised countries, most studies using this method come up with a value of $5m–10m.

Life-cycle hypothesis

An attempt to explain the way that people split their INCOME between spending and saving, and the way that they borrow. Over their lifetime, a typical person's spending varies by far less than their income because of "CONSUMPTION smoothing". On average, young people have low incomes but big spending commitments: on investing in their human capital through education and training, building a family, buying a home, and so on. So they do not save much and often borrow heavily. As they get older their income generally rises, they pay off their mortgage, the children leave home and they prepare for retirement, so they sharply increase their saving and INVESTMENT. In retirement, their income is largely or entirely from state benefits and the SAVINGS and investments they made when working; they spend most or all of their income, and, by selling off ASSETS, often spend more than their income.

Broadly, this theory is supported by the data, though some economists argue that young people do not spend as much as they should on, say, being educated, because lenders are reluctant to extend CREDIT to them. One puzzle is that people often have substantial assets left when they die. Some economists say this is because they want to leave a generous inheritance for their relatives; others say that people are simply far too optimistic about how long they will live. (See also PERMANENT INCOME HYPOTHESIS and RELATIVE INCOME HYPOTHESIS.)

Liquidity

How easily an ASSET can be spent, if so desired. Cash is wholly liquid. The liquidity of other assets is usually less; how much less may be measured by the ease with which they can be exchanged for cash (that is, liquidated). Public FINANCIAL MARKETS try to maximise the liquidity of assets such as BONDS and EQUITIES by providing a central meeting place (the exchange) in which would-be buyers and sellers can easily find each other. Financial market-makers (middlemen such as investment BANKS) can also increase liquidity by using some of their CAPITAL to buy SECURITIES from those who want to sell, when there is no other buyer offering a decent PRICE. They do this in the expectation that if they hold the asset for a while they will be able to find somebody to buy it. Typically, the higher the volume of trades happening in a marketplace, the greater is its liquidity. Moreover, highly liquid markets attract more liquidity-seeking traders, further increasing liquidity.

In a similar way, there can be vicious cycles in which liquidity dries up. The amount of liquidity in financial markets can vary enormously from one moment to the next, and can sometimes evaporate entirely, especially if market makers become too RISK AVERSE to put their capital at risk in this way. This was the case in the CREDIT CRUNCH of 2007, and even more so following the BANKRUPTCY of Lehman Brothers in 2008, plunging the global economy into crisis.

Liquidity preference

The proportion of their ASSETS that FIRMS and individuals choose to hold in varying degrees of LIQUIDITY. The more cash they have, the greater is their desire for liquidity.

Liquidity premium

Because LIQUIDITY can disappear, investors have to pay a premium if they want to be sure they can sell an ASSET at the time of their choosing. The size of that liquidity premium can vary enormously over time depending on the mood of the market.

Liquidity trap

When MONETARY POLICY becomes impotent. Cutting the rate of INTEREST is supposed to be the escape route from economic RECESSION, boosting the MONEY SUPPLY, increasing DEMAND and thus reducing UNEMPLOYMENT. But KEYNES argued that sometimes cutting the rate of interest, even to zero, would not help. People, BANKS and FIRMS could become so RISK AVERSE that they preferred the liquidity of cash to offering CREDIT or using the credit that is on offer. In such circumstances, the economy would be trapped in recession, despite the best efforts of monetary policymakers.

KEYNESIANS reckon that in the 1930s the economies of both the United States and the UK were caught in a liquidity trap. In the late 1990s, the Japanese economy suffered a similar fate. But monetarism has no place for liquidity traps. Monetarists pin the blame for the Great DEPRESSION and Japan's more recent troubles on other factors and reckon that ways could have been found to make monetary policy work.

Lock-in

See PATH DEPENDENCE.

Long run

When we are all dead, according to KEYNES. Unimpressed by the thrust of CLASSICAL ECONOMICS, which said that economies have a long-run tendency to settle in EQUILIBRIUM at FULL EMPLOYMENT, he wanted economists to try to explain why in the short run economies are so often in DISEQUILIBRIUM, or in equilibrium at high levels of UNEMPLOYMENT.

Long tail

In 2004, inspired by a statistical feature identified in the 1940s, Chris Anderson, editor of *Wired* magazine, coined the phrase "the long tail" to describe the niche strategy of a new wave of (mostly) internet-based businesses, such as Amazon, which sold many different items often in small quantities. This was in contrast to traditional mass-production strategies based on selling a few items in large quantities. Anderson argued that products that are in low DEMAND or have low sales volume can collectively make up a market share that rivals or exceeds the few current bestsellers and blockbusters, if the store or distribution channel is large enough. Internet economics, such as the low cost of ADVERTISING and distribution, created an opportunity for many more profitable long tail products.

Lump of labour fallacy

One of the best-known fallacies in ECONOMICS is the notion that there is a fixed amount of work to be done – a lump of LABOUR – which can be shared out in different ways to create fewer or more jobs. For instance, suppose that everybody worked 10% fewer hours. FIRMS would need to hire more workers. Hey presto, UNEMPLOYMENT would shrink.

In 1891 D.F. Schloss, an economist, described such thinking as the lump of labour fallacy because, in reality, the amount of work to be done is not fixed. GOVERNMENT-imposed restrictions on the amount of work people may do can actually reduce the EFFICIENCY of the labour market, thereby increasing unemployment. Shorter hours will create more jobs only if weekly pay is also cut (which workers are likely to resist), otherwise costs per unit of OUTPUT will rise. Not all labour costs vary with the number of hours worked. FIXED costs, such as recruitment and training, can be substantial, so it will cost a firm more to hire two part-time workers than one full-timer. Thus a cut in the working week may raise AVERAGE costs per unit of output and cause firms to buy fewer total hours of labour. A better way to reduce unemployment may be to stimulate DEMAND and so increase output; another is to make the labour market more flexible, not less.

Lump-sum tax

A tax that is the same amount for everybody, regardless of INCOME or wealth. Some economists argue that this is the most efficient form of TAXATION, as it does not distort incentives and thus it has no DEADWEIGHT COST. This is because each person knows that whatever they do they will have to pay the same amount. It is also cheap to administer, as there is no complex process of measuring each person's income and ASSETS in order to calculate their tax bill. However, because rich and poor people pay the same, the tax may be perceived as unfair – as Margaret Thatcher found out when she introduced a lump-sum "poll tax", a decision that was later to play a large part in her ousting as British prime minister.

Luxuries

Goods and SERVICES that have a high ELASTICITY of DEMAND. When the PRICE of, say, a Caribbean holiday rises, the number of vacations demanded falls sharply. Likewise, demand for Caribbean holidays rises significantly as AVERAGE INCOME increases, certainly by more than demand for many NORMAL GOODS. Contrast this with necessities, such as milk or bread, which people usually demand in similar quantities whatever their income and whatever the price.

Macroeconomics

The big picture: analysing economy-wide phenomena such as GROWTH, INFLATION and UNEMPLOYMENT. Contrast with MICROECONOMICS, the study of the behaviour of individual markets, workers, households and FIRMS. Although economists generally separate themselves into distinct macro and micro camps, macroeconomic phenomena are the product of all the microeconomic activity in an economy. The precise relationship between macro and micro is not particularly well understood, which has often made it difficult for a GOVERNMENT to deliver well-run MACROECONOMIC POLICY.

Macroeconomic policy

Top-down policy by GOVERNMENT and CENTRAL BANKS, usually intended to maximise GROWTH while keeping down INFLATION and UNEMPLOYMENT. The main instruments of macroeconomic policy are changes in the rate of INTEREST and MONEY SUPPLY, known as MONETARY POLICY, and changes in TAXATION and PUBLIC SPENDING, known as FISCAL POLICY. The fact that unemployment and inflation often rise sharply, and that growth often slows or GDP falls, may be evidence of poorly executed macroeconomic policy. However, BUSINESS CYCLES may simply be an unavoidable fact of economic life that macroeconomic policy, however well conducted, can never be sure of conquering.

Manufacturing

Making things like cars or frozen food has shrunk in importance in most developed countries during the past half century as SERVICES have grown. In the United States and the UK, the proportion of workers in manufacturing has shrunk since 1900 from around 40% to barely 20%. More than two-thirds of OUTPUT in OECD countries, and up to four-fifths of employment, is now in the services sector. At the same time, manufacturing has grown in importance in developing countries.

Many people think that manufacturing somehow matters more than any other economic activity and is in some way superior to surfing the internet or cutting somebody's hair. This is probably nothing more than nostalgia for times past when making things in factories was what real men did, just as 150 years ago growing things in fields was what real men did. Mostly, the shift from manufacturing to services (as with the earlier shift from agriculture to manufacturing) reflects progress into jobs that create more UTILITY, this time for real women as well as real men, which may explain why it is happening first in richer countries.

Marginal

The difference made by one extra unit of something. Marginal revenue is the extra revenue earned by selling one more unit of something. The marginal PRICE is how much extra a consumer must pay to buy one extra unit. Marginal UTILITY is how much extra utility a person gets from consuming (or doing) an extra unit of something. The marginal product of LABOUR is how much extra OUTPUT a firm would get by employing an extra worker, or by getting an existing worker to put in an extra hour on the job. The marginal PROPENSITY to consume (or to save) measures by how much a household's CONSUMPTION (SAVINGS) would increase if its INCOME rose by, say, $1. The marginal tax rate measures how much extra tax you would have to pay if you earned an extra dollar.

The marginal cost (or whatever) can be very different from the AVERAGE cost (or whatever), which simply divides total costs (or whatever) by the total number of units produced (or whatever). A common finding in MICROECONOMICS is that small incremental changes can matter enormously. In general, thinking "at the margin" often leads to better economic decision-making than thinking about the averages.

Alfred MARSHALL, the father of NEO-CLASSICAL ECONOMICS, based many of his theories of economic behaviour on marginal rather than average behaviour. For instance, given certain plausible assumptions, a PROFIT-maximising FIRM will increase production up to the point where marginal revenue equals marginal cost. This is because if marginal revenue exceeded marginal cost, the firm could increase its profit by producing an extra unit of output. Alternatively, if marginal cost exceeded marginal revenue, the firm could increase its profit by producing fewer units of output.

In all walks of life, a basic rule of rational economic decision-making is this: do something only if the marginal utility you get from it exceeds the marginal cost of doing it.

Market capitalisation

The market value of a company's SHARES: the quoted share PRICE multiplied by the total number of shares that the company has issued.

Market failure

When a market left to itself does not allocate resources efficiently. Interventionist politicians usually allege market failure to justify their interventions.

Economists have identified four main sorts or causes of market failure:

- The abuse of market power, which can occur whenever a single buyer or seller can exert significant influence over PRICES or OUTPUT (see MONOPOLY and MONOPSONY).
- EXTERNALITIES, when the market does not take into account the impact of an economic activity on outsiders. For example, the market may ignore the costs imposed on outsiders by a firm polluting the environment.
- PUBLIC GOODS, such as national defence. How much defence would be provided if it were left to the market?
- Where there is incomplete or ASYMMETRIC INFORMATION or uncertainty.

Abuse of market power is best tackled through ANTITRUST policy. Externalities can be reduced through REGULATION, a tax or SUBSIDY, or by USING PROPERTY rights to force the market to take into account the WELFARE of all who are affected by an economic activity. The SUPPLY of public goods can be ensured by compelling everybody to pay for them through the tax system.

Market forces

Shorthand for the pressures from buyers and sellers in a market, rather than those coming from a GOVERNMENT planner or from REGULATION.

❝ *Markets can remain irrational longer than you can remain solvent.*
John Maynard Keynes, economist

Market power

When one buyer or seller in a market has the ability to exert significant influence over the quantity of goods and SERVICES traded or the PRICE at which they are sold. Market power does not exist when there is PERFECT COMPETITION, but it does when there is a MONOPOLY, MONOPSONY or OLIGOPOLY.

Marshall, Alfred

A British economist (1842–1924) who developed some of the most important concepts in MICROECONOMICS. In his best-known work, *Principles of Economics*, he retained the emphasis on the importance of costs, which was standard in CLASSICAL ECONOMICS. But he added to it, helping to create NEO-CLASSICAL ECONOMICS, by explaining that the OUTPUT and PRICE of a product are determined by both SUPPLY and DEMAND, and that MARGINAL costs and benefits are crucial. He was the first economist to explain that demand falls as price increases, and that therefore the DEMAND CURVE slopes downwards from left to right. He was also first with the concept of PRICE ELASTICITY of demand and CONSUMER SURPLUS.

Marshall Plan

Probably the most successful programme of INTERNATIONAL AID and NATION BUILDING in history. It was named after General George Marshall, an American secretary of state, who at the end of the second world war proposed giving aid to western Europe to rebuild its war-torn economies. North America gave around 1% of its GDP in total between 1948 and 1952; most of it came from the United States and the rest from Canada. The Americans left it to the Europeans to work out the details on allocating aid, which may be why, according to most economic analyses, it achieved more success than latter-day aid programmes in which most of the decisions on how the MONEY is spent are made by the donors. The main institution through which aid was administered was the

Organisation for European Economic Co-operation (OEEC), which in 1961 became the OECD. Nowadays, whenever there is a proposal for the international community to rebuild an economy damaged by war, such as Iraq's in 2003, you are sure to hear the phrase "new Marshall Plan".

Marx, Karl

Much followed, and much misunderstood, German economist (1818–83). His two best-known works were the *Communist Manifesto*, written in 1848 with Friedrich Engels, and *Das Kapital*, in four volumes published between 1867 and 1910. Most of his economic assumptions were drawn from orthodox CLASSICAL ECONOMICS, but he used them to reach highly unorthodox conclusions. Although claimed and blamed as the inspiration of some of the most virulently anti-market GOVERNMENTS the world has ever seen, he was not wholly against CAPITALISM. Indeed, he praised it for rescuing millions of people from "the idiocy of rural life". Even so, he thought it was doomed. A shortage of DEMAND would concentrate economic power and wealth in ever fewer hands, producing an ever-larger and more miserable proletariat. This would eventually rise up, creating a "dictatorship of the proletariat" and leading in time to a "withering away" of the state. Marx thought that this version of history was inevitable. So far, history has proved him wrong, largely because capitalism has delivered a much better deal to the masses than he believed it would.

Mean

See AVERAGE.

Mean reversion

The tendency for subsequent observations of a random variable to be closer to its mean than the current observation. For example, if the current number is 7, the AVERAGE is 5, and there is mean reversion, the next observation is likelier to be 6 than 8.

Median

See AVERAGE.

Medium term

Somewhere between SHORT-TERMISM, which is bad, and the LONG RUN lies the hallowed ground of the medium term – far enough away to discourage myopic behaviour by decision-makers but close enough to be meaningful. But not many GOVERNMENTS say exactly how long they think the medium term is.

Menu costs

How much it costs to change PRICES. Just as a restaurant has to print a new menu when it changes the price of its food, so many other FIRMS face a substantial outlay each time they cut or raise what they charge. Such menu costs mean that firms may be reluctant to change their prices every time there is a shift in the balance of SUPPLY and DEMAND, so there will be STICKY PRICES and the market for their OUTPUT will be in DISEQUILIBRIUM. The internet may sharply reduce menu costs as it allows prices to be changed at the click of a mouse, which may improve EFFICIENCY by keeping markets more often in EQUILIBRIUM.

Mercantilism

The conventional economic wisdom of the 17th century that made a partial come-back in recent years (not least within the GOVERN-MENT of China). Mercantilists feared that MONEY would become too scarce to sustain high levels of OUTPUT and employment; their favoured solution was cheap MONEY (low INTEREST RATES). In a forerunner to the 20th-century debate between KEYNESIANS and monetarists, they were opposed by advocates of CLASSICAL ECONOMICS, who argued that cheap and plentiful money could result in INFLATION. The original mercantilists, such as John Law, a Scots financier (and convicted murderer), believed that a country's economic prosperity and political power came from its stocks of precious metals. To maximise these stocks they argued against FREE TRADE, favouring protectionist policies designed to minimise IMPORTS and maximise EXPORTS, creating a TRADE SURPLUS that could be used to acquire more precious metal. This was contested for the classicists by Adam SMITH and David Hume, who argued that a country's wealth came not from its stock of precious metals but rather from its stocks of productive resources (LAND, LABOUR, CAPITAL, and so on) and how efficiently they are used. Free trade increased EFFICIENCY by allowing countries to specialise in things in which they have a COMPARATIVE ADVANTAGE.

Mergers and acquisitions

When two businesses join together, either by merging or by one company taking over the other. There are three sorts of mergers between FIRMS: HORIZONTAL INTEGRATION, in which two similar firms tie the knot; VERTICAL INTEGRATION, in which two firms at different stages in the SUPPLY chain get together; and DIVERSIFICATION, when two companies with nothing in common jump into bed. These can be a voluntary marriage of equals; a voluntary takeover of one firm by another; or a hostile takeover, in which the management of the target firm resists the advances of the buyer but is eventually forced to accept a deal by its current owners. For reasons that are not at all clear, merger activity generally happens in waves. One possible explanation is that when SHARE PRICES are low, many firms have a MARKET CAPITALISATION that is low relative to the value of their ASSETS. This makes them attractive to buyers (see TOBIN).

In theory, the different sorts of mergers have different sorts of potential benefits. However, the damning lesson of merger waves stretching back over the past 50 years is that, with one big exception – the spate of LEVERAGED BUY-OUTS in the United States during the 1980s – they have often failed to deliver benefits that justify the costs. Whether the merger wave at the start of the 21st century, which was driven in part by globalisation, will prove to have been more successful remains to be seen.

Microeconomics

The study of the individual pieces that together make an economy. Contrast with MACROECONOMICS, the study of economy-wide phenomena such as GROWTH, INFLATION and UNEMPLOYMENT. Microeconomics considers issues such as how households reach decisions about CONSUMPTION and SAVING, how FIRMS set a PRICE for their OUTPUT, whether PRIVATISATION improves EFFICIENCY, whether a particular market has enough COMPETITION in it and how the market for LABOUR works.

Microfinance

FINANCIAL SERVICES for poor people, particularly in DEVELOPING COUNTRIES. Since the 1970s, there has been rapid GROWTH in the supply of microcredit – the provision of small loans to poor people, especially women, to fund small businesses that help them help themselves to escape from POVERTY. Increasingly, other financial services, from SAVINGS accounts to INSURANCE, are being offered as well as microcredit. Initially, microfinance relied heavily on charitable donations to provide the initial CAPITAL to lend, though repayment rates have generally been high, demonstrating that being poor does not make someone a high-RISK CREDITOR. More recently, there has been a rapid growth in for-PROFIT microfinance. Its critics say that it is wrong to make a profit from the very poor. Its advocates argue that being profitable enables them to attract far more capital, which is made available to the poor, than could ever be raised through CHARITY.

Minimum wage

A minimum rate of pay that firms are legally obliged to pay their workers. Most industrial countries have a minimum wage, although certain sorts of workers are often exempted, such as young people or part-timers. Most economists reckon that a minimum wage, if it is doing what it is meant to do, will lead to higher UNEMPLOYMENT than there would be without it. The main justification offered by politicians for having a minimum wage is that the wage that would be decided by buyers and sellers in a free market would be so low that it would be immoral for people to work for it. So the minimum wage should be above the market-clearing wage, in which case fewer workers would be demanded at that wage than would be hired at the market wage. How many fewer will depend on how far the minimum wage is above the market wage.

Some economists have challenged this simple SUPPLY and DEMAND model. Several empirical studies have suggested that a minimum wage moderately above the free-market wage would not harm employment much and could (in rare circumstances) potentially raise it. These studies are not widely accepted among economists. Whatever it does for those in work, a minimum wage cannot help the majority of the very poorest people in most countries, who typically have no job in which to earn a minimum wage.

Misery index

The sum of a country's INFLATION and UNEMPLOYMENT rates. The higher the score, the greater is the economic misery.

Mixed economy

A market economy in which both private-sector FIRMS and firms owned by GOVERNMENT take part in economic activity. The proportions of public and private enterprise in the mix vary a great deal among countries. In the early 1980s, the public role in most mixed economies started to decline, as NATIONALISATION gave way to PRIVATISATION. However, this trend was reversed, at least temporarily, during the global economic crisis that began in 2007, as many governments took ownership stakes in leading BANKS and some other firms.

Mobility

The easier it is for the FACTORS OF PRODUCTION to move to where they are most valuable, the more efficient the allocation of the world's scarce resources is likely to be and the faster GDP will grow. Apart from continental drift, land is immobile. CAPITAL has long been extremely mobile within countries, and, with the rise of GLOBALISATION, it is now able to move easily around the world. ENTERPRISE is mobile, although to what extent depends on the particular ENTREPRENEUR. Some members of the LABOUR market zoom around the world to work; others will not move to the next town.

CAPITAL CONTROLS are the main obstacle to capital mobility, and these have been mostly removed or reduced since 1980. The sources of labour immobility are more numerous and complex, including immigration controls, transport costs, language barriers and a reluctance to move away from family or friends. Workers are far more mobile within the United States than they are within the EUROPEAN UNION or within individual EU countries. Some economists reckon that the willingness of workers to move to where the work is helps to explain the stronger economic performance and lower UNEMPLOYMENT of the United States. The higher INCOMES available in rich countries have also led poorer countries to complain of a "brain drain" as their most talented workers move abroad. However, their absence is often eased by substantial sums of MONEY sent home as REMITTANCES to family members.

Can you sometimes have too much mobility? Certainly, some DEVELOPING COUNTRIES have suffered from HOT MONEY rushing into and then out of their markets.

In general, the possibility that a factor of production may suddenly move elsewhere can create serious economic problems. For instance, an employer may think twice about investing in training an employee if it fears that the employee may suddenly take a job with another firm. Similarly, entrepreneurs are unlikely to take the RISK of pursuing a new idea if they fear that their capital may disappear at any moment, hence the importance of having access to long-term capital, such as by issuing BONDS and EQUITIES.

Mode

See AVERAGE.

Modelling

When economists make a number of simplified assumptions about how the economy, or some part of it, behaves, and then see what this implies in various different scenarios. Milton FRIED-MAN argued that economic models should not be judged on the basis of the validity of their assumptions, but on the accuracy of their predictions. An expert billiards player, he said, may not know the laws of physics, but acts as if he knows such laws. So his behaviour could be predicted accurately with a model that assumes he knows the laws of physics. Likewise, the behaviour of people making economic decisions may be accurately predicted by a model that assumes their goal is, say, PROFIT MAXIMISA-TION, even if they are not actually conscious of this being their goal.

The more complex the thing being modelled, the harder it is to get right. Economic FORECASTING has a poor overall track record. The more microeconomic the thing being modelled, the more likely it is that a model can be designed that will deliver accurate predictions.

Modern portfolio theory

One of the most important and influential economic theories about finance and INVESTMENT. Modern portfolio theory is based upon the simple idea that DIVERSIFICATION can produce the same total RETURNS for less RISK. Combining many financial ASSETS in a portfolio is less risky than putting all your investment eggs in one basket.

The theory has four basic premises:

- Investors are RISK AVERSE.
- SECURITIES are traded in efficient markets.
- Risk should be analysed in terms of an investor's overall portfolio, rather than by looking at individual assets.

■ For every level of risk, there is an optimal portfolio of assets that will have the highest EXPECTED RETURNS.

All of this seems straightforward now, except perhaps the bit about efficient markets. But it was shocking when it was put forward in the early 1950s by Harry Markowitz, who later won the Nobel Prize for it. According to Markowitz, when he explained his theory to the high priests of the CHICAGO SCHOOL, "Milton FRIEDMAN argued that portfolio theory was not ECONOMICS". It is now. (See ARBITRAGE PRICING THEORY, CAPITAL ASSET PRICING MODEL, SHARPE RATIO and BLACK-SCHOLES.)

Monetarism

Control the MONEY SUPPLY, and the rest of the economy will take care of itself. A school of economic thought that developed in opposition to post-1945 KEYNESIAN policies of DEMAND management, echoing earlier debates between MERCANTILISM and CLASSICAL ECONOMICS. Monetarism is based on the belief that INFLATION has its roots in the GOVERNMENT printing too much MONEY. It is closely associated with Milton FRIEDMAN, who argued, based on the QUANTITY THEORY OF MONEY, that government should keep the money supply fairly steady, expanding it slightly each year mainly to allow for the natural GROWTH of the economy. If it did this, MARKET FORCES would efficiently solve the problems of INFLATION, UNEMPLOYMENT and RECESSION.

Monetarism had its heyday in the early 1980s, when economists, governments and investors pounced eagerly on every new money-supply statistic, particularly in the United States and the UK. Many CENTRAL BANKS had set formal targets for money-supply growth, so every wiggle in the data was scrutinised for clues to the next move in the rate of INTEREST. Since then, the notion that faster money-supply growth automatically causes higher inflation has fallen out of favour. The money supply is useful as a policy target only if the relationship between money and nominal GDP, and hence inflation, is stable and predictable. The way the money supply affects PRICES and OUTPUT depends on how fast it circulates through the economy. The trouble is that its VELOCITY OF CIRCULATION can suddenly change. During the 1980s, the link between different measures of the money supply and inflation proved to be less clear than monetarist theories had suggested, and most central banks stopped setting binding monetary targets. Instead, many have adopted explicit inflation targets.

Monetary neutrality

Changes in the MONEY SUPPLY have no effect on real economic variables such as OUTPUT, real INTEREST RATES and UNEMPLOY-MENT. If the CENTRAL BANK doubles the money supply, the PRICE level will double too. Twice as many dollars means half as much bang for the buck. This theory, a core belief of CLASSICAL ECONOMICS, was first put forward in the 18th century by David Hume. He set out the classical dichotomy that economic variables come in two varieties, nominal and real, and that the things that influence nominal variables do not necessarily affect the real economy. Today few economists think that pure monetary neutrality exists in the real world, at least in the short run. INFLATION does affect the real economy because, for instance, there may be STICKY PRICES or MONEY ILLUSION.

Monetary policy

What a CENTRAL BANK does to control the MONEY SUPPLY, and thereby manage DEMAND. Monetary policy involves OPEN-MAR-KET OPERATIONS, reserve requirements and changing the short-term rate of INTEREST (the DISCOUNT RATE). It is one of the two main tools of MACROECONOMIC POLICY, the side-kick of FISCAL POLICY, and is easier said than done well. (See MONETARISM.)

Money

Makes the world go round and comes in many forms, from shells and beads to GOLD coins to plastic or paper. It is better than BARTER in enabling an economy's scarce resources to be allocated efficiently. Money has three main qualities:

- as a medium of exchange, buyers can give it to sellers to pay for goods and SERVICES;
- as a unit of account, it can be used to add up apples and oranges in some common value;
- as a store of value, it can be used to transfer purchasing power into the future.

A farmer who exchanges fruit for money can spend that money in the future; if he holds on to his fruit it might rot and no longer be useful for paying for something. INFLATION undermines the usefulness of money as a store of value, in particular, and also as a unit of account for comparing values at different points in time. HYPERINFLATION may destroy confidence in a particular form of money even as a medium of exchange. Measures of LIQUIDITY describe how easily an ASSET can be exchanged for money (the easier this is, the more liquid is the asset).

Money illusion

When people are misled by INFLATION into thinking that they are getting richer, when in fact the value of MONEY is declining. Whether, and how much, people are fooled by inflation is much debated by economists. Money illusion, a phrase coined by KEYNES, is used by some economists to argue that a small amount of inflation may not be a bad thing and could even be beneficial, helping to "grease the wheels" of the economy. Because of money illusion, workers like to see their nominal WAGES rise, giving them the illusion that their circumstances are improving, even though in real (inflation-adjusted) terms they may be no better off. During periods of high inflation double-digit pay rises (as well as, say, big increases in the value of their homes) can make people feel richer even if they are not really better off. When inflation is low, GROWTH in real incomes may hardly register.

Money markets

Any market where MONEY and other liquid ASSETS (such as TREASURY BILLS) can be lent and borrowed for between a few hours and a few months. Contrast with CAPITAL MARKETS, where longer-term CAPITAL changes hands.

Money supply

The amount of MONEY available in an economy. In the heyday of MONETARISM in the early 1980s, economists pounced upon the monthly (in some countries, even weekly) MONEY-SUPPLY numbers for clues about future INFLATION. CENTRAL BANKS aim to manage DEMAND by controlling the supply of money through OPEN-MARKET OPERATIONS, RESERVE REQUIREMENTS and changing the rate of INTEREST (to be exact, the DISCOUNT RATE).

One difficulty for policymakers lies in how to measure the relevant MONEY SUPPLY. There are several different methods, reflecting the different LIQUIDITY of various sorts of money. Notes and coins are completely liquid; some BANK deposits cannot be withdrawn until after a waiting period. M3 (M4 in the UK) is known as broad money, and consists of cash, current-account deposits in banks and other financial institutions, SAVINGS deposits and time-restricted deposits. M1 is known as narrow money, and consists mainly of cash in circulation and current-account deposits. M0 (in the UK) is the most liquid measure, including only cash in circulation, cash in banks' tills and banks' operational deposits held at the Bank of England.

Although it is a poor predictor of inflation, monetary GROWTH can be a handy LEADING INDICATOR of economic activity. In many countries, there is a clear link between the growth of the real broad-money supply and that of real GDP.

Monopolistic competition

Somewhere between PERFECT COMPETITION and MONOPOLY, also known as imperfect competition. It describes many real-world markets. Perfectly competitive markets are extremely rare, and few FIRMS enjoy a pure monopoly; OLIGOPOLY is more common. In monopolistic competition, there are fewer firms than in a perfectly competitive market and each can differentiate its products from the rest somewhat, perhaps by ADVERTISING or through small differences in design. These small differences form BARRIERS TO ENTRY. As a result, firms can earn some excess PROFITS, although not as much as a pure monopoly, without a new entrant being able to reduce PRICES through COMPETITION. Prices are higher and OUTPUT lower than under perfect competition.

Monopoly

When the production of a good or service with no close substitutes is carried out by a single firm with the MARKET POWER to decide the PRICE of its OUTPUT. Contrast with PERFECT COMPETITION, in which no single firm can affect the price of what it produces. Typically, a monopoly will produce less, at a higher price, than would be the case for the entire market under perfect competition. It decides its price by calculating the quantity of output at which its MARGINAL revenue would equal its marginal cost, and then sets whatever price would enable it to sell exactly that quantity.

In practice, few monopolies are absolute, and their power to set prices or limit SUPPLY is constrained by some actual or potential near-competitors (see MONOPOLISTIC COMPETITION). An extreme case of this occurs when a single firm dominates a market but has no pricing power because it is in a CONTESTABLE MARKET; that is, if it does not operate efficiently, a more efficient rival firm will take its entire market away. ANTITRUST policy can curb monopoly power by encouraging competition or, when there is a NATURAL MONOPOLY and thus COMPETITION would be inefficient, through REGULATION of prices. Furthermore, the mere possibility of antitrust action may encourage a monopoly to self-regulate its behaviour, simply to avoid the trouble an investigation would bring.

Monopsony

A market dominated by a single buyer. A monopsonist has the MARKET POWER to set the PRICE of whatever it is buying (from raw materials to LABOUR). Under PERFECT COMPETITION, by contrast, no individual buyer is big enough to affect the market price of anything.

Moral hazard

One of two main sorts of MARKET FAILURE often associated with the provision of INSURANCE. The other is ADVERSE SELECTION. Moral hazard means that people with insurance may take greater

RISKS than they would do without it because they know they are protected, so the insurer may get more claims than it bargained for. (See also DEPOSIT INSURANCE, LENDER OF LAST RESORT, IMF and WORLD BANK.) Many economists think that widespread moral hazard in the FINANCIAL SYSTEM – the result of insurance provided by BANKS to GOVERNMENTS – deserves much of the blame for creating the BUBBLES that, when they burst, helped trigger the global economic crisis that began in 2007.

Most-favoured nation

Equal treatment, at least, in international trade. If country A grants country B the status of most-favoured nation, it means that B's EXPORTS will face TARIFFS that are no higher (and also no lower) than those applied to any other country that A calls a most-favoured nation. This will be the most favourable tariff treatment available to IMPORTS.

Most-favoured nation treatment is one of the most important building blocks of the international trading system. The WORLD TRADE ORGANISATION requires member countries to accord the most favourable tariff and regulatory treatment given to the product of any one member to the "like products" of all other members. Before the GENERAL AGREEMENT ON TARIFFS AND TRADE, there was often a most-favoured nation clause in bilateral trade agreements, which helped the world move towards FREE TRADE. In the 1930s, however, there was a backlash against this, and most-favoured nations were treated less favourably. This shift pushed the world economy towards division into regional TRADE AREAS. In the United States, most-favoured nation status has to be re-ratified periodically by Congress, a process that has often given rise to considerable controversy, particularly when it comes to favouring China.

Multiplier

Shorthand for the way in which a change in spending produces an even larger change in INCOME. For instance, suppose a GOVERNMENT loosens FISCAL POLICY, increasing net PUBLIC SPENDING by pumping an extra $10 billion into education. This has an immediate effect by increasing the income of teachers and of people who sell educational supplies or build or maintain schools. These people will in turn spend some of their extra MONEY, putting more cash into the pockets of others, who spend some of it, and so on.

In theory, this process could continue indefinitely, in which case the multiplier would have an infinite value. In practice, most people save some of their extra income rather than spend it. How much they spend will depend on their MARGINAL PROPENSITY to consume. The value of the multiplier can be calculated by this formula:

$$\text{multiplier} = 1 \div (1 - \text{marginal propensity to consume})$$

If the marginal propensity to consume is 0.5 (50 cents of an extra dollar), the multiplier is 2. In practice, it is often hard to measure the multiplier effect, or to predict how it will respond to, say, changes in MONETARY POLICY or fiscal policy.

NAFTA

Short for North American Free-Trade Agreement. In 1993, the United States, Mexico and Canada agreed to lower the barriers to trade among the three economies. The formation of this regional TRADE AREA was opposed by many politicians in all three countries. In the United States and Canada, in particular, there were fears that NAFTA would result in domestic job losses to cheaper locations in Mexico. Most studies have found that, in practice, the economic gains far outweighed any costs. Even so, the agreement remains controversial to such an extent that in 2008, during his campaign for the presidency, Barack Obama talked about renegotiating it.

NAIRU

The non-accelerating-inflation rate of unemployment (see NATURAL RATE OF UNEMPLOYMENT).

Nash equilibrium

An important concept in GAME THEORY, a Nash EQUILIBRIUM occurs when each player is pursuing their best possible strategy in the full knowledge of the strategies of all other players. Once a Nash equilibrium is reached, nobody has any incentive to change their strategy. It is named after John Nash, a mathematician and Nobel Prize-winning economist.

National debt

The total outstanding borrowing of a country's GOVERNMENT (usually including national and local government). It is often described as a burden, although public DEBT may have economic benefits (see BALANCED BUDGET, FISCAL POLICY and GOLDEN RULE). Certainly, debt incurred by one generation may become a heavy burden for later generations, especially if the MONEY borrowed is not invested wisely. The national debt is a total of all the money ever raised by a government that has yet to be paid off; this is very different from an annual public-sector budget DEFICIT. In 1999, the American government celebrated a huge budget surplus, yet the country still had a national debt equal to nearly half its GDP. It has got bigger since.

National income

Shorthand for everything that is produced, earned or spent in a country (see GDP and GNP).

Nationalisation

When a GOVERNMENT takes ownership of a private-sector business. Nationalisation was a fashionable part of the mix in countries with a MIXED ECONOMY between 1945 and 1980, after which the PRIVATISATION of state-owned FIRMS became increasingly popular. The amount of public ownership in different countries has always varied considerably. Nationalisation has taken place for various reasons, ranging from socialist ideology to attempts to remedy examples of MARKET FAILURE (as in the case of purchases by governments in many countries of shares in leading BANKS during the global economic crisis that began in 2007).

The performance of nationalised firms has often, but not

always, been poor compared with their private-sector counterparts. State-owned businesses often enjoy a legally protected MONOPOLY, and the lack of COMPETITION means the firms face little pressure to be efficient. Politicians often interfere in important management decisions, making it harder to take unpopular actions on pay, factory closures and job cuts, particularly when there are strong public-sector trade UNIONS and a union-friendly government. Politically imposed financial constraints may also force public-sector firms to underinvest. Although privatisation has not been universally beneficial, on balance it has increased economic EFFICIENCY.

Nation building

Creating a country that works out of one that does not – because the old order has collapsed (as in the former Soviet bloc), or been destroyed by war (Iraq), or never really functioned in the first place (Afghanistan). To transform a failed country can involve establishing order through the rule of law and creating legitimate GOVERNMENT and other effective social institutions, as well as a credible currency and a functioning market economy. Nation building is rarely easy, and often fiendishly difficult, especially where there are deep ethnic, religious or political divisions in the POPULATION or the country has no history of ever functioning effectively. Outside expertise, such as from the WORLD BANK, and MONEY (as in, most famously, the MARSHALL PLAN) can help, but they are no guarantee of success.

Natural monopoly

When a MONOPOLY occurs because it is more efficient for one firm to serve an entire market than for two or more FIRMS to do so, because of the sort of ECONOMIES OF SCALE available in that market. A common example is water distribution, in which the main cost is laying a network of pipes to deliver water. One firm can do the job at a lower AVERAGE cost per customer than two firms with competing networks of pipes. Monopolies can arise unnaturally by a firm acquiring sole ownership of a resource that is essential to the production of a good or service, or by a GOVERNMENT granting a firm the legal right to be the sole producer. Other unnatural monopolies occur when a firm is much more efficient than its rivals for reasons other than economies of scale. Unlike some other sorts of monopoly, natural monopolies have little chance of being driven out of a market by more efficient new entrants. Thus REGULATION of natural monopolies may be needed to protect their captive consumers.

Natural rate of unemployment

A controversial phrase, which actually means little more than the lowest rate of UNEMPLOYMENT at which the jobs market can be in stable EQUILIBRIUM. KEYNESIANS, encouraged by the PHILLIPS CURVE, assumed that a GOVERNMENT could lower the rate of unemployment if it was willing to accept a little more INFLATION. However, economists such as Milton FRIEDMAN and Edmund Phelps, both of whom later won the NOBEL PRIZE IN ECONOMICS, argued that this supposed inflation-for-jobs trade-off was in fact a trap. Governments that tolerated higher inflation in the hope of lowering unemployment would find that joblessness dipped only briefly before returning to its previous level, while inflation would rise and stay high. Instead, they argued, unemployment has an equilibrium or natural rate, determined not by the amount of DEMAND in an economy but by the structure of the LABOUR market. This is the lowest level of unemployment at which inflation will remain stable. When unemployment is above the natural rate demand can potentially be increased to bring it to the natural rate, but attempting to lower it even further will only cause inflation to accelerate. Hence the natural rate is also known as the non-accelerating-inflation rate of unemployment, or NAIRU.

At first, the NAIRU became synonymous with the view that MACROECONOMIC POLICY could not conquer unemployment. It was often used to justify policy inaction even when unemployment rose to more than 10% of workers in industrialised countries during the 1980s and 1990s, even though economists' estimates of the NAIRU differed hugely. More recently, economists looking for ways to reduce unemployment have started to ask whether, and under what circumstances, the natural rate might change. Most solutions have stressed the need to make more people employable at the prevailing level of wages, in particular by increasing LABOUR MARKET FLEXIBILITY. Economists still disagree over what jobless rate at any particular point in time is the NAIRU, but nobody any longer thinks that the natural rate is fixed. Indeed, some think the concept has no meaning at all.

Negative income tax

A way of building redistribution into the TAXATION system by taking money from people with high incomes and paying it to people with low incomes. Because it takes place automatically through the tax system, it may attach less stigma to the receipt of financial help than some other forms of WELFARE assistance. However, it may also discourage recipients from working to increase their INCOME (see UNEMPLOYMENT TRAP), which is why some countries have introduced a form of negative income tax that is available only to the working poor. In the United States, this is known as the earned income tax credit.

Neo-classical economics

The school of ECONOMICS that developed the free-market ideas of CLASSICAL ECONOMICS into a full-scale model of how an economy works. The best-known neo-classical economist was Alfred MARSHALL, the father of MARGINAL analysis. Neo-classical thinking, which mostly assumes that markets tend towards EQUI-LIBRIUM, was attacked by KEYNES and became unfashionable during the KEYNESIAN-dominated decades after the second world war. But, thanks to economists such as Milton FRIEDMAN, many neo-classical ideas have since become widely accepted and uncontroversial.

Net present value

A measure used to help decide whether or not to proceed with an INVESTMENT. Net means that both the costs and benefits of the investment are included. To calculate net present value (NPV), first add together all the expected benefits from the investment, now and in the future. Then add together all the expected costs. Then work out what these future benefits and costs are worth now by adjusting future cash flow using an appropriate DISCOUNT RATE. Then subtract the costs from the benefits. If the NPV is negative, the investment cannot be justified by the EXPECTED RETURNS. If the NPV is positive, it can, although it pays to make comparisons with the NPVs of other investment opportunities before going ahead.

Network effect

When the value of a good to a consumer changes because the number of people using it changes. For instance, owning a phone becomes more valuable as more people are plugged into the tele-phone network. Network effects are sometimes called network

EXTERNALITIES, although this implies, often wrongly, that the benefits from being part of a network are a sort of MARKET FAILURE. They give a huge COMPETITIVE ADVANTAGE to the firm that owns the network. This INCUMBENT ADVANTAGE arises because a new entrant must persuade people to join a network that starts with fewer members, and thus may be less valuable to them than the network they are currently in. This is why markets for products with network effects are often dominated by only a few FIRMS or a single MONOPOLY. Some economists argue that many recent technological INNOVATIONS, notably the internet, have large positive network effects, which make possible much higher PRODUCTIVITY and GROWTH than in the past.

Neuroeconomics

A school of ECONOMICS that tries to explain the economic decisions people take by studying the chemical processes of the brain. Since the late 1990s, neuroeconomists have studied economic decisions using recently developed techniques such as magnetic resonance imaging (MRI), which show that different bits of the old grey matter are associated with different sorts of emotional and decision-making activity. Already they have examined issues such as people's reasons for trusting one another, apparently irrational RISK-taking, the relative valuation of short-term and long-term costs and benefits, altruistic or charitable behaviour, and addiction.

Releases of dopamine, the brain's pleasure chemical, may indicate economic UTILITY or value, they say. There is also growing interest in new evidence from neuroscience which tentatively suggests that two conditions of the brain compete in decision-making: a cold, objective state and a hot, emotional state in which the ability to make sensible trade-offs disappears. The potential interactions between these two brain states are ideal subjects for economic modelling.

Some economists are sceptical, arguing that economists do not need brains (as it were). Studying what people decide – their REVEALED PREFERENCE – is sufficient. Yet today's neuroeconomists are not the first dismal scientists to dream of peering inside the human brain. In 1881, Francis Edgeworth proposed the creation of a "hedonimeter", which would measure the utility that each individual gained from his decisions. Alas, the technology to make this instrument was not available then, but it seems more plausible today.

Neutrality

See FISCAL NEUTRALITY and MONETARY NEUTRALITY.

New economy

In the last years of the 20th century, some economists argued that developments in information technology and GLOBALISATION had given birth to a new economy (first in the United States), which had a higher rate of PRODUCTIVITY and GROWTH than the old economy it replaced. Some went further, adding that in the new economy INFLATION was dead, the BUSINESS CYCLE abolished and the traditional rules of ECONOMICS were redundant. These claims were highly controversial. Other economists pointed out that similar predictions had been made during earlier periods of rapid technological change, yet the nature of economics was not fundamentally altered. With the bursting of the dotcom stockmarket BUBBLE in 2000, the phrase fell into disuse, although productivity continued to soar, thanks not least to new technology, especially in the United States.

New growth theory

See GROWTH.

New trade theory

Although most economists support FREE TRADE, in the 1970s a growing number of them became increasingly puzzled by the large differences between the predictions of free-trade theory and real-world trade flows. Their solution to this puzzle is known as new trade theory.

One mystery was that trade was growing fastest between industrial countries with similar economies and endowments of the FACTORS OF PRODUCTION. In many new industries, there was no clear COMPARATIVE ADVANTAGE for any country. Patterns of production and trade often seemed matters of chance. Trade between two countries would often consist mostly of similar goods; for example, one country would sell cars to another country from which it would import different models of cars.

One explanation, associated in particular with Nobel Prize-winning economist Paul Krugman of the Massachusetts Institute of Technology, drew on Adam SMITH's idea that the DIVISION OF LABOUR lowers unit costs. ECONOMIES OF SCALE within FIRMS are incompatible with the PERFECT COMPETITION assumed by traditional trade theory. A more realistic assumption is that many markets have MONOPOLISTIC COMPETITION. When a monopolistically competitive market expands, it does so through a mixture of more firms (greater product variety) and bigger firms, with bigger-scale economies. Free trade expands market size beyond national borders and so allows firms to reap bigger economies of scale, to the benefit of consumers, workers and shareholders.

The upside may be greater the more similar are the trading economies. This may explain why trade LIBERALISATION is easier to achieve between similar countries. Thus, for example, the free-trade agreement between the United States and Canada produced only minor local complaints, whereas its subsequent expansion to include the very different economy of Mexico was much more controversial (see NAFTA).

NGO

Short for non-government organisation. Although such groups have existed for generations (in the early 1800s, the British and Foreign Anti-Slavery Society played a powerful part in abolishing slavery laws), recent social and economic shifts have given these typically non-PROFIT organisations new life. In 2007, there were an estimated 5m NGOs worldwide, including at least 1m in both the United States and India.

NGOs have grown rapidly in both number and size for several reasons:

- GOVERNMENTS have struggled increasingly to meet social needs, and so NGOs have stepped in to fill the gap as providers of SERVICES.

- Even when governments have tried to address a particular social need, they have done so ineffectively, and more creative SOCIAL ENTREPRENEURS within NGOs have found better solutions.

- Citizens have increasingly sought to improve how they hold governments and FIRMS to account for their impact on society and to encourage them to do better, and (mostly) NGOs have been their preferred organisational form for doing so.

Governments have been increasingly at the sharp end of pressure from campaigning NGOs. Arguably, however, it is intergovernmental institutions such as the WORLD BANK, the IMF, other UN agencies and the WORLD TRADE ORGANISATION (WTO) that have felt it more, owing to their lack of political leverage. Few parliamentarians will face direct pressure from the IMF or the WTO, but every policymaker faces pressure from citizens' groups with special interests. Add to this the poor public image that these technocratic, faceless bureaucracies have developed, and it is hardly surprising that they are popular targets for NGO "swarms". How governments and intergovernmental organisations respond to NGOS could have huge implications, including for the world's economies.

Equally important will be how NGOs themselves respond to greater scrutiny and to growing concern about how accountable they are, and to whom. Nor is it just their accountability, or lack of it, that is attracting scrutiny. So, too, is their EFFICIENCY, or, more often, inefficiency. The growth of the NGO sector has drawn attention to its economic importance – over 10% of jobs in the United States now are with non-profits – which in turn has raised questions about how well it uses the economic resources it controls. Compared with for-profit firms, NGOs are often small, lacking in TRANSPARENCY and inefficient. They often lack both the resources to grow large and (however poorly they perform) the market pressure to go out of business.

Nevertheless, in recent years a growing number of NGOs have become SOCIAL ENTERPRISES, engaging in business activities to generate INCOME to fund their activities. In many cases, this has improved their efficiency. Also, the rise of PHILANTHROCAPITAL-ISM has seen a new wave of wealthy philanthropists apply their money and business skills to trying to improve the performance of NGOs, often working in partnership with social entrepreneurs.

Nobel Prize in Economics

The sixth annual prize established in memory of Alfred Nobel. Strictly speaking, this is not a fully fledged Nobel Prize, as it was not mentioned in Nobel's will, unlike the five prizes established earlier for peace, literature, medicine, chemistry and physics. Still, the title of Nobel laureate and the $1m award stumped up each year by Sweden's CENTRAL BANK make it worth winning. Since 1969, when its first (joint) winners hailed from Norway and the Netherlands, it has been won mostly by American economists, many of them of the CHICAGO SCHOOL.

Nominal value

The value of anything expressed simply in the MONEY of the day. Since INFLATION means that money can lose its value over time, nominal figures can be misleading when used to compare values in different periods. It is better to compare their real value, by adjusting the nominal figures to remove the inflationary distortions.

Non-price competition

Trying to win business from rivals other than by charging a lower PRICE. Methods include ADVERTISING, slightly differentiating your product or improving its quality, or offering free gifts or discounts on subsequent purchases. Non-price competition is particularly common when there is an OLIGOPOLY, perhaps because it can give an impression of fierce rivalry while the FIRMS are actually colluding to keep prices high.

Non-profit

See NGO.

Normal goods

When average INCOME increases, the DEMAND for normal goods increases, too. The opposite of INFERIOR GOODS.

Normative economics

ECONOMICS that tries to change the world, by suggesting policies for increasing economic WELFARE. The opposite of POSITIVE ECONOMICS, which is content to try to describe the world as it is, rather than prescribe ways to make it better.

NPV

See NET PRESENT VALUE.

Null hypothesis

A statement that is being put to the test. In ECONOMETRICS, economists often start with a null hypothesis that a particular variable equals a particular number, then crunch their data to see if they can prove or disprove it, according to the laws of STATISTICAL SIGNIFICANCE. The null hypothesis chosen is often the reverse of what the experimenter actually believes; it may be put forward to allow the data to contradict it.

OECD

The Organisation for Economic Co-operation and Development, a Paris-based club for industrialised countries and the best of the rest. It was formed in 1961, building on the Organisation for European Economic Co-operation (OEEC), which had been established under the MARSHALL PLAN. By 2003, its membership had risen to 30 countries, from an original 20. Together, OECD countries produce two-thirds of the world's goods and SERVICES. The OECD provides a policy talking shop for GOVERNMENTS. It produces forests-worth of documents discussing public policy ideas, as well as detailed empirical analysis. It also publishes reports on the economic performance of individual countries, which usually contain lots of valuable INFORMATION even if they are rarely critical of the policies implemented by a member government.

Offshore

Where the usual rules of a person or firm's home country do not apply. It can be literally offshore, as in the case of investors moving their MONEY to a Caribbean island TAX HAVEN. Or it can be merely legally offshore, as in the case of certain financial transactions that take place within, say, the City of London, which are deemed for regulatory purposes to have taken place offshore.

Offshoring

See OUTSOURCING.

Oil

Sharp increases in the price of oil have had huge economic consequences over the years. In the 1970s, driven up by the OPEC CARTEL, oil PRICES were a big contributor to INFLATION and STAGFLATION problems in the leading industrial economies. Many MANUFACTURING operations were rendered obsolete, and were replaced eventually by new plant that was far more efficient in its consumption of oil, or relied on other fuels.

More recently, the oil price surged to a record high in 2008. This time OPEC was not the primary cause. Economists disagreed on what was responsible: rising DEMAND, certainly, especially from fast-growing DEVELOPING COUNTRIES such as China, but also, according to some, rampant SPECULATION by HEDGE FUNDS and other financial investors. There was talk, though not much evidence, that global oil production had peaked. Two main beneficiaries of these high prices were SOVEREIGN WEALTH FUNDS established by oil-producing countries, which could suddenly afford to invest in some of the world's most respected FIRMS, and companies developing alternative energy, especially environmentally friendly, non-climate-changing "clean tech". Oil prices plunged again in late 2008, as the global economic crisis took its toll both on demand and on financial speculators, though this fall may well prove to have been temporary.

Okun's law

A description of what happens to UNEMPLOYMENT when the rate of GROWTH of GDP changes, based on empirical research by Arthur Okun (1928–80). It predicts that if GDP grows at around 3% a year, the jobless rate will be unchanged. If it grows faster, the unemployment rate will fall by half of what the growth rate exceeds 3% by; that is, if GDP grows by 5%, unemployment will fall by 1 PERCENTAGE POINT. Likewise, a lesser, say 2%, increase in

GDP would be associated with a half a percentage point increase in the jobless rate.

This relationship is not carved in stone, as it merely reflects the American economy during the period studied by Okun. Even so, in most economies Okun's Law is a reasonable rule of thumb for estimating the likely impact on jobs of changes in OUTPUT.

Oligopoly

When a few FIRMS dominate a market. Often they can together behave as if they were a single MONOPOLY, perhaps by forming a CARTEL. Or they may collude informally, by preferring gentle NON-PRICE COMPETITION to a bloody PRICE war. Because what one firm can do depends on what the other firms do, the behaviour of oligopolists is hard to predict. However, the evidence suggests that cartels are inherently unstable. When oligopolists do compete on price, they may produce as much and charge as little as if they were in a market with PERFECT COMPETITION.

OPEC

The Organisation of Petroleum Exporting Countries, a CARTEL set up in 1960 that wrought havoc in industrialised countries during the 1970s and early 1980s by forcing up OIL PRICES (which quadrupled in a few weeks during 1973–74 alone), resulting in high INFLATION and slow GROWTH. A lot of productive capital equipment that had been viable at lower oil prices proved to be unprofitable to run at the higher prices and was shut down. Some economists reckon that MARKET FORCES would have driven up oil prices anyway and that OPEC merely capitalised on the opportunity. Since the early 1980s, OPEC's influence has waned. Many firms have switched to production methods that need less oil, or less energy altogether. Non-OPEC producers such as the UK have brought new oil fields on stream. And some individual members of the cartel have broken ranks by failing to co-ordinate their oil production with other members. Increasingly, OPEC has found itself responding to sharp surges and falls in oil prices, rather than driving them.

Open economy

An economy that allows the unrestricted flow of people, CAPITAL, goods and SERVICES across its borders; the opposite of a CLOSED ECONOMY.

Open-market operations

CENTRAL BANKS buying and selling SECURITIES in the open market, as a way of controlling INTEREST RATES or the growth of the MONEY SUPPLY. By selling more securities, they can mop up surplus MONEY; buying securities adds to the money supply. The securities traded by central banks are mostly GOVERNMENT BONDS and TREASURY BILLS, although they sometimes buy or sell commercial securities.

Opportunity cost

The true cost of something is what you give up to get it. This includes not only the MONEY spent in buying (or doing) the something, but also the economic benefits (UTILITY) that you did without because you bought (or did) that particular something and thus can no longer buy (or do) something else. For example, the opportunity cost of choosing to train as a lawyer is not merely the tuition fees, PRICE of books, and so on, but also the fact that you are no longer able to spend your time holding down a sala-ried job or developing your skills as a footballer. These lost opportunities may represent a significant loss of utility. Going for a walk may appear to cost nothing, until you consider the opportunity forgone to use that time earning money. Everything you do has an opportunity cost (see SHADOW PRICE).

ECONOMICS is primarily about the efficient use of scarce resources, and the notion of opportunity cost plays a crucial part in ensuring that resources are indeed being used efficiently.

Optimal currency area

A geographical area within which it would pay to have a single currency. An optimal currency area can come in many sizes. Some may span several countries and others may be smaller than an individual country.

The benefits of having one currency are lower foreign exchange and currency HEDGING costs and more transparent pricing (because every PRICE is expressed in the same currency). But unless the single currency is used within an optimal currency area, these benefits may be dwarfed by the costs. A single currency means a single MONETARY POLICY and no opportunity for one part of the currency area to change its EXCHANGE RATE with the other parts. This can be a big problem if a country or region is likely to suffer from ASYMMETRIC SHOCKS that affect it differently from the rest of the single-currency area, because it will no longer be able to respond by loosening its national monetary policy or devaluing its currency. This may not be an insuperable problem if workers in the affected country are able and willing to move freely to other countries; if WAGES and prices are flexible and can adjust to the shock; or if FISCAL POLICY can shift resources to areas hurt by a shock from areas that are not hurt.

For a currency area to be optimal, ideally asymmetric shocks should be rare, implying that the economies involved are on similar BUSINESS CYCLES and have similar structures. Moreover, the single monetary policy should affect all the constituent parts in the same way (an INTEREST RATE cut should not, say, reduce UNEMPLOYMENT in one part and increase INFLATION in another). There should be no cultural, linguistic or legal barriers to LABOUR mobility across frontiers; there should be wage flexibility; and there should be some system for transferring resources to regions that are suffering. In practice, few of the parts of the world that have a single currency are optimal currency areas, probably including the EURO ZONE, although having a single currency often makes them become gradually more alike and thus more optimal.

Optimum

As good as it gets, given the constraints you are operating within. For the concept of optimum to mean anything, there must be both a goal, say, to maximise economic WELFARE, and a set of constraints, such as an available stock of scarce economic resources. Optimising is the process of doing the best you can in the circumstances.

Option

See DERIVATIVES and BLACK-SCHOLES.

Output

The fruit of economic activity: whatever is produced by using the FACTORS OF PRODUCTION. See GDP.

Output gap

How far an economy's current OUTPUT is below what it would be at full CAPACITY. On average, INFLATION rises when output is above potential and falls when output is below potential. However, in the short run, the relationship between inflation and the output gap can deviate from the longer-term pattern and can thus be misleading. Alas for policymakers: because nobody really knows what an economy's potential output is, the size and even the direction of the output gap can easily be misdiagnosed, which can contribute to serious errors in MACROECONOMIC POLICY.

Outsourcing

Shifting activities that used to be done inside a FIRM to an outside company, which can do them more cost-effectively. Big firms have outsourced a growing amount of their business since the early 1990s, including increasingly offshoring work to cheaper employees at firms in countries such as India. This has become politically controversial in countries that lose jobs as a result of offshoring. However, a firm that outsources can improve its EFFICIENCY by focusing on those activities in which it can create the most value; the firm to which it outsources can also increase efficiency by specialising in that activity. That, at least, is the theory. In practice, managing the outsourcing process can be tricky, particularly for more complex activities.

Outward investment

Investing abroad; the opposite of INWARD INVESTMENT.

Overheating

When an economy is growing too fast and its productive CAP-ACITY cannot keep up with DEMAND. It often boils over into INFLATION.

Overshooting

The common tendency of PRICES in FINANCIAL MARKETS initially to move further than would seem strictly necessary in response to changes in the fundamentals that should, in theory, determine value. One reason may be that in the absence of perfect INFORMATION, investors move in herds, rushing in and out of markets on rumour. Eventually, as investors become better informed, the price usually returns to a more appropriate level. Overshooting is especially common during significant realignments of EXCHANGE RATES, but there are plenty of other examples. For instance, following the abolition of CAPITAL CONTROLS by some DEVELOPING COUNTRIES, the prices of EQUITIES in those countries initially soared to what proved to be unjustified levels as foreign CAPITAL rushed in, before settling in the longer term at more sustainable valuations.

Over the counter

In the case of drugs, those that can be purchased without a prescription from a doctor. In the case of financial SECURITIES, those that are bought or sold through a private dealer or BANK rather than on a financial exchange.

Paradox of thrift

One of the most interesting insights of KEYNES, the paradox states that if everyone saves more MONEY during times of RECESSION, aggregate DEMAND will fall and will in turn lower total SAVINGS in the POPULATION because of the decrease in CONSUMPTION and GROWTH. This is one example, though there are others, of individuals, by doing what is rational at the personal level, producing an outcome in aggregate which is worse for everyone.

Pareto efficiency

A situation in which nobody can be made better off without making somebody else worse off is "Pareto optimal". Named after Vilfredo Pareto (1843–1923), an Italian economist. If an economy's resources are being used inefficiently, it ought to be possible to make somebody better off without anybody else becoming worse off. In reality, change often produces losers as well as winners. Pareto efficiency does not help judge whether this sort of change is economically good or bad.

Paris Club

The name given to the arrangements through which countries reschedule their official DEBT; that is, money borrowed from other GOVERNMENTS rather than BANKS or private FIRMS. The Paris Club's base is in Avenue Kléber in Paris and it has 19 members. Other institutions such as the WORLD BANK attend in an informal role. Rescheduling requires the consensus agreement of members and must not favour one CREDITOR nation over another. Private debt rescheduling takes place through the London Club.

Patents

In 1899 the commissioner of the American Office of Patents recommended that his office be abolished because "everything that can be invented has been invented". The fact that there has been so much INNOVATION during the subsequent 100 years may owe something to the existence of patents. Economists reckon that if people are going to spend the time and MONEY needed to think up and develop new products, they need to be fairly confident that if the idea works they will earn a decent PROFIT. Patents help achieve this by granting the inventor a temporary monopoly over the idea, to stop it being stolen by imitators who have not borne any of the development RISK and costs. Like any MONOPOLY, patents create inefficiency because of the lack of COMPETITION to produce and sell the product. So economists debate how long patent protection should last. There is also debate about which sorts of innovation require the encouragement of a potential monopoly to make them happen. Furthermore, the pace of innovation in some industries has sharply reduced the number of years during which a patent is valuable. Some economists say that this shows that patents do not play a large part in the process of innovation.

Path dependence

History matters. Where you have been in the past determines where you are now and where you can go in future. Indeed, even small, apparently trivial, differences in the path you have taken can have huge consequences for where you are and can go. In economics, path dependence refers to the way in which apparently insignificant events and choices can have huge consequences for the development of a market or an economy.

Economists disagree over how widespread path dependence is, and whether it is a form of MARKET FAILURE. One focus of this debate is the QWERTY keyboard. Some argue that the QWERTY design was deliberately made slow to use so as to overcome a jamming-at-speed problem in early typewriters. Much faster alternative layouts of keys have failed to prosper, even though the anti-jamming rationale for QWERTY has been defunct for years. Others say that the QWERTY system is as efficient a layout of keys as any other and that its success is a triumph of MARKET FORCES. Having invested in learning to make and use the QWERTY keyboard, it makes no economic sense to switch to an alternative that is no better than QWERTY.

Peak pricing

When CAPACITY is fixed and DEMAND varies during a time period, it may make sense to charge above-AVERAGE PRICES when demand peaks. Because this will divert some peak demand to cheaper off-peak periods, it will reduce the total amount of capacity needed at the peak and reduce the amount of capacity lying idle at off-peak times, thus resulting in a more efficient use of resources. Peak pricing is common in SERVICES with substantial fixed capacity, such as electricity supply and rail transport, as anybody who pays higher fares to travel during rush hours knows only too well.

Percentage point

A unit of size, a one-hundredth of the total. Not to be confused with percentage change. When something increases by 1 percentage point this may be quite different from a 1% increase. For instance, if GDP grew last year by 1% and this year by 2%, the growth rate this year increased by 1 percentage point compared with last year (the difference between 1% and 2%) and also by 100% (2% is double 1%). A 1% increase would mean that the growth rate this year was only 1.01%.

Percentile

Part of the "ile" family that signposts positions on a scale of numbers (see also QUARTILE). The top percentile on, say, the distribution of INCOME, is the richest 1% of the POPULATION.

Perfect competition

The most competitive market imaginable. Perfect COMPETITION is rare and may not even exist. It is so competitive that any individual buyer or seller has a negligible impact on the market PRICE. Products are homogeneous. INFORMATION is perfect. Everybody is a price taker. FIRMS earn only normal PROFIT, the bare minimum profit necessary to keep them in business. If firms earn more than that (excess profits), the absence of BARRIERS TO ENTRY means that other firms will enter the market and drive the price level down until there are only normal profits to be made. OUTPUT will be maximised and price minimised. Contrast with MONOPOLISTIC COMPETITION, OLIGOPOLY and, above all, MONOPOLY.

Permanent income hypothesis

Over their lives, people try to spread their spending more evenly than their INCOME. The permanent income hypothesis, developed by Milton FRIEDMAN, says that a person's spending decisions are guided by what they think over their lifetime will be their AVERAGE (also known as permanent) income. A sharp increase in short-term income will not result in an equally sharp increase in short-term CONSUMPTION. What if somebody unexpectedly comes into MONEY, say by winning the lottery? The permanent income hypothesis suggests that people will save most of any such windfall gains. Reality may be somewhat different. (See LIFE-CYCLE HYPOTHESIS.)

Philanthrocapitalism

A movement in which wealthy business leaders give away a large part of their personal fortunes and use their business talents to ensure that the MONEY is used effectively to solve society's problems. The best known philanthrocapitalist is Bill Gates, the co-founder of Microsoft, who has given away billions of dollars through the Bill & Melinda Gates Foundation, mostly to improve the quality of schools in the United States and to combat deadly diseases in DEVELOPING COUNTRIES. Some economists question whether this giving will be any more effective than INTERNATIONAL AID, and argue that instead the wealthy should be taxed more heavily. Others argue that the relative absence of AGENCY COSTS in personal philanthropy, combined with the business talents of the philanthropist, can be more effective in some activities than traditional GOVERNMENT spending.

Whereas in the past philanthropy was often an alternative to government action, today even the largest personal fortunes are dwarfed by government BUDGETS, and philanthrocapitalists such as Gates generally engage in public-private partnerships with government. They also increasingly partner with NGOs, especially those formed by SOCIAL ENTREPRENEURS, and with large FIRMS, some of which are also playing a more active role in addressing society's thorniest problems through their corporate social responsibility or corporate citizenship strategies – a process that Gates calls "creative CAPITALISM".

Phillips curve

In 1958, an economist from New Zealand, A.W.H. Phillips (1914–75) proposed that there was a trade-off between INFLATION and UNEMPLOYMENT: the lower the unemployment rate, the higher was the rate of inflation. GOVERNMENTS simply had to choose the right balance between the two evils. He drew this conclusion by studying nominal wage rates and jobless rates in the UK between 1861 and 1957, which seemed to show the relationship of unemployment and inflation as a smooth curve.

Economies did seem to work like this in the 1950s and 1960s, but then the relationship broke down. Now economists prefer to talk about the NAIRU, the lowest rate of unemployment at which inflation does not accelerate.

Pigou effect

Named after Arthur Pigou (1877–1959), a sort of WEALTH EFFECT resulting from DEFLATION. A fall in the price level increases the real value of people's SAVINGS, making them feel wealthier and thus causing them to spend more. This increase in DEMAND can lead to higher employment.

Plaza Accord

On September 22nd 1985, finance ministers from the world's five biggest economies – the United States, Japan, West Germany, France and the UK – announced the Plaza Accord at the eponymous New York hotel. Each country made specific promises on economic policy: the United States pledged to cut the federal DEFICIT; Japan promised a looser MONETARY POLICY and a range of financial-sector reforms; and Germany proposed tax cuts. All countries agreed to intervene in currency markets as necessary to get the dollar down. Perhaps not surprisingly, not all the promises were kept (least of all the American one on deficit cutting), but even so the plan turned out to be spectacularly successful. By the end of 1987, the dollar had fallen by 54% against both the D-mark and the yen from its peak in February 1985. This sharp drop led to a new fear: of an uncontrolled dollar plunge. So in 1987 another big international plan, the Louvre Accord, was hatched to stabilise the dollar. Again specific policy pledges were made (the United States to tighten FISCAL POLICY, Japan to loosen monetary policy). Again the participants promised currency intervention if major currencies moved outside an agreed, but unpublished, set of ranges. The dollar promptly rose.

Population

At the beginning of the 20th century the population of the world was 1.7 billion. At the end of that century, it had soared to 6 billion. Recent estimates suggest that it will be nearly 8.4 billion by 2030 and 9.5 billion by 2050. Almost all of this increase is forecast to occur in the developing regions of Africa, Asia and Latin America. For what economists have had to say about this, see DEMOGRAPHICS.

Positional goods

Things that the Joneses buy. Some things are bought for their intrinsic usefulness, such as a hammer or a washing machine. Positional goods are bought because of what they say about the person who buys them. They are a way for a person to establish or signal their status relative to people who do not own them: fast cars, holidays in the most fashionable resorts, clothes from trendy designers. By necessity, the quantity of these goods is somewhat fixed, because to increase SUPPLY too much would mean that they were no longer positional. What would owning a Rolls-Royce say about you if everybody owned one? Fears that the rise of positional goods would limit GROWTH, since by definition they had to be in scarce supply, have so far proved misplaced. ENTREPRE-NEURS have come up with ever more ingenious ways for people to buy status, thus helping developed economies to keep growing.

Positive economics

ECONOMICS that describes the world as it is, rather than trying to change it. The opposite of NORMATIVE ECONOMICS, which suggests policies for increasing economic WELFARE.

Poverty

The state of being poor, which depends on how you define it. One approach is to use some absolute measure. For instance, the poverty rate refers to the number of households whose INCOME is less than three times what is needed to provide an adequate diet. (Though what constitutes adequate may change over time.) Another is to measure relative poverty. For instance, the number of people in poverty can be defined as all households with an income of less than, say, half the AVERAGE household income. Or the (relative) poverty line may be defined as the level of income below which are, say, the poorest 10% of households. In each case, the dividing line between poverty and not-quite poverty is somewhat arbitrary.

As countries get richer, the number of people in absolute poverty usually gets smaller. This is not necessarily true of the numbers in relative poverty. The way that relative poverty is defined means that it is always likely to identify a large number of impoverished households. However rich a country becomes, there will always be 10% of households poorer than the rest, even though they may live in mansions and eat caviar (albeit smaller mansions and less caviar than the other 90% of households).

Poverty trap

Another name for the UNEMPLOYMENT TRAP. At the macro level, a country that is too poor to achieve sustained economic GROWTH.

PPP

See PURCHASING POWER PARITY.

Precautionary motive

Keeping some MONEY handy, just in case. One of three motives for holding money identified by KEYNES, along with the transactional motive (having the cash to pay for planned purchases) and the speculative motive (you think ASSET PRICES are going to fall, so you sell your ASSETS for cash). As uncertainty about the outlook for the economy increases, so does precautionary holding of money.

Predatory lending

Lending that exploits vulnerable borrowers. There is much disagreement among economists over when lending becomes predatory rather than extending access to CREDIT to a needy borrower. See FINANCIAL LITERACY, SUB-PRIME and USURY.

Predatory pricing

Charging low PRICES now so you can charge much higher prices later. The predator charges so little that it may sustain losses over a period of time, in the hope that its rivals will be driven out of business. Clearly, this strategy makes sense only if the predatory firm is able eventually to establish a MONOPOLY. Some advocates of anti-DUMPING policies say that cheap IMPORTS are examples of predatory pricing. In practice, the evidence gives little support for this view. Indeed, in general, predatory pricing is rare. It is certainly much less common in practice than it might appear from the propaganda of FIRMS that are under pricing pressure from more efficient competitors.

Preference

What consumers want (see REVEALED PREFERENCE).

Present value

See NET PRESENT VALUE.

Price

In EQUILIBRIUM, what balances SUPPLY and DEMAND. The price charged for something depends on the tastes, INCOME and ELASTICITY of demand of customers. It depends on the amount of COMPETITION in the market. Under PERFECT COMPETITION, all FIRMS are price takers. Where there is a MONOPOLY, or firms have some MARKET POWER, the seller has some control over the price, which will probably be higher than in a perfectly competitive market. By how much more will depend on how much market power there is, and on whether the firm(s) with the market power are committed to PROFIT MAXIMISATION. In some cases, firms may charge less than the profit-maximising price for strategic or other reasons (see PREDATORY PRICING).

Price discrimination

When a FIRM charges different customers different PRICES for the same product. For producers, the perfect world would be one in which they could charge each customer a different price: the price that each customer would be willing to pay. This would maximise PRODUCER SURPLUS. This cannot happen, not least because sellers do not know how much any individual would pay.

Yet some price discrimination is possible if an overall market can be segmented into somewhat separate markets and the EQUI-LIBRIUM price in each of these markets is different, perhaps because of differences in consumer tastes, perhaps because in some segments the firm enjoys some MARKET POWER. But this will work only if the market segments can be kept apart. If it is possible and profitable to buy the product in a low-price segment and resell it in a high-price segment, then price discrimination will not last for long.

Price/earnings ratio

A crude method of judging whether SHARES are cheap or expensive; the ratio of the market PRICE of a share to the company's earnings (PROFIT) per share. The higher the price/earnings (P/E) ratio, the more investors are buying a company's shares in the expectation that it will make larger profits in future than now. In other words, the higher the P/E ratio, the more optimistic investors are being.

Price elasticity

A measure of the responsiveness of DEMAND to a change in PRICE. If demand changes by more than the price has changed, the good is price-elastic. If demand changes by less than the price, it is price-inelastic. Economists also measure the ELASTICITY of demand to changes in the INCOME of consumers.

Price mechanism

The process by which markets set PRICES.

Price regulation

When PRICES of, say, a PUBLIC UTILITY are regulated, giving producers an incentive to maximise their PROFITS by reducing their costs as much as possible. Contrast with RATE OF RETURN REGULATION.

Principal–agent theory

See AGENCY COSTS.

Prisoner's dilemma

A favourite example in GAME THEORY, which shows why co-operation is difficult to achieve even when it is mutually beneficial. Two prisoners have been arrested for the same offence and are held in different cells. Each has two options: confess, or say nothing. There are three possible outcomes. One could confess and agree to testify against the other as state witness, receiving a light sentence while his fellow prisoner receives a heavy sentence. They can both say nothing and may be lucky and get light sentences or even be let off, owing to lack of firm evidence. Or they may both confess and probably get lighter individual sentences than one would have received had he said nothing and the other had testified against him. The second outcome would be the best for both prisoners. However, the risk that the other might confess and turn state witness is likely to encourage both to confess, landing both with sentences that they might have avoided had they been able to co-operate in remaining silent. In an OLIGOPOLY, FIRMS often behave like these prisoners, not setting PRICES as high as they could do if they only trusted the other firms not to undercut them. As a result, they are worse off.

Private equity

When a FIRM'S SHARES are held privately and not traded in the public markets. Private equity includes shares both in mature private companies and, as VENTURE CAPITAL, in newly started businesses. As it is less liquid than publicly traded EQUITY, investors in private equity expect on average to earn a higher EQUITY RISK PREMIUM from it.

Private equity first boomed during the 1980s, when private equity firms such as KKR undertook high-profile LEVERAGED BUYOUTS. After crashing at the end of that decade, and recovering slowly, it boomed again at the start of the 21st century, reaching an unprecedented scale, only to suffer a sharp (but perhaps temporary) decline as access to CREDIT evaporated during the economic crisis that began in 2007.

Some economists argue that private equity creates PROFIT by taking on extra RISK by borrowing to buy firms and by cutting costs aggressively; others say that it improves economic EFFICIENCY by reducing the AGENCY COSTS in the firms owned by private equity through much more effective corporate governance than is typical in public companies.

Privatisation

Selling state-owned businesses to private investors. This policy was associated initially with Margaret Thatcher's GOVERNMENT in the 1980s, which privatised numerous companies, including PUBLIC UTILITY businesses such as British Telecom, British Gas, and electricity and water companies. During the 1990s, privatisation became a favourite policy of governments all over the world.

There were several reasons for the popularity of privatisation. In some instances, the aim was to improve the performance of publicly owned companies. Often NATIONALISATION had failed to achieve its goals and had become increasingly associated with poor service to customers. Sometimes privatisation was part of transforming a state-owned MONOPOLY into a competitive market, by combining ownership transfer with DEREGULATION and LIBERALISATION. Sometimes it offered a way to raise new CAPITAL for the firm to invest in improving its service, MONEY that was not available in the public sector because of constraints on PUBLIC SPENDING. Indeed, perhaps the main attraction of privatisation to many politicians was that the proceeds from it could ease the pressure on the public purse. As a result, they could avoid (in the short term) doing the more painful things necessary to improve the fiscal position, such as raising taxes or cutting public spending.

Probability

How likely something is to happen, usually expressed as the ratio of the number of ways the outcome may occur to the number of total possible outcomes for the event. For instance, each time you throw a dice there are six possible outcomes, but in only one of these can a six come up. Thus the probability of throwing a six on any given throw is one in six. The fact that you threw a six last time does not alter the one-in-six probability of throwing a six next time (see RISK).

Producer prices

See FACTORY PRICES.

Producer surplus

The difference between what a supplier is paid for a good or service and what it cost to SUPPLY. Added to CONSUMER SURPLUS, it provides a measure of the total economic benefit of a sale.

Production function

A mathematical way to describe the relationship between the quantity of inputs used by a FIRM and the quantity of OUTPUT it produces with them. If the amount of inputs needed to produce one more unit of output is less than was needed to produce the last unit of output, the firm is enjoying increasing RETURNS to scale (or increasing MARGINAL product). If each extra unit of output requires a growing amount of inputs to produce it, the firm faces diminishing returns to scale (diminishing marginal product).

Productivity

The relationship between inputs and OUTPUT, which can be applied to individual FACTORS OF PRODUCTION or collectively. LABOUR productivity is the most widely used measure and is usually calculated by dividing total output by the number of workers or the number of hours worked. Total factor productivity attempts to measure the overall productivity of the inputs used by a FIRM or a country.

Alas, the usefulness of productivity statistics is questionable. The quality of different inputs can change significantly over time. There can also be significant differences in the mix of inputs.

Furthermore, firms and countries may use different definitions of their inputs, especially CAPITAL.

That said, much of the difference in countries' living standards reflects differences in their productivity. Usually, the higher their productivity is the better, but this is not always so. In the UK during the 1980s, labour productivity rose sharply, leading some economists to talk of a "productivity miracle". Others disagreed, saying that productivity had risen because UNEMPLOYMENT had risen – in other words, the least productive workers had been removed from the figures on which the AVERAGE was calculated.

There was a similar debate in the United States starting in the late 1990s. Initially, economists doubted that a productivity miracle was taking place. But by 2003, they conceded that during the previous five years the United States enjoyed the fastest productivity growth in any such period since the second world war. Over the whole period from 1995, labour productivity growth averaged almost 3% a year, twice the average rate over the previous two decades. That did not stop economists debating why the miracle had occurred.

Profit

The main reason FIRMS exist. In economic theory, profit is the reward for RISK taken by ENTERPRISE, the fourth of the FACTORS OF PRODUCTION – what is left after all other costs, including RENT, WAGES and INTEREST. Put simply, profit is a firm's total revenue minus total cost.

Economists distinguish between normal profit and excess profit. Normal profit is the OPPORTUNITY COST of the ENTREPRENEUR, the amount of profit just sufficient to keep the firm in business. If profit is any lower than that, enterprise would be better off engaged in some other economic activity. Excess profit, also known as super-normal profit, is profit above normal profit and is usually evidence that the firm enjoys some market power that allows it to be more profitable than it would be in a market with perfect competition.

Profit margin

A firm's PROFIT expressed as a percentage of its turnover or sales.

Profit maximisation

The presumed goal of FIRMS. In practice, business people often trade off making as much PROFIT as possible against other goals, such as building business empires, being popular with staff and enjoying life. The growing popularity in recent years of paying bosses with SHARES in their firm may have reduced the AGENCY COSTS that arise because they are the hired hands of shareholders, thus making them more likely to pursue profit maximisation.

Progressive taxation

TAXATION that takes a larger proportion of a taxpayer's INCOME the higher the income is. (See VERTICAL EQUITY.)

Propensity

ECONOMICS abounds with propensities to do various things: consume, save, invest, import, and so on. In each case, it is important to distinguish between the AVERAGE propensity and the MARGINAL one. The average propensity to consume is simply total CONSUMPTION divided by total INCOME. The marginal propensity to consume measures how much of each extra dollar of income is consumed: the percentage change in consumption divided by the percentage change in income. The value of the marginal propensity to consume, which determines the MULTI-PLIER, is harder to predict than the value of the average propensity to consume.

Property rights

Essential to any market economy. To trade, it is essential to know that the person selling a good or service owns it and that ownership will pass to the buyer. The stronger and clearer property rights are, the more likely it is that trade will take place and that PRICES will be efficient. If there are no property rights over something, there can be severe consequences. A solution to the costly EXTERNALITY of clean air being polluted may be to establish property rights over the air, so that the owner can charge the polluter to pump smoke into the atmosphere.

Private property rights are often more economically efficient than common ownership. When people do not own something directly, they may have little incentive to look after it. (See TRAGEDY OF THE COMMONS.) Strikingly, in Russia after COMMUNISM, the establishment of a well-functioning market economy proved difficult, partly because it was unclear who owned many of the country's resources, and those property rights that did exist often counted for little. Businesses would often have their products stolen by criminal gangs or be forced to hand over most of their PROFIT in protection money. It is no coincidence that an effective judicial system, as well as property rights for it to enforce, is a feature of advanced market economies.

That said, nowhere are property rights absolute. For instance, TAXATION is a clear example of the state infringing taxpayers' ownership of their MONEY. GOVERNMENTS sometimes exercise their right of "eminent domain" (known as compulsory purchase in some countries) to take control of privately owned land. The economic cost of infringing property rights underlines how important it is that governments think carefully about the consequences for economic growth of their tax policies.

Prospect theory

A theory of "irrational" economic behaviour. Prospect theory holds that there are recurring biases driven by psychological factors that influence people's choices under uncertainty. In particular, it assumes that people are more motivated by losses than by gains and as a result will devote more energy to avoiding loss than to achieving gain. The theory is based on the experimental work of two psychologists, Daniel Kahneman (who won the NOBEL PRIZE IN ECONOMICS for it) and Amos Tversky (1937–96). It is an important component of BEHAVIOURAL ECONOMICS.

Protectionism

Opposition to FREE TRADE. Although intended to protect a country's economy from foreign competitors, it usually makes the protected country worse off than if it allowed international trade to proceed without hindrance from trade barriers such as QUOTAS and TARIFFS.

Public goods

Things that can be consumed by everybody in a society, or nobody at all. They have three characteristics. They are:

- non-rival – one person consuming them does not stop another person consuming them;
- non-excludable – if one person can consume them, it is impossible to stop another person consuming them;

■ non-rejectable – people cannot choose not to consume them even if they want to.

Examples include clean air, a national defence system and the judiciary. The combination of non-rivalry and non-excludability means that it can be hard to get people to pay to consume them, so they might not be provided at all if left to MARKET FORCES. Thus public goods are regarded as an example of MARKET FAILURE, and in most countries they are provided at least in part by GOVERNMENT and paid for through compulsory TAXATION. (See also GLOBAL PUBLIC GOODS.)

Public spending

Spending by national and local GOVERNMENT and some government-backed institutions. See FISCAL POLICY, GOLDEN RULE and BUDGET.

Public–private

When private FIRMS, NGOs or individuals such as philanthropists partner with GOVERNMENT. This has become increasingly popular since the early 1980s as governments have tried to obtain some of the benefits of the private sector without going as far as full PRIVATISATION. Some of the biggest EFFICIENCY gains have come when SERVICES have been allocated to private firms through competitive bidding. The gains have been smallest, and arguably even negative, in cases when the main contribution of the private firm has been to raise finance. That is because governments can usually borrow more cheaply than private firms, so when they ask them to raise money the question that springs to mind is: are they doing this to make their public borrowing look smaller?

More recently, the rise of NGOs and PHILANTHROCAPITALISM has led to new sorts of public–private partnerships that draw on

the entrepreneurship of philanthropists and SOCIAL ENTREPRE-
NEURS to develop more innovative solutions than are often forth-
coming when problems are addressed by government acting
alone. In the DIVISION OF LABOUR at the heart of these partnerships, government often benefits most when it concentrates on
providing the funds while its private-sector partners focus on
doing things in efficient, innovative ways.

Public utility

A firm providing essential services to the public, such as water,
electricity and postal services, usually involving elements of
natural monopoly. Food is essential, but because it is provided in
a competitive market, food supply is not usually regarded as a
public utility. Because public utilities have some monopoly power,
they are typically subject to some regulation by government, such
as price controls and perhaps an obligation to provide their services to everybody, even those who cannot afford to pay a market
price (the universal service obligation). Public utilities are often
owned by the state, although this has become less common as a
result of PRIVATISATION.

Purchasing power parity

A method for calculating the correct value of a currency, which
may differ from its current market value. Purchasing power parity
(PPP) is helpful when comparing living standards in different
countries, as it indicates the appropriate EXCHANGE RATE to use
when expressing incomes and PRICES in different countries in a
common currency.

By correct value, economists mean the exchange rate that
would bring DEMAND and SUPPLY of a currency into EQUILIB-
RIUM over the long-term. The current market rate is only a

short-run equilibrium. It says that goods and SERVICES should cost the same in all countries when measured in a common currency. It is the exchange rate that equates the price of a basket of identical traded goods and services in two countries.

PPP is often very different from the current market exchange rate. Some economists argue that once the exchange rate is pushed away from its PPP, trade and financial flows in and out of a country can move into DISEQUILIBRIUM, resulting in potentially substantial trade and current account DEFICITS or surpluses. Because it is not just traded goods that are affected, some economists argue that PPP is too narrow a measure for judging a currency's true value. They prefer the fundamental equilibrium exchange rate (FEER), which is the rate consistent with a country achieving an overall balance with the outside world, including both traded goods and services and CAPITAL flows. (See BIG MAC INDEX.)

Q theory

See TOBIN.

Quantity theory of money

The foundation stone of MONETARISM. The theory says that the quantity of MONEY available in an economy determines the value of money. Increases in the MONEY SUPPLY are the main cause of INFLATION. This is why Milton FRIEDMAN claimed "inflation is always and everywhere a monetary phenomenon".

The theory is built on the Fisher equation, MV = PT, named after Irving Fisher (1867–1947). M is the stock of money, V is the VELOCITY OF CIRCULATION, P is the average PRICE level and T is the number of transactions in the economy. The equation says, simply and obviously, that the quantity of money spent equals the quantity of money used. The quantity theory, in its purest form, assumes that V and T are both constant, at least in the short-run. Thus any change in M leads directly to a change in P. In other words, increase the money supply and you simply cause inflation.

In the 1930s KEYNES challenged this theory, which was orthodoxy until then. Increases in the money supply seemed to lead to a fall in the velocity of circulation and to increases in real INCOME, contradicting the classical dichotomy (see MONETARY NEUTRALITY). Later, monetarists such as Friedman conceded that V could change in response to variations in M, but did so only in stable, predictable ways that did not challenge the thrust of the theory. Even so, monetarist policies did not perform well when they were applied in many countries during the 1980s, as even Friedman has since conceded.

Quartile

Part of the "ile" family that signposts positions on a scale of numbers (see also PERCENTILE). The top quartile on, say, the distribution of INCOME, is the richest 25% of the POPULATION.

Queueing

MARKET FAILURE? Not necessarily. Usually a queue reflects a PRICE that is set too low, so that DEMAND exceeds SUPPLY, so some customers have to wait to buy the product. But a queue may also be the result of deliberate rationing by a producer, perhaps to attract attention – by a restaurant that wants to appear popular, say. Customers may regard a queue, such as a waiting list for health treatment, as a fairer way to distribute the product than using the PRICE MECHANISM.

Quota

A form of PROTECTIONISM. A country imposes limits on the number of goods that can be imported from another country. For instance, France may limit the number of cars imported from Japan to, say, 20,000 a year. As a result of limiting SUPPLY, the PRICE of the imported good is higher than it would be under FREE TRADE, thus making life easier for domestic producers.

Random walk

Impossible to predict the next step. EFFICIENT MARKET THEORY says that the PRICES of many financial ASSETS, such as SHARES, follow a random walk. In other words, there is no way of knowing whether the next change in the price will be up or down, or by how much it will rise or fall. The reason is that in an efficient market, all the INFORMATION that would allow an investor to predict the next price move is already reflected in the current price. This belief has led some economists to argue that investors cannot consistently outperform the market. But some economists argue that asset prices are predictable (they follow a non-random walk) and that markets are not efficient.

Rate of return

A way to measure economic success, albeit one that can be manipulated quite easily. It is calculated by expressing the economic gain (usually PROFIT) as a percentage of the CAPITAL used to produce it. Deciding what number to use for profit is rarely simple. Likewise, adding up how much capital was used can be tricky, especially if it is expanded to include INTANGIBLE ASSETS and HUMAN CAPITAL. When firms are evaluating a project to decide whether to go ahead with it, they estimate the project's expected rate of return and compare it with their COST OF CAPITAL. (See NET PRESENT VALUE and DISCOUNT RATE.)

Rate of return regulation

An approach to REGULATION often used for a PUBLIC UTILITY to stop it exploiting MONOPOLY power. A public utility is forbidden to earn above a certain rate of return decided by the regulator. In practice, this often encourages the utility to be inefficient, slow to innovate and quick to spend MONEY on such things as big offices and executive jets, to keep down its PROFIT and thus the rate of return. Contrast with PRICE REGULATION.

Ratings

A guide to the riskiness of a FINANCIAL INSTRUMENT provided by a ratings agency, such as Moody's, Standard & Poor's and Fitch IBCA. These measures of CREDIT quality are mostly offered on marketable GOVERNMENT and corporate DEBT. A triple-A or A++ rating represents a low risk of DEFAULT, and a C or D rating an extreme risk of, or actual, default. Debt PRICES and YIELDS often (but not always) reflect these ratings. A triple-A BOND has a low yield. High-yielding bonds, also known as junk bonds, usually have a rating that suggests a high risk of default.

A series of FINANCIAL MARKET crises from the mid-1990s onwards led to growing debate about the reliability of ratings, and whether they were slow to give warning of impending trouble. After the ENRON debacle, which again the ratings agencies had failed to predict, some critics argued that the big three agencies had formed a cosy OLIGOPOLY and that encouraging more COM-PETITION was the way to improve ratings. Such criticisms intensi-fied during the global economic crisis that began in 2007, not least because financial SECURITIES linked to SUB-PRIME mortgages were rated too favourably, giving investors confidence that proved to have been seriously misplaced.

Rationality

See ECONOMIC MAN.

Rational expectations

How some economists believe that people think about the future. Nobody can predict the future perfectly; but rational expectations theory assumes that, over time, unexpected events (SHOCKS) will cancel out each other and that on average people's EXPECTATIONS about the future will be accurate. This is because they form their expectations on a rational basis, using all the INFORMATION available to them optimally, and learn from their mistakes. This is in contrast to other theories of how people look ahead, such as ADAPTIVE EXPECTATIONS, in which people base their predictions on past trends and changes in trends, and BEHAVIOURAL ECONOMICS, which assumes that expectations are somewhat irrational as a result of psychological biases.

The theory of rational expectations, for which Robert Lucas won the NOBEL PRIZE IN ECONOMICS, initially became popular with monetarists because it seemed to prove that KEYNESIAN policies of demand management would fail. With rational expectations, people learn to anticipate GOVERNMENT policy changes and act accordingly; since macroeconomic FINE TUNING requires that governments be able to fool people, this implies that it is usually futile. Subsequently, this conclusion has been challenged, not least by behavioural economics. However, rational and near-rational expectations have remained part of the mainstream of economic thought.

❝❝ *An economist is an expert who will know tomorrow why the things he predicted yesterday didn't happen today.*
Laurence Peter, Canadian academic and humorist

Rationing

Although economists say that rationing is what the PRICE MECH-ANISM does, what most people think of as rationing is an alternative to letting PRICES determine how scarce economic resources, goods and SERVICES are distributed (see also QUEUEING). Non-price rationing is often used when the distribution decided by MARKET FORCES is perceived to be unfair. Rationing may lead to the creation of a black market, as people sell their rations to those willing to pay a high price (see BLACK ECONOMY).

Real balance effect

Falling INFLATION and INTEREST RATES lead to higher spending (see WEALTH EFFECT).

Real exchange rate

An EXCHANGE RATE that has been adjusted to take account of any difference in the rate of INFLATION in the two countries whose currency is being exchanged.

Real interest rate

The INTEREST RATE less the rate of INFLATION.

Real options theory

A newish theory of how to take INVESTMENT decisions when the future is uncertain, which draws parallels between the real economy and the use and valuation of financial options. It is becoming increasingly fashionable at business schools and even in the boardroom.

Traditional investment theory says that when a FIRM evaluates a proposed project, it should calculate the project's NET PRESENT VALUE (NPV) and if it is positive, go ahead.

Real options theory assumes that firms also have some choice in when to invest. In other words, the project is like an option: there is an opportunity, but not an obligation, to go ahead with it. As with financial options, the interesting question is when to exercise the option: certainly not when it is out of the money (the cost of investing exceeds the benefit). Financial options should not necessarily be exercised as soon as they are in the money (the benefit from exercising exceeds the cost). It may be better to wait until they are deep in the money (the benefit is far above the cost). Likewise, companies should not necessarily invest as soon as a project has a positive NPV. It may pay to wait.

Most firms' investment opportunities have embedded in them many managerial options. For instance, consider an OIL company whose bosses think they have discovered an oil field, but they are uncertain about how much oil it contains and what the PRICE of oil will be once they start to pump. Option one: to buy or lease the land and explore? Option two: if they find oil, to start to pump? Whether to exercise these options will depend on the oil price and what it is likely to do in future. Because oil prices are highly volatile, it might not make sense to go ahead with production until the oil price is far above the price at which traditional investment theory would say that the NPV is positive and give the investment the green light.

Options on real ASSETS behave rather like financial options (a SHARE option, say). The similarities are such that they can, at least in theory, be valued according to the same methodology. In the case of the oil company, for instance, the cost of LAND corresponds to the down-payment on a call (right to buy) option, and the extra investment needed to start production to its strike price (the money that must be paid if the option is exercised). As with financial options, the longer the option lasts before it expires and the more volatile is the price of the underlying asset (in this case, oil) the more the option is worth. That is the theory. In practice, pricing financial options is often tricky, and valuing real options is harder still.

Real terms

A measure of the value of MONEY that removes the effect of INFLATION. Contrast with NOMINAL VALUE.

Recession

Broadly, a period of slow or negative economic growth, usually accompanied by rising UNEMPLOYMENT. Economists have two more precise definitions of a recession. The first, which can be hard to prove, is when an economy is growing at less than its long-term trend rate of GROWTH and has spare CAPACITY. The second is two consecutive quarters of falling GDP.

Reciprocity

Doing as you are done by. A grants B certain privileges on the condition that B grants the same privileges to A. Most international economic agreements, for example on trade, include binding reciprocity requirements.

Redlining

Not lending to people in certain poor or troubled neighbourhoods – drawn with a red line on a map – simply because they live there, regardless of their CREDIT-worthiness judged by other criteria.

Reflation

Policies to pump up DEMAND and thus boost the level of economic activity. Monetarists fear that such policies may simply result in higher INFLATION.

Regional policy

A policy intended to boost economic activity in a specific geographical area that is not an entire country and, typically, is in worse economic shape than nearby areas. It can include offering FIRMS incentives to provide jobs in the region, such as SOFT LOANS, grants, lower taxes, cheap LAND and buildings, subsidised LABOUR and worker training.

Is it necessary? A region's problems should be somewhat self-correcting. After all, simple theories of SUPPLY and DEMAND would suggest that firms will move to areas of low WAGES and high UNEMPLOYMENT to take advantage of cheaper labour and surplus workers, or that workers will move away from such areas to where more and better-paid jobs exist. But some economic theories suggest that rather than moving to areas where wages are lowest, firms often cluster together with other successful businesses. Regional policy may need to be extremely generous to tempt firms to give up the advantages of being in a cluster.

Regression analysis

Number-crunching to discover the relationship between different economic variables. The findings of this statistical technique should always be taken with a pinch of salt. How big a pinch can vary considerably and is indicated by the degree of STATISTICAL SIGNIFICANCE and R SQUARED. The relationship between a dependent variable (GDP, say) and a set of explanatory variables

(DEMAND, INTEREST RATES, CAPITAL, UNEMPLOYMENT, and so on) is expressed as a regression equation.

Regressive tax

A tax that takes a smaller proportion of INCOME as the taxpayer's income rises, for example, a fixed-rate vehicle tax that eats up a much larger slice of a poor person's income than a rich person's income. This goes against the principle of VERTICAL EQUITY, which many people think should be at the heart of any fair tax system.

Regulation

Rules governing the activities of private-sector enterprises. Regulation is often imposed by GOVERNMENT, either directly or through an appointed regulator. However, some industries and professions impose rules on their members through self-regulation.

Regulation is often introduced to tackle MARKET FAILURE. EXTERNALITIES such as pollution have inspired rules limiting factory emissions. Regulations on the selling of financial products to individuals have been introduced as protection against unscrupulous financial FIRMS with better INFORMATION than their customers. RATE OF RETURN regulation and PRICE regulation have been used to combat NATURAL MONOPOLY, sometimes instead of NATIONALISATION. Some regulation has been motivated by politics rather than ECONOMICS, for instance, restrictions on the number of hours people can work or the circumstances in which an employer can dismiss employees.

Even when introduced for sound economic reasons, regulation can generate more costs than benefits. Regulated firms or individuals may face substantial compliance costs. Firms may devote substantial resources to REGULATORY ARBITRAGE, which would leave consumers no better off. Regulation may lead to MORAL HAZARD if people believe that the government is keeping an eye on the behaviour of the regulated business and so do less monitoring of their own. Regulation may be badly designed and thus lock an industry into an inefficient EQUILIBRIUM. Rigid regulation may hold back INNOVATION. There is also the danger of REGULATORY CAPTURE. In short, then, REGULATORY FAILURE may be even worse for an economy than market failure.

The global economic crisis that began in 2007 reinvigorated the debate about the relative severity of market failure and regulatory failure, both prevalent at the time.

Regulatory arbitrage

Exploiting loopholes in REGULATION, and perhaps making the regulation useless in the process. This is often done by international investors that use DERIVATIVES to find ways around a country's financial regulations.

Regulatory capture

Gamekeeper turns poacher or, at least, helps poacher. The theory of regulatory capture was set out by Richard Posner, an economist and lawyer at the University of Chicago, who argued:

Regulation is not about the public interest at all, but is a process, by which interest groups seek to promote their private interest ... Over time, regulatory agencies come to be dominated by the industries regulated.

Most economists are less extreme, arguing that REGULATION often does good but is always at risk of being captured by the regulated firms.

Regulatory failure

When REGULATION generates more economic costs than economic benefits.

Regulatory risk

A RISK faced by private-sector firms that regulatory changes will hurt their business. In competitive markets, regulatory risk is usually small. But in NATURAL MONOPOLY industries, such as electricity distribution, it may be huge. To ensure that regulatory risk does not deter private firms from offering their services, a GOVERNMENT wishing to change its REGULATIONS may have good reason to compensate private firms that suffer losses as a result of the change.

Relative income hypothesis

People often care more about their relative well-being than their absolute well-being. Someone who prefers a $100 a week pay rise when a colleague gets $50 to both of them getting a $200 increase, for example. Poor people may consume more of their INCOME than rich people do because they want to reduce the gap in their CONSUMPTION levels. The relative income hypothesis, set out by James Duesenberry, says that a household's consumption depends partly on its income relative to other families. Contrast with PERMANENT INCOME HYPOTHESIS.

Remittances

Money sent home, typically to relatives, by migrant workers abroad. According to the WORLD BANK, remittances from over 190m migrant workers totalled $305 billion in 2008. These

financial inflows can be extremely valuable to receiving econo-
mies, in many cases more valuable than INTERNATIONAL AID.
India receives the largest amount of remittances in absolute terms,
around $27 billion, ahead of China, Mexico and the Philippines.
Other economies receive less, but are far more dependent on
these inflows. For instance, remittances represent nearly 25% of
GDP for Honduras and 20% for Haiti, compared with just 3% for
Mexico.

Rent

Confusingly, rent has two different meanings for economists. The
first is the commonplace definition: the INCOME from hiring out
LAND or other durable goods. The second, also known as economic rent, is a measure of MARKET POWER: the difference
between what a FACTOR OF PRODUCTION is paid and how much
it would need to be paid to remain in its current use. A soccer star
may be paid $50,000 a week to play for his team when he would
be willing to turn out for only $10,000, so his economic rent is
$40,000 a week. In PERFECT COMPETITION, there are no economic
rents, as new FIRMS enter a market and compete until PRICES fall
and all rent is eliminated. Reducing rent does not change production decisions, so economic rent can be taxed without any adverse
impact on the real economy, assuming that it really is rent.

Rent-seeking

Cutting yourself a bigger slice of the cake rather than making the
cake bigger. Trying to make more MONEY without producing more
for customers. Classic examples of rent-seeking, a phrase coined
by an economist, Gordon Tullock, include:

- a protection racket, in which the gang takes a cut from the
  shopkeeper's PROFIT;

- a CARTEL of FIRMS agreeing to raise PRICES;
- a UNION demanding higher WAGES without offering any increase in PRODUCTIVITY;
- lobbying the GOVERNMENT for tax, spending or regulatory policies that benefit the lobbyists at the expense of taxpayers or consumers or some other rivals.

Whether legal or illegal, as they do not create any value, rent-seeking activities can impose large costs on an economy.

Replacement cost

What it would cost today to replace a FIRM's existing ASSETS.

Replacement rate

The fertility rate required in a country to keep its POPULATION steady. In rich countries, this is usually reckoned to be 2.1 children per woman, the extra 0.1 reflecting the likelihood that some children will die before their parents. In poorer countries with higher infant mortality, the replacement rate may be much higher. In many countries, since the early 1990s the fertility rate has fallen below the replacement rate. There has been much debate about why, and much agreement that, if this trend continues, those countries may face long-term problems such as a relatively growing proportion of retired older people having to be supported by a relatively shrinking proportion of younger people.

Repo

An agreement in which one party sells a security to another party and agrees to buy it back on a specified date for a specified price. CENTRAL BANKS deal in short-term repos to provide LIQUIDITY to the FINANCIAL SYSTEM, buying SECURITIES from BANKS with cash on the condition that the banks will repurchase them a few weeks later.

Required return

The minimum EXPECTED RETURN you require from an INVEST-MENT to be willing to go ahead with it.

Rescheduling

Changing the payment schedule for a DEBT by agreement between borrower and lender. This is usually done when the borrower is struggling to make payments under the original schedule. Rescheduling can involve reducing INTEREST payments but extending the period over which they are collected; putting back the date of repayment of the loan; reducing interest payments but increasing the amount that has to be repaid eventually; and so on. The rescheduling may or may not require the lender to bear some financial loss. The rescheduling of loans to countries usually takes place through the PARIS CLUB and London Club.

Reservation wage

The lowest WAGE for which a person will work.

Reserve currency

A foreign currency held by a GOVERNMENT or CENTRAL BANK as part of a country's RESERVES. Outside the United States the dollar is the most widely used reserve currency. Everywhere the EURO is increasingly widely used.

Reserve ratio

The fraction of its deposits that a BANK holds as RESERVES.

Reserves

MONEY in the hand, available to be used to meet planned future payments or if some other need arises. FIRMS may put their reserves in a BANK, as a deposit. For a bank, reserves are those deposits it retains rather than lending them out.

Reserve requirements

Regulations governing the minimum amount of RESERVES that a BANK must hold against deposits.

Residual risk

When you buy an ASSET you become exposed to a bundle of different RISKS. Many of these risks are not unique to the asset you own but reflect broader possibilities, such as that the stockmarket AVERAGE will rise or fall, that INTEREST RATES will be cut or increased, or that the GROWTH rate will change in an entire economy or industry. Residual risk, also known as alpha, is what is left after you take out all the other shared risk exposures. Exposure to this risk can be reduced by DIVERSIFICATION. Contrast with SYSTEMATIC RISK.

Restrictive practice

A general term for anything done by a firm, or FIRMS, to inhibit COMPETITION. Generally against the law. (See ANTITRUST and CARTEL.)

Returns

The rewards for doing business. Returns usually refer to PROFIT and can be measured in various ways (see RATE OF RETURN and TOTAL RETURNS).

Revealed preference

An example of a popular joke among economists: two economists see a Ferrari. "I want one of those," says the first. "Obviously not," replies the other. To get a smile out of this it is necessary (but not, alas, sufficient) to know about revealed preference. This is the notion that what you want is revealed by what you do, not by what you say. Actions speak louder than words. If the economist had really wanted a Ferrari he would have tried to buy one, if he did not own one already.

Economists have three main approaches to modelling DEMAND and how it will change if PRICES or INCOMES change:

- The cardinal approach involves asking consumers to say how much UTILITY they get from consuming a particular good, aggregating this across all goods and SERVICES, and calculating how demand would change on the assumption that people will consume the combination of things that maximises their total utility.

- The ordinal approach does not require consumers to say how much utility they get in absolute terms from consuming a particular good. Instead, it asks them to indicate the relative utility they get from consuming one item compared with another, that is, to say if they prefer one basket of goods to another, or are indifferent between them.

- The third approach is revealed preference. To model demand it is only necessary to be able to compare an individual's

CONSUMPTION decisions in situations with different prices and/or incomes and to assume that consumers are consistent in their decisions over time (that is, if they prefer wine to beer in one period they will still prefer wine in the next).

Ricardian equivalence

The controversial idea, suggested by David RICARDO, that GOVERNMENT DEFICITS do not affect the overall level of DEMAND in an economy. This is because taxpayers know that any deficit has to be repaid later, and so increase their SAVINGS in anticipation of a tax bill. Thus government attempts to stimulate an economy by increasing PUBLIC SPENDING and/or cutting taxes will be rendered impotent by the private-sector reaction.

Ricardo, David

The third of 17 children of a wealthy banker, David Ricardo (1772–1823) was disinherited at the age of 21 after he married a Quaker against the wishes of his parents. He became a stockbroker and did so well that he retired at 42 to concentrate on writing and politics.

A friend of fellow CLASSICAL ECONOMISTS Thomas Malthus and Jean-Baptiste Say (see SAY'S LAW), he developed many economic theories that are still in use today. The most influential was COMPARATIVE ADVANTAGE, the theory underpinning the case for FREE TRADE. In his 1817 book, *The Principles of Political Economy and Taxation*, he outlined a theory of distribution of OUTPUT in an economy. In this he argued that the allocation of FACTORS OF PRODUCTION to any area of economic activity is determined by the level of economic RENT that can be earned from it. As this gradually falls because of DIMINISHING RETURNS, CAPITAL and other resources shift to more profitable projects. He examined the split between WAGES and PROFIT, arguing that "there can be no rise in the value of LABOUR without a fall of profits". He also claimed that changes in the GOVERNMENT DEFICIT did not affect the level of DEMAND in the economy (RICARDIAN EQUIVALENCE).

Risk

The chance of things not turning out as expected. Risk taking lies at the heart of CAPITALISM and is responsible for a large part of the GROWTH of an economy. In general, economists assume that people are willing to be exposed to increased risks only if, on average, they can expect to earn higher returns than if they had less exposure to risk. How much higher these EXPECTED RETURNS need to be depends partly on the PROBABILITY of an undesirable outcome and partly on whether the risk taker is RISK AVERSE, RISK NEUTRAL or RISK SEEKING.

During the second half of the 20th century, economists greatly improved their understanding of risk and developed theories of RISK MANAGEMENT, which suggest when it makes sense to use INSURANCE, DIVERSIFICATION or HEDGING to change risk exposures.

In FINANCIAL MARKETS the most commonly used measure of risk is the VOLATILITY (or STANDARD DEVIATION) of the PRICE of, or more appropriately the TOTAL RETURNS on, an ASSET. Often added to the risk profile are other statistical measures such as skewness and the possibility of extreme changes on rare occasions. (See STRESS TESTING, SCENARIO ANALYSIS and VALUE AT RISK.)

Risk averse

Someone who thinks RISK is a four-letter word. Risk-averse investors are those who, when faced with two INVESTMENTS with the same EXPECTED RETURN but two different risks, prefer the one with the lower risk.

Risk-free rate

The RATE OF RETURN earned on a RISK-free ASSET. This is a crucial component of MODERN PORTFOLIO THEORY, which assumes the existence of both risky and risk-free assets. The risk-free asset is usually assumed to be a GOVERNMENT BOND, and the risk-free rate is the YIELD on that bond, although in fact even a TREASURY BILL is not entirely without risk. In modern portfolio theory, the risk-free rate is lower than the EXPECTED RETURN on the risky asset, because the issuer of the risky asset has to offer RISK-AVERSE investors the expectation of a higher return to persuade them to forgo the risk-free asset.

Risk management

The process of bearing the RISK you want to bear, and minimising your exposure to the risk you do not want. This can be done in several ways: not doing things that carry a particular risk; HEDGING; DIVERSIFICATION; and buying INSURANCE.

Risk neutral

Someone who is insensitive to RISK. Risk-neutral investors are indifferent between an INVESTMENT with a certain outcome and a risky investment with the same EXPECTED RETURNS but an uncertain outcome. Such people are few and far between.

Risk premium

The extra RETURN that investors require to hold a risky ASSET instead of a risk-free one; the difference between the EXPECTED RETURN from a risky investment and the RISK-FREE RATE. (See EQUITY RISK PREMIUM.)

Risk seeking

Someone who cannot get enough RISK. Risk-seeking (also known as risk-loving) investors prefer an INVESTMENT with an uncertain outcome to one with the same EXPECTED RETURNS and certainty that it will deliver them.

R squared

An indicator of the reliability of a relationship identified by REGRESSION ANALYSIS. An R^2 of 0.8 indicates that 80% of the change in one variable is explained by a change in the related variable.

Safe harbour

Protection from the rough seas of REGULATION. Laws and regulations often include a safe harbour clause that sets out the circumstances in which otherwise regulated FIRMS or individuals can do something without regulatory oversight or interference.

Satisficing

Settling for what is good enough, rather than the best that is possible. This may occur in any situation in which decision-makers are trying to pursue more than one goal at a time. CLASSICAL ECONOMICS and NEO-CLASSICAL ECONOMICS assume that individuals, FIRMS and GOVERNMENTS try to achieve the OPTIMUM, best possible outcome from their decisions. Satisficing assumes they decide for each goal a level of achievement that would be good enough and try to find a way to achieve all of these sub-optimal goals at once. This approach to decision-making is common in BEHAVIOURAL ECONOMICS. It can be regarded as a realist's theory of how decisions are taken. The concept was invented by Herbert Simon (1916–2001), a Nobel Prize-winning economist, in his book, *Models of Man*, in 1957.

Savings

Any INCOME that is not spent. Ultimately, savings are the source of INVESTMENT in an economy, although domestic savings may be supplemented by CAPITAL from foreign savers or themselves be invested abroad.

In an economic sense, savings include purchases of SHARES or other financial SECURITIES. However, many official measures of a country's savings ratio – total savings expressed as a percentage of total income – leave out such financial transactions. At times when the DEMAND for financial securities is unusually high, this can give a misleading impression of how much saving is taking place.

How much individuals save varies significantly among different age groups (see LIFE-CYCLE HYPOTHESIS) and nationalities. Everywhere, people of all ages save more as their income rises. The supply of savings rises when INTEREST RATES rise; a rise in interest rates causes demand for funds to invest to fall; a rise in demand for investment funds may cause interest rates, and thus the COST OF CAPITAL, to rise. The level of savings is also influenced by changes in wealth (see WEALTH EFFECT) and by TAXATION policies.

Say's law

SUPPLY creates its own DEMAND. So argued a French economist, Jean-Baptiste Say (1767–1832), and many classical and neo-classical economists since. KEYNES argued against Say, making the case for the use of FISCAL POLICY to boost demand if there is not enough of it to produce FULL EMPLOYMENT.

Scalability

The ease with which the SUPPLY of an economic product or process can be expanded to meet increased DEMAND. Recent technological advances have led some economists to talk about the growing importance of instant scalability. For example, once a piece of software has been written it can be made available in an instant over the internet to unlimited numbers of users for almost no cost. This potentially allows a new product to enter and win market share far more quickly than ever before, intensifying COMPETITION and perhaps accelerating the process of creative destruction (see SCHUMPETER).

Scarcity

Supplies of the FACTORS OF PRODUCTION are not unlimited. This is why choices have to be made about how best to use them, which is where ECONOMICS comes in. MARKET FORCES operating through the PRICE MECHANISM usually offer the most efficient way to allocate scarce resources, with GOVERNMENT planning playing at most a minor role. Scarcity does not imply POVERTY. In economic terms, it means simply that needs and wants exceed the resources available to meet them, which is as common in rich countries as in poor ones.

Scenario analysis

Testing your plans against various possible scenarios to see what might happen should things not go as you hope. Scenario analysis is an important technique in RISK MANAGEMENT, helping FIRMS and especially financial institutions to make sure that they do not take on too much RISK. Its usefulness does of course depend on risk managers coming up with the right scenarios.

Schumpeter, Joseph

After growing up in the Austro-Hungarian empire, in which he worked as an itinerant lawyer, Joseph Schumpeter (1883–1950) became an academic in 1909. He was appointed Austrian minister of finance in 1919, presiding over a period of HYPERINFLATION. He then became president of a small Viennese BANK, which collapsed. He returned to academia in Bonn in 1925 and in the 1930s joined the faculty of Harvard.

In 1911, while teaching at Czernowitz (now in Ukraine), he wrote the *Theory of Economic Development*. In this he set out his theory of entrepreneurship, in which GROWTH occurred, usually in spurts, because COMPETITION and declining PROFIT inspired ENTREPRENEURS to innovate. This developed into a theory of the trade cycle (see BUSINESS CYCLE) and into a notion of dynamic competition characterised by his phrase "creative destruction". In CAPITALISM, he argued, there is a tendency for FIRMS to acquire a degree of MONOPOLY power. At this point, competition no longer takes place through the PRICE MECHANISM but instead through INNOVATION. Perhaps because monopolies often become lazy, successful innovation may come from new entrants to a market, who take it away from the incumbent, thus blowing "gales of creative destruction" through the economy. Eventually, the new entrants grow fat on their monopoly PROFITS, until the next gale of creative destruction blows them away.

Ever controversial, and often wrong, in his 1942 book, *Capitalism, Socialism and Democracy*, he predicted the downfall of capitalism at the hands of an intellectual elite. Time may yet prove him right.

SDR

Short for special drawing rights. Created in 1967, the SDR is the IMF's own currency. Its value is based on a portfolio of widely used currencies.

Search costs

The cost of finding what you want. The economic cost of buying something is not simply the price you pay. Finding what you want and ensuring that it is competitively priced can be expensive, be it the financial cost of physically getting to a marketplace or the OPPORTUNITY COST of time spent fact-finding. Search costs mean that people often take decisions without all the relevant INFORMATION, which can result in inefficiency. Technological changes such as the internet may sharply reduce search costs and thus lead to more efficient decision-making.

Seasonally adjusted

There are seasonal patterns in many economic activities; for instance, there is less construction in winter than in summer, and spending in shops soars as Christmas approaches. To reveal underlying trends, statistics reflecting only part of the year are often adjusted to iron out seasonal variations.

Secondary market

A market in second-hand FINANCIAL INSTRUMENTS. BONDS and SHARES are first sold in the primary market, for instance through an initial public offering. After that, their new owners often sell them in the secondary market. The existence of liquid secondary markets can encourage people to buy in the primary market, as they know they are likely to be able to sell easily should they wish.

Second-best theory

As we do not live in a perfect world, how useful are economic theories based on the assumption that we do? Second-best theory, set out in 1956 by Richard Lipsey and Kelvin Lancaster (1924–99), looks at what happens when the assumptions of an economic model are not fully met. They found that in situations where not all the conditions are met, the second-best situation – that is, meeting as many of the other conditions as possible – may not result in the OPTIMUM solution. Indeed, reckoned Lipsey and Lancaster, in general, when one optimal equilibrium condition is not satisfied all of the other equilibrium conditions will change.

Potentially, the second-best EQUILIBRIUM may be worse than a new equilibrium brought about by GOVERNMENT intervention, either to restore equilibrium to the market that is in DISEQUILIB-RIUM, or to move the other markets away from their second-best conditions.

Economists have seized on this insight to justify all sorts of interventions in the economy, ranging from taxing certain goods and subsidising others to restricting FREE TRADE. Whenever there is MARKET FAILURE, second-best theory says it is always possible to design a government policy that would increase economic WELFARE. Alas, the history of government intervention suggests that although the second best may be improved on in theory, in practice second best is often least worst.

Securities

Financial contracts, such as BONDS, SHARES or DERIVATIVES, that grant the owner a stake in an ASSET. Such securities account for most of what is traded in the FINANCIAL MARKETS.

Securitisation

Turning an expected future cash flow into tradable, BOND-like securities. Creating such ASSET-backed securities became a lucrative business for financial FIRMS during the 1990s, as they invented new securities based on cash flow ranging from future mortgage and credit-card payments to BANK loans, movie revenue and even the royalties on songs by David Bowie (so-called Bowie-bonds).

Securitisation has many benefits, at least in theory. Issuers gain instant access to MONEY for which they would otherwise have to wait months or years, and they can shed some of the RISK that their expected revenue will not materialise. By selling securitised loans (known as collateralised debt obligations, or CDOs), banks are able to finance their customers without tying up large amounts of CAPITAL. Investors can hold a new sort of asset, (supposedly) less risky than unsecured bonds, giving them the risk-reducing benefit of DIVERSIFICATION. But there are dangers. The future cash flow underlying the securities may flow earlier or later than promised, or not at all.

This downside became all too clear during the global economic crisis that began in 2007, in which many securitised assets performed far worse than their ratings suggested they would, resulting in massive losses that paralysed the FINANCIAL SYSTEM. The first asset-backed securities to go badly wrong were tied to SUB-PRIME mortgages on millions of American homes. It remains to be seen if securitisation will ever again be as popular as it was during the gung-ho years before the CREDIT CRUNCH of 2007.

Seller's market

A market in which the seller seems to have the upper hand and so can charge a higher PRICE than in a buyer's market.

Seignorage

Traditionally, the PROFIT rulers made from allowing metals to be turned into coins. Now it refers in a loosely defined way to the power of a country whose notes and coins are held by another country as a RESERVE CURRENCY.

Seniority

The order in which CREDITORS are entitled to be repaid. In the event of a BANKRUPTCY, senior DEBT must be paid off before junior debt. Because junior debt has a lower chance of being repaid than senior debt, it carries more RISK, and thus typically has a higher YIELD.

Sequencing

Shorthand for implementing economic reforms in the right order. In recent years, this has become a hot topic in DEVELOPMENT ECONOMICS. Some economists argue that introducing the right policies alone is not enough to revive a malfunctioning economy; reforms must be implemented in the right sequence. Thus they debate when in the reform process there should be, say, PRIVATI-SATION of state enterprises, and in which order, or the lifting of CAPITAL CONTROLS or other trade barriers. Other economists dispute whether there is a right sequence.

Services

Products of economic activity that you can't drop on your foot, ranging from hairdressing to websites. In most countries, the share of economic activity accounted for by services rose steadily during the 20th century at the expense of AGRICULTURE and MANUFAC-TURING. More than two-thirds of OUTPUT in OECD countries, and up to four-fifths of employment, is now in the services sector.

Shadow banking

The highly interconnected network of investment BANKS, HEDGE FUNDS, mortgage originators, and the like, that played a significant part in causing the CREDIT CRUNCH of 2007, the BUBBLE that preceded it and the economic crisis that came after. These institutions took on many of the same risks as banks, yet were free of (most of) the regulations that were designed to stop banks creating dangerous amounts of SYSTEMIC RISK in the FINANCIAL SYSTEM. Yet the importance of shadow banks to the financial system was so great that it was widely believed that the biggest of them, at least, would never be allowed to fail by GOVERNMENT, thus creating a MORAL HAZARD that led them to take on excessive RISK, with ultimately disastrous consequences. As their role in the economic crisis became clear, moves were made to subject shadow banks to more stringent REGULATION.

Shadow price

The true economic PRICE of an activity: the OPPORTUNITY COST. Shadow prices can be calculated for those goods and SERVICES that do not have a market price, perhaps because they are set by GOVERNMENT. Shadow pricing is often used in COST-BENEFIT ANALYSIS, where the whole purpose of the analysis is to capture all the variables involved in a decision, not merely those for which market prices exist.

Shareholder value

Putting shareholders first; the notion that all business activity should aim to maximise the total value of a company's SHARES. Some critics argue that concentrating on shareholder value will be harmful to a company's other STAKEHOLDERS, such as employees, suppliers and customers.

Shares

Financial SECURITIES, each granting part ownership of a company. In return for risking their CAPITAL by giving it to the company's management to develop the business, shareholders get the right to a slice of whatever is left of the company's revenue after it has met all its other obligations. This MONEY is paid as a DIVIDEND, although most companies retain some of their residual revenue for INVESTMENT purposes. Shareholders have voting rights, including the right to vote in the election of the company's board of directors. Shares are also known as equities. They can be traded in the public FINANCIAL MARKETS or held as PRIVATE EQUITY.

Sharpe ratio

A rough guide to whether the rewards from an INVESTMENT justify the RISK, invented by Bill Sharpe, a winner of the NOBEL PRIZE IN ECONOMICS and co-creator of the CAPITAL ASSET PRICING MODEL. You simply divide the past RETURN on the investment (less the RISK-FREE RATE) by its STANDARD DEVIATION, the simplest measure of risk. The higher the Sharpe ratio is the better, that is, the greater is the return per unit of risk. However, as it is a backward-looking measure, based on what an investment has done in the past, the Sharpe ratio does not guarantee similar performance in future.

Shock

An unexpected event that affects an economy (see ASYMMETRIC SHOCK).

Shorting

Selling a SECURITY, such as a SHARE, that you do not currently own, in the expectation that its PRICE will fall by the time the security has to be delivered to its new owner. If the price does fall, you can buy the security at the lower price, deliver it to whoever you sold it to and make a PROFIT. The RISK is that the price rises, leaving you with a loss. Sometimes an investor will borrow a security in order to short it. When an investor sells a security without such borrowing, it is called naked shorting.

Shorting can be controversial, and naked shorting more so. During the CREDIT CRUNCH that began in 2007, BANKS accused short sellers of making matters worse by shorting their shares. For a while, regulators in leading economies banned the shorting of shares of some financial FIRMS. Critics of this ban argued that shorting provides LIQUIDITY to the market, and banning it made matters worse by reducing liquidity at a time when the credit crunch made it especially valuable.

Short-termism

Doing things that make you better off in the short run but worse off in the end. After the bursting of the stockmarket BUBBLE and the failure of ENRON at the start of the 2000s, and again during the economic crisis that began in 2007, accusations of short-termism were made against the financial markets-based CAPITAL-ISM of the United States and the UK. Investors, it was claimed, had become too focused on short-term PROFITS and changes in SHARE prices, and failed to probe deeply enough into long-term performance. As a result, managers did things that made their profits look as good as possible in the short run, often to the detriment of their company's long-term health. How managers were paid often exacerbated this tendency, resulting in massive AGENCY COSTS in the long run for investors, as many firms engaged in misleading and even fraudulent accounting practices to inflate short-term profits, as well as taking excessive RISKS. In the 1980s and early 1990s, there were also complaints about short-termism, albeit in a somewhat different and arguably less convincing form, namely that short-termism caused lower levels of INVESTMENT by businesses than in countries where the stockmarket was less important, such as Germany and Japan.

How to reduce short-termism is unclear, especially given KEYNES's observation about the lack of appeal of the LONG RUN. However, focusing on how managers and institutional investors are compensated, to minimise the incentives for short-termist behaviour, offers plenty of potential.

Signalling

A solution to one of the biggest sources of MARKET FAILURE: ASYMMETRIC INFORMATION. Often the biggest problem facing sellers is how to convince buyers that what they are selling is as good as they say it is. This problem arises in situations where the qualities of the thing being sold cannot be observed easily by buyers, who thus fear that sellers may be conning them. In such situations, an answer may be for sellers to do something that shows they mean what they say about quality. This something is what economists call signalling.

Going to a leading university might be worth far more for what it signals to prospective employers about your abilities than for what you learn as a student. Likewise, the fact that a FIRM is willing to spend a lot of MONEY ADVERTISING its product may say far more about what it thinks of the product than any information included in the actual ad. To be useful, signals must impose more costs on those who use them to send false messages than any gains to be had from lying.

Simple interest

INTEREST calculated only on the initial amount borrowed or invested. Contrast with COMPOUND INTEREST.

Smith, Adam

The founder of ECONOMICS as we know it. Born in Kirkcaldy, Fife, Adam Smith (1723–90) was educated at Glasgow and Oxford, and in 1751 became professor of logic at Glasgow University. Eight years later he made his name by publishing the *Theory of Moral Sentiments*. His 1776 book, *An Inquiry into the Nature and Causes of the Wealth of Nations*, is the bible of CLASSICAL ECONOMICS – though it should be read in conjunction with his *Theory of Moral Sentiments*. He emphasised the role of specialisation (the DIVISION OF LABOUR), TECHNICAL PROGRESS and CAPITAL INVESTMENT as the main engines of economic GROWTH. Above all, he stressed the importance of the INVISIBLE HAND, the way in which self-interest pursued in free markets leads to the most efficient use of economic resources and makes everybody better off in the process.

Social benefits/costs

The overall impact of an economic activity on the WELFARE of society. Social benefits/costs are the sum of private benefits/costs arising from the activity and any EXTERNALITIES.

Social capital

The amount of community spirit or trust that an economy has gluing it together. The more social capital there is, the more productive the economy will be. Yet, curiously, one of the best-known books to address the role of social capital, *Bowling Alone*, by Robert Putnam of Harvard University, pointed out that Americans were far less likely to be members of community organisations, clubs or associations in the 1990s than they were in the 1950s. He illustrated his thesis by charting the decline of bowling leagues. Yet the American economy has gone from strength to strength. This has led some economists to question whether social capital is really as important as the theory suggests, and others to argue that membership of bowling leagues and other community organisations is simply not a good indicator of the amount of social capital in a country.

Social enterprise

Organisations that trade in goods and SERVICES to support a social mission. These include non-PROFIT organisations or NGOs that trade as an alternative or in addition to receiving grant funding and, increasingly, for-profit companies that seek to achieve social goals while at the same time "doing well by doing good". A growing number of "blended value" companies measure their performance according to a "double bottom line" (that considers profits and social impact) or a "triple bottom line" (profit, social and environmental impact).

Social entrepreneur

Someone who recognises a social problem and uses entrepreneurial approaches to solve it. Whereas business ENTREPRENEURS ultimately judge their performance by their ability to create a profitable business, social entrepreneurs measure success according to the impact they have on society. In recent years, the number of social entrepreneurs has soared, both within the non-PROFIT/NGO sector and increasingly within mission-driven for-profit businesses, such as MICROFINANCE FIRMS. Some economists believe that social entrepreneurs are increasing the EFFICIENCY and PRODUCTIVITY of the social sector, which has often been inefficient because of the lack of entrepreneurship in GOVERNMENT and the established NGO sector. Some leading social entrepreneurs have been helped to grow by philanthropic donations from wealthy practitioners of PHILANTHROCAPITALISM.

Socialism

The exact meaning of socialism is much debated, but in theory it includes some collective ownership of the means of production and a strong emphasis on equality, of some sort.

Social market

The name given to the economic arrangements devised in Germany after the second world war. This blended market CAPITALISM, strong LABOUR protection and UNION influence, and a generous WELFARE state. The phrase has also been used to describe attempts to make capitalism more caring, and to the use of market mechanisms to increase the EFFICIENCY of the social functions of the state, such as the education system or prisons. More broadly, it refers to the study of the different social institutions underpinning every market economy.

Soft currency

A currency that is expected to drop in value relative to other currencies.

Soft dollars

The value of research services that brokerage companies provide "free" to INVESTMENT managers in exchange for the investment managers' business. Economists disagree on whether or not such hidden payments are economically inefficient.

Soft loan

A loan provided at below the market INTEREST RATE. Soft loans are used by international agencies to encourage economic activity in DEVELOPING COUNTRIES and to support non-commercial activities.

Soft paternalism

In traditional hard paternalism, the nanny state orders its citizens to do what it believes is in their best interests. In soft paternalism, which draws on the insights of BEHAVIOURAL ECONOMICS, the GOVERNMENT merely gives citizens a nudge in the right direction. One thing behavioural economics has found is that people will make different decisions depending on how a choice is framed – for instance, they may be far less likely to opt in to something than to opt out of it. Thus one popular policy among soft paternalists is to try to increase retirement SAVINGS (a goal shared by most governments) by automatically deducting money from workers' salaries unless they opt out, rather than doing so only if they opt in to the scheme. The choice facing the workers, and their right to choose, would be the same: they are free to be in or out of the retirement scheme. Yet, the soft paternalists believe, a government could raise retirement savings significantly with this helpful nudge. Might this approach offer a "third way" between authoritarian and LAISSEZ-FAIRE government?

Sovereign risk

The RISK that a GOVERNMENT will default on its DEBT or on a loan guaranteed by it.

Sovereign wealth fund

A state-owned INVESTMENT fund. The first sovereign wealth fund was the Kuwait Investment Authority, established in 1953 to invest the newly independent country's OIL revenues. In 2008, the biggest was the Abu Dhabi Investment Authority (ADIA) with ASSETS of around $625 billion, twice the size of the second biggest, the Norwegian GOVERNMENT's fund. Many new sovereign wealth funds have been created in recent years, not least by the government of China. Rising COMMODITY PRICES in some cases and ballooning foreign exchange RESERVES in others led to a sharp increase in the amount of MONEY managed by sovereign wealth funds. By 2008, together they controlled assets of nearly $10 trillion, equivalent to 15% of all publicly traded SHARES and BONDS in the world. Their growing appetite for investing in leading companies from the United States and Europe, together with the lack of democratic credentials of many of the governments controlling them, made sovereign wealth funds increasingly controversial. Some critics described them as the driving force of a "new MERCANTILISM". However, this controversy eased, at least temporarily, as the global economic crisis that began in 2007 intensified. Tumbling commodity prices hit some of the most prominent sovereign wealth funds, as did large losses on some of their highest profile investments, such as in shares of Wall Street BANKS.

Speculation

An attitude to INVESTMENT that is often criticised. According to critics, speculation involves buying or selling a financial ASSET with the aim of making a quick PROFIT. This is contrasted with long-term investment, in which an asset is retained despite short-term fluctuations in its value. Speculators can play a valuable role in financial markets as their appetite for frequent buying and selling provides LIQUIDITY to the markets. This benefits longer-term investors, too, as it enables them to get a good PRICE when they do eventually sell.

Speculative motive

See PRECAUTIONARY MOTIVE.

Spot price

The PRICE quoted for a transaction that is to be made on the spot; that is, paid for now for delivery now. Contrast spot markets with forward contracts and futures markets (see DERIVATIVES), where payment and/or delivery will be made at some future date. Also contrast with long-term contracts, in which a price is agreed for repeated transactions over an extended time period and which may not involve immediate payment in full.

Spread

The difference between one item and another. A much used term in FINANCIAL MARKETS. Examples are the differences between:

- the bid (what a dealer will pay) and ask or offer (what a dealer will sell for) PRICE of a SHARE or other SECURITY;
- the price an underwriter pays for an issue of BONDS from a

company and the price the underwriter charges the public;
- the YIELD on two different bonds.

Stabilisation

GOVERNMENT policies intended to smooth the economic cycle, expanding DEMAND when UNEMPLOYMENT is high and reducing it when INFLATION threatens to increase. Doing this by FINE TUNING has mostly proved harder than KEYNESIAN policymakers expected, and it has become unfashionable. However, the use of automatic stabilisers remains widespread. For instance, social handouts from the state usually increase during tough times, and taxes increase (FISCAL DRAG), boosting government revenue, when the economy is growing.

Stability and Growth Pact

Budgetary rules agreed to by EURO ZONE countries as a condition of joining the EURO. The pact stipulates that all the countries will run a balanced BUDGET in normal times. A GOVERNMENT that runs a fiscal DEFICIT bigger than 3% of GDP must take swift corrective action. And if any country breaches the 3% limit for more than three years in a row, it becomes liable to fines of billions of euros. The pact was supposed to be a powerful political symbol that euro-using countries would not cheat each other. However, Portugal became the first country to break the deficit limit by notching up 4.1% in 2001. When, in 2002, France and Germany also exceeded the 3% limit, some EU members were outraged and others lobbied for the pact to be modified or even scrapped. In 2005 the rules were relaxed, ostensibly to make it more enforceable, though critics said it would have the opposite effect in practice.

Stagflation

A term coined in the 1970s for the twin economic problems of STAGNATION and rising INFLATION. Until then, these two economic blights had not appeared simultaneously. Indeed, policymakers believed the message of the PHILLIPS CURVE: that UNEMPLOYMENT and inflation were alternatives.

Stagnation

A prolonged recession, but not as severe as a depression.

Stakeholders

All the parties that have an interest, financial or otherwise, in a company, including shareholders, CREDITORS, bondholders, employees, customers, management, the community and GOVERNMENT. How these different interests should be catered for, and what to do when they conflict, is much debated. In particular, there is growing disagreement between those who argue that companies should be run primarily in the interests of their shareholders, in order to maximise SHAREHOLDER VALUE, and those who argue that the wishes of shareholders should sometimes be traded off against those of other stakeholders.

Standard deviation

A measure of how far a variable moves over time away from its AVERAGE (mean) value.

Standard error

A measure of the possible error in a statistical estimate.

Statistical significance

There are lies, damned lies and statistics, said Benjamin Disraeli, a British prime minister. Certainly, even if the result of number crunching is statistically significant, it does not mean it is true. But it does mean it is much more likely to be true than false. Statistical significance means that the PROBABILITY of getting that result by chance is low. The most commonly used measure of statistical significance is that there must be a 95% chance that the result is right and only a 1 in 20 chance of the result occurring randomly.

Sterilised intervention

When a GOVERNMENT or CENTRAL BANK buys or sells some of its RESERVES of foreign currency, this can affect the country's MONEY SUPPLY. Selling reserves decreases the supply of the domestic currency; buying reserves increases the domestic money supply. Governments or central banks can sterilise (that is, cancel out) this effect of foreign exchange intervention on the money supply by buying or selling an equivalent amount of SECURITIES. For example, if the government increases reserves by buying foreign currency, the domestic money supply will increase, unless it sells securities such as treasury bills to mop up the extra DEMAND.

Sticky prices

Petrol-pump PRICES do not change every time the OIL price changes, and holiday prices and standard hotel rates are fixed for months. Sticky prices are slow to change in response to changes in SUPPLY or DEMAND. As a result there is, at least temporarily, DISEQUILIBRIUM in the market. The causes of stickiness include MENU COSTS, inadequate INFORMATION, consumers' dislike of frequent price changes and long-term contracts with fixed prices.

Prices change only when the cost of leaving them unchanged exceeds the expense of adjusting them. In FINANCIAL MARKETS, prices move all the time because the cost of quoting the wrong price can be huge. In other industries, the penalty may be much less severe. Small disequilibria in, say, the pricing of hotel rooms will not make much difference. So hotel prices are often sticky.

Stochastic process

A process that exhibits random behaviour. For instance, Brownian motion, which is often used to describe changes in SHARE PRICES in an EFFICIENT MARKET (the RANDOM WALK), is a stochastic process.

Stocks

Another term for SHARES. What are called ordinary shares in the UK are known as common stock in the United States. It is also another word for inventories of goods held by a firm to meet future DEMAND.

Stress-testing

A process for exploring how a portfolio of ASSETS and/or liabilities would fare in extreme adverse conditions. A useful tool in RISK MANAGEMENT.

Structural adjustment

A programme of policies designed to change the structure of an economy. Usually, the term refers to adjustment towards a market economy, under a programme approved by the IMF and/or WORLD BANK, which often supply structural adjustment funds to ease the pain of transition. Such policies are much criticised in the developing world, sometimes with good reason.

Structural unemployment

The hardest sort of UNEMPLOYMENT to cure because it is caused by the structure of an economy rather than by changes in the economic cycle. Contrast with cyclical unemployment, which can, in theory if not always in practice, be cut without sparking INFLATION by stimulating faster economic GROWTH. Structural unemployment can be reduced only by changing the economic structures causing it, for instance by removing rules that limit LABOUR MARKET FLEXIBILITY.

Sub-prime

The popular bogeyman of the CREDIT CRUNCH that arrived in 2007. During the previous few years, there had been a sharp increase in the amount of CREDIT (particularly mortgages) extended to borrowers who did not meet established "prime" underwriting guidelines. Such borrowers were known to be riskier than prime borrowers, and so sub-prime debt was lent at higher interest rates than prime debt and, when securitised into CDOs, typically traded in the financial markets at a higher YIELD than investment-grade securities. In practice, sub-prime debt turned out to be far riskier than most people had thought. Initially heralded as a much-needed extension of credit to poorer people who had previously been denied access to mainstream finance, sub-prime came to be shorthand for a black hole at the heart of the FINANCIAL SYSTEM.

Subsidy

MONEY paid, usually by GOVERNMENT, to keep PRICES below what they would be in a free market, or to keep alive businesses that would otherwise go bust, or to make activities happen that otherwise would not take place. Subsidies can be a form of PROTECTIONISM by making domestic goods and SERVICES artificially competitive against IMPORTS. By distorting markets, they can impose large economic costs.

Substitute goods

Goods for which an increase (or fall) in DEMAND for one leads to a fall (or increase) in demand for the other – Coca-Cola and Pepsi, perhaps.

Substitution effect

When the PRICE of petrol falls people buy more of it. There are two reasons:

- The INCOME EFFECT: cheaper petrol means that real purchasing power rises, so consumers have more to spend on everything, including petrol.
- The substitution effect: petrol has become cheaper relative to everything else, so people switch some of their CONSUMPTION out of goods that are now relatively more expensive and buy more petrol instead.

Sunk costs

When what is done cannot be undone. Sunk costs are costs that have been incurred and cannot be reversed, for example spending on ADVERTISING or researching a product idea. They can be a

BARRIER TO ENTRY. If potential entrants would have to incur similar costs, which would not be recoverable if the entry failed, they may be scared off.

Supply

One of the two words economists use most, along with DEMAND. These are the twin driving forces of the market economy. Supply is the amount of a good or service available at any particular PRICE. The law of supply is that, other things remaining the same, the quantity supplied will increase as the price increases. The actual amount supplied will be determined, ultimately, by what the market price is, which depends on the amount demanded as well as what suppliers are willing to produce. What suppliers are willing to supply depends on several things:

- the cost of the FACTORS OF PRODUCTION;
- technology;
- the price of other goods and SERVICES (which, if high enough, might tempt the supplier to switch production to those products); and
- the ability of the supplier accurately to forecast demand and plan production to make the most of the opportunity.

Supply curve

A graph of the relationship between the PRICE of a good and the amount supplied at different prices. (See also DEMAND CURVE.)

Supply-side policies

Increasing economic GROWTH by making markets work more efficiently. In the 1980s, Ronald Reagan and Margaret Thatcher championed supply-side policies as they attacked KEYNESIAN DEMAND management. Pumping up demand without making markets work better would simply lead to higher INFLATION; economic growth would increase only when markets were able to operate more freely. Thus they pursued policies of DEREGULATION, LIBERALISATION and PRIVATISATION and encouraged FREE TRADE. To reduce UNEMPLOYMENT, they tried to increase the EFFICIENCY of the jobs market by cutting the rate of INCOME TAX and attacking legal and other impediments to LABOUR MARKET FLEXIBILITY. The results of these programmes are much debated. In particular, the belief, apparently supported by the LAFFER CURVE, that cutting tax rates would increase tax revenue did not always stand up well to real-world testing. Even so, it is now recognised that supply-side reforms are a crucial element in an effective economic policy.

Sustainable growth

A term much used by environmentalists, meaning economic GROWTH that can continue in the long term without non-renewable resources being used up or pollution becoming intolerable. Mainstream economists use the term, too, to describe a rate of growth that an economy can sustain indefinitely without causing a rise in INFLATION.

Swap

See derivatives.

Systematic risk

The RISK that remains after DIVERSIFICATION, also known as market risk or undiversifiable risk. It is systematic risk that determines the return earned on a well-diversified portfolio of ASSETS.

Systemic risk

The RISK of damage being done to the health of the FINANCIAL SYSTEM as a whole. A constant concern of BANK regulators is that the collapse of a single bank could bring down the entire financial system. This is why regulators often organise a rescue when a bank gets into financial difficulties. However, the expectation of such a rescue may create a MORAL HAZARD, encouraging banks to behave in ways that increase systemic risk. Another concern of regulators is that the RISK MANAGEMENT methods used by banks are so similar that they may increase systemic risk by creating a tendency for CROWD behaviour. In particular, problems in one market may cause banks in general to liquidate positions in other markets, causing a vicious cycle of LIQUIDITY being withdrawn from the financial system as everybody rushes for the emergency exit at once. (See CAPITAL ASSET PRICING MODEL.)

In 2008, American financial regulators were confronted with the greatest systemic risk since at least the 1930s, as the CREDIT CRUNCH that began the previous year pushed leading financial institutions to the brink of BANKRUPTCY. Regulators intervened to prevent the bankruptcy first of Bear Stearns, an investment bank, and then two GOVERNMENT-SPONSORED ENTERPRISES, Fannie Mae and Freddie Mac. However, in September, they decided to allow another big investment bank, Lehman Brothers, to file for bankruptcy, apparently judging that its failure did not pose a systemic risk. Within days that judgment was to prove catastrophically wrong, prompting a massive bail-out of the global financial system that cost many times more than it would have done to prevent Lehman Brothers from going bust.

Tangible assets

ASSETS you can touch: buildings, machinery, GOLD, works of art, and so on. Contrast with INTANGIBLE ASSETS.

Tariff

Often used to describe a tax on goods produced abroad imposed by the GOVERNMENT of the country to which they are exported. Many countries have reduced such tariffs as part of the process of freeing up world trade.

Taxation

Prostitution may be the oldest profession, but tax collection was surely not far behind. In its early days, taxation did not always involve handing over money. The ancient Chinese paid with pressed tea, and Jivara tribesmen in Brazil stumped up shrunken heads. As the PRICE of their citizenship, ancient Greeks and Romans could be called on to serve as soldiers and had to supply their own weapons. The origins of modern taxation can be traced to wealthy subjects paying money to their king in lieu of military service.

The other early source of tax revenue was trade, with tolls and customs duties being collected from travelling merchants. The big advantage of these taxes was that they fell mostly on visitors rather than residents.

INCOME TAX, the biggest source of GOVERNMENT funds today in most countries, is a comparatively recent invention, probably because the notion of annual INCOME is itself a modern concept. Governments preferred to tax things that were easy to measure and on which it was thus easy to calculate the liability. This is why early taxes concentrated on tangible items such as LAND and property, physical goods, commodities and ships, as well as things such as the number of windows or fireplaces in a building.

In the 20th century, particularly the second half, governments around the world took a growing share of their country's NATIONAL INCOME in tax, mainly to pay for increasingly more expensive defence efforts and for a modern WELFARE state. INDIRECT TAXATION on CONSUMPTION, such as VALUE-ADDED tax, has become increasingly important as DIRECT TAXATION on income and wealth has become increasingly unpopular.

But big differences among countries remain. One is the overall level of tax. For example, in the United States tax revenue amounts to around one-third of its GDP, whereas in Sweden it is closer to half. Others are the preferred methods of collecting it (direct versus indirect), the rates at which it is levied and the definition of the TAX BASE to which these rates are applied. Countries have different attitudes to PROGRESSIVE TAXATION and REGRESSIVE TAXATION. There are also big differences in the way responsibility for taxation is divided among different levels of government.

Arguably, any tax is a bad tax. But PUBLIC GOODS and other government activities have to be paid for somehow, and economists often have strong views on which methods of taxation are more or less efficient. Most economists agree that the best tax is one that has as little impact as possible on people's decisions about whether to undertake a productive economic activity. High rates of tax on LABOUR may discourage people from working, and so result in lower tax revenue than there would be if the tax rate were lower, an idea captured in the LAFFER CURVE. Certainly, the MARGINAL rate of tax may have a bigger effect on incentives than the overall TAX BURDEN.

LAND TAX is regarded as the most efficient by some economists and tax on expenditure by others, as it does all the taking after the wealth creation is done. Some economists favour a neutral tax system that does not influence the sorts of economic activities that take place. Others favour using tax, and tax breaks, to guide economic activity in ways they favour, such as to minimise pollution and to increase the attractiveness of employing people rather than CAPITAL.

Some economists argue that the tax system should be characterised by both HORIZONTAL EQUITY and VERTICAL EQUITY, because this is fair, and because when the tax system is fair people may find it harder to justify TAX AVOIDANCE and TAX EVASION. However, who ultimately pays (the TAX INCIDENCE) may be different from who is initially charged, if that person can pass it on, say by adding the tax to the price he charges for his OUTPUT. Taxes on companies, for example, are always paid in the end by humans, be they workers, customers or shareholders.

Tax arbitrage

Creating FINANCIAL INSTRUMENTS or transactions that allow the parties involved to exploit loopholes in or differences between their tax exposures, so that all involved pay less tax.

Tax avoidance

Doing everything possible within the law to reduce your tax bill. Learned Hand, an American judge, once said: "There is nothing sinister in so arranging one's affairs as to keep taxes as low as possible ... nobody owes any public duty to pay more than the law demands." Contrast with TAX EVASION.

Tax base

The thing or amount to which a tax rate applies. To collect INCOME TAX, for example, you need a meaningful definition of INCOME. Definitions of the tax base can vary enormously, over time and among countries, especially when tax breaks are taken into account. As a result, a country with a comparatively high tax rate may not have a high TAX BURDEN if it has a more narrowly defined tax base than other countries. In recent years, the political unpopularity of high tax rates has lead many governments to lower rates and at the same time broaden the tax base, often leaving the tax burden unchanged.

Tax burden

Total tax paid in a period as a proportion of total INCOME in that period. It can refer to personal, corporate or NATIONAL INCOME.

Tax competition

Low-tax policies pursued by some countries in the hope of attracting international businesses and CAPITAL. Economists usually favour COMPETITION in any form. But some say that tax competition is often a beggar-thy-neighbour policy, which can reduce another country's TAX BASE, or force it to change its mix of taxes, or stop it taxing in the way it would like.

Economists who favour tax competition often cite a 1956 article by Charles Tiebout (1924–68) entitled "A Pure Theory of Local Expenditures". In it he argued that, faced with a choice of different combinations of tax and GOVERNMENT services, taxpayers will choose to locate where they get closest to the mixture they want. Variations in tax rates among different countries are good, because they give taxpayers more choice and thus more chance of being satisfied. This also puts pressure on governments to be efficient. Thus measures to harmonise taxes are a bad idea.

There is at least one big caveat to this theory. Tiebout assumed, crucially, that taxpayers are highly mobile and able to move to wherever their preferred combination of taxes and benefits is on offer. But many taxpayers, including the great majority of workers, are not able to move easily. Tax competition may make it harder to redistribute from rich to poor through the tax system by allowing the rich to move to where taxes are not redistributive.

Tax efficient

From the point of view of the taxpayer, the way of undertaking an economic activity that results in the lowest (legitimate) tax bill.

Tax evasion

Paying less tax than you are legally obliged to. Contrast with TAX AVOIDANCE. There may be a thin line between the two, but as Denis Healey, a former British chancellor, once put it, "The difference between tax avoidance and tax evasion is the thickness of a prison wall."

Tax haven

A country or designated zone that has low or no taxes, or highly secretive BANKS, and often a warm climate and sandy beaches, which make it attractive to foreigners bent on TAX AVOIDANCE or even TAX EVASION.

Tax incidence

Where a tax really bites. Who ultimately pays a tax is often not the same as who the taxman collects the tax from, because the cost of the tax can be passed on. For example, by demanding higher WAGES if INCOME TAX rises, workers can transfer some of the TAX BURDEN to their employer's customers or shareholders.

Taylor rule

A popular rule of thumb for MONETARY POLICY, stipulating how much a CENTRAL BANK should change the INTEREST RATE in response to a divergence of actual GDP from potential GDP and of actual INFLATION from the target rate. At its simplest, it recommends a relatively high interest rate when inflation is above its target or employment is above its FULL-EMPLOYMENT level (see NAIRU), and a relatively low interest rate when inflation is below target or employment is less than full. The rule was first proposed by economist John Taylor in 1993.

Technical progress

A crucial ingredient of economic GROWTH. Economists often used to take a certain rate of technological progress for granted, but in new ENDOGENOUS growth theory they make more effort to measure accurately and better understand what causes differences in the rate of technical change.

Terms of trade

The weighted AVERAGE of a country's export PRICES relative to its import prices.

Third way

An economic philosophy espoused by some leftish political leaders in the late 20th century, including Bill Clinton and Tony Blair. According to the rhetoric, it is not CAPITALISM and not SOCIALISM, but a third (pragmatic) way. Many have therefore found it rather hard to pin down. It was earlier used to describe Sweden's economic model.

Tick

The minimum PRICE change possible in a financial marketplace.

Time value of money

The idea that a dollar today is worth more than a dollar in the future, because the dollar in the hand today can earn INTEREST during the time until the future dollar is received.

Time series

Several measurements of a variable taken at regular intervals, such as daily, monthly, quarterly, and so on. They are often used by economists in search of trends that they hope will let them predict future movements in the variable.

Tobin, James

A Nobel Prize-winning economist, James Tobin (1918–2002) theorised that FIRMS would continue to invest as long as the value of their SHARES exceeded the replacement cost of their ASSETS. The ratio of the market value of a firm to the net replacement cost of the firm's assets is known as "Tobin's Q". If Q is greater than 1, it should pay the firm to expand, as the PROFIT it should expect to make from its assets (reflected in the share price) exceeds the cost of the assets. If Q is less than 1, the firm would be better off selling its assets, which are worth more than shareholders currently expect the firm to earn in profit by retaining them.

Tobin also gave his name to the "Tobin tax", a (so far unimplemented) proposal to reduce speculative cross-border flows of CAPITAL by levying a small tax on foreign exchange transactions.

Total return

The sum of all the different benefits from investing in an ASSET, including INCOME paid to the investor and any change in the market value of the asset. The total return is often expressed as a percentage of the amount invested.

Trade

See FREE TRADE.

Trade area

In a globalising economy, it is perhaps surprising that countries increasingly trade with their nearest neighbours. One explanation is geography: as countries have lowered their TARIFF barriers, the relatively greater importance of transport costs makes proximity matter more. According to NEW TRADE THEORY, this also produces gains from ECONOMIES OF SCALE. But another reason for the fast growth in trade among nearby countries may be less benign. The proliferation of regional trade agreements may be causing neighbours to trade with each other when it would be more efficient for them to export to and import from afar.

Since the second world war, more than 300 regional trade agreements have been notified to the GENERAL AGREEMENT ON TARIFFS AND TRADE (GATT) or the WORLD TRADE ORGANISATION (WTO), most of which are still in force. Roughly half of these, including some revisions of previous deals, have been set up since 1990. The best-known are the EUROPEAN UNION, the North American Free-Trade Agreement (NAFTA) and Mercosur in South America. There are dozens of other examples.

Economists have generally been unenthusiastic about regionalism, for two reasons. First, they worry that preferential tariffs will cause trade to flow in inefficient ways, a process known as trade diversion. In a perfect world, trade patterns should be determined by COMPARATIVE ADVANTAGE: the comparative cost of making different goods yourself as opposed to buying them from various countries. If the United States imports Mexican televisions merely because the Mexican goods are tariff-free, even if Malaysia has a comparative advantage in television MANUFACTURING, the main benefit of trade will be lost.

The second concern is that regionalism will impede efforts to liberalise trade throughout the world. One prominent critic, Jagdish Bhagwati, an economist at Columbia University in New York, has famously said that regional trade areas are "stumbling blocks" rather than "building blocks" in the freeing of global trade. There is no clear-cut theoretical answer to the question of whether regional trade agreements are good or bad, and the empirical findings are hotly disputed. In general, though, it seems likely that it is better to have regional groups that are open to the rest of the world than groups that are closed.

Trade cycle

See BUSINESS CYCLE.

Trade deficit/surplus

An excess of IMPORTS over EXPORTS is a trade deficit. An excess of exports over imports is a trade surplus. (See BALANCE OF PAYMENTS.)

Trade unions

See UNIONS.

Trade-weighted exchange rate

A country's EXCHANGE RATE with the currencies of its trading partners weighted by the amount of trade done by the country in each currency.

Tragedy of the commons

A 19th-century amateur mathematician, William Forster Lloyd, modelled the fate of a common pasture shared among rational, UTILITY-maximising herdsmen. He showed that as the POPULATION increased the pasture would inevitably be destroyed. This tragedy may be the fate of all sorts of common resources, because no individual, firm or group has meaningful PROPERTY RIGHTS that would make them think twice about using so much of it that it is destroyed.

Once a resource is being used at a rate near its sustainable capacity, any additional use will reduce its value to its current users. Thus they will increase their usage to maintain the value of the resource to them, resulting in a further deterioration in its value, and so on, until no value remains. Contemporary examples include overfishing and the polluting of the atmosphere. (See PUBLIC GOODS and EXTERNALITY.)

Transaction costs

The costs incurred during the process of buying or selling, on top of the PRICE of what is changing hands. If these costs can be reduced, the PRICE MECHANISM will operate more efficiently.

Transfers

Payments that are made without any good or service being received in return. Much PUBLIC SPENDING goes on transfers, such as pensions and WELFARE benefits. Private-sector transfers include charitable donations and prizes to lottery winners.

Transfer pricing

The PRICES assumed, for the purposes of calculating tax liability, to have been charged by one unit of a multinational company when selling to another (foreign) unit of the same FIRM. Firms spend a fortune on advisers to help them set their transfer prices so that they minimise their total tax bill. For instance, by charging low transfer prices from a unit based in a high-tax country that is selling to a unit in a low-tax country, a firm can record a low PROFIT in the first country and a high profit in the second. In theory, however, transfer prices are supposed to be set according to the arm's-length principle: that they should be the same as would be charged if the sale was to a business unconnected in any way to the selling firm. But when there is no genuinely independent market with which to compare transfer prices, what an arm's length price would be can be a matter of great debate and an opportunity for firms that want to lower their tax bill.

Transition economies

Former communist economies that, with varying degrees of enthusiasm, have embraced CAPITALISM.

Transmission mechanism

The process by which changes in the MONEY SUPPLY affect the level of total DEMAND in an economy.

Transparency

A buzz word for the idea that the more INFORMATION is disclosed about an economic activity the better. Many regulators, private lenders, politicians and economists reckoned that the ASIAN CRISIS of the late 1990s would not have been so severe, or even have happened, had Asian GOVERNMENTS, BANKS and other companies made available more and better data about their financial condition. Likewise, the collapse of ENRON provoked demands for greater transparency, to help improve corporate governance in the United States and other industrialised countries. Some economists reckon that transparency is one of the most effective methods of REGULATION. Rather than risk REGULATORY CAPTURE, why not simply maximise disclosure and leave it to the market to decide whether what the information reveals is acceptable?

Treasury bills

A form of short-term GOVERNMENT DEBT. Treasury bills usually mature after three months. They are used for managing fluctuations in the government's short-run cash needs. Most government borrowing takes the form of longer-term BONDS.

Trough

Transition point between economic RECESSION and recovery.

Trust

One of the most valuable economic ASSETS, hard to create but easy to destroy – a crucial ingredient of a country's SOCIAL CAPITAL. People are more likely to do business together when they trust each other. Trust can reduce MARKET FAILURE that otherwise results from ASYMMETRIC INFORMATION. When there is a lack of trust, people may have to spend heavily on monitoring others' behaviour to ensure they do what they say they will do. This cost may be so high that it is not worth going ahead with a business deal. When trust is absent, people may be less flexible in their dealings with each other. Countries can overcome some of the problems of a lack of trust by passing laws requiring good behaviour, but only to the extent that people trust that the laws will be enforced. One way in which companies seek to demonstrate that they can be trusted is by investing heavily in a BRAND.

Uncertainty

See INFORMATION.

Underground economy

See BLACK ECONOMY.

Unemployment

The number of people of working age without a job is usually expressed as an unemployment rate, a percentage of the workforce. This rate generally rises and falls in step with the BUSINESS CYCLE – cyclical unemployment. But some joblessness is not caused by the cycle, being STRUCTURAL UNEMPLOYMENT. There are also voluntary unemployment and involuntary unemployment. Some people who are not in work have no interest in getting a job and probably should not be regarded as part of the workforce. Others choose to be out of work briefly while they look for, or are waiting to start, a new job. This is known as FRICTIONAL UNEMPLOYMENT. In the 1950s, the PHILLIPS CURVE seemed to show that policymakers could reduce unemployment by having higher INFLATION. Economists now say there is a NAIRU (non-accelerating inflation rate of unemployment). In most markets, PRICES change to keep SUPPLY and DEMAND in EQUILIBRIUM; in the LABOUR market, WAGES are often sticky, being slow to fall when demand declines or supply increases. In these situations, unemployment often increases. One way to tackle this may

be to boost demand. Another is to increase LABOUR MARKET
FLEXIBILITY.

Unemployment trap

When unemployed people who receive benefits, either from the
GOVERNMENT or from private CHARITY, are deterred from taking
a new job because the reduction or removal of benefit if they do
will make them worse off. Also known as the poverty trap, it can
be addressed, to an extent, by continuing to pay benefit for a while
to unemployed people returning to work. (See WELFARE TO
WORK.)

Unions

In developed countries, at least, trade union membership and
influence has declined over the past three decades. Fewer WAGES
are now set by collective bargaining, and far fewer working days
are lost to strikes. Unions, which are in effect a CARTEL of workers,
probably make UNEMPLOYMENT higher than it would be without
them, as collective bargaining often pushes wages above the level
that would bring LABOUR SUPPLY and DEMAND into EQUILIB-
RIUM. These higher wages increase supply and reduce demand,
with the result that there are more jobless people. Unions thus
deepen a conflict between those in the labour market who are
insiders, that is, union members, and those who are outsiders,
typically non-unionised, poorly paid or jobless people. However,
unions can combat the excessive MARKET POWER of some FIRMS,
particularly when the firms (or a GOVERNMENT) dominate a particular job market. They can support workers who are badly
treated by management, as well as promoting safer workplaces.
They sometimes provide an efficient, and thus valuable, channel
for communication between workers and managers, particularly

in countries such as Germany, where conflict between management and unions is viewed as unhealthy.

Usury

Charging INTEREST, or, at least, an exorbitant rate of interest. Plato and Aristotle reckoned that charging interest was "contrary to the nature of things"; Cato considered it on a par with homicide. For many centuries, the Catholic Church regarded as sinful the charging of any interest by lenders and it was not allowed in Catholic countries, although Jews were exempted, provided they did not charge excessive rates. According to Pope Benedict XIV in 1745, interest should be regarded as a sin because "the CREDITOR desires more than he has given". In most modern economies, interest is recognised as a crucial part of the economic system, a reward to the lender for the RISK taken in making a loan. Even so, many countries have some form of usury law imposing limits on how high interest charges can be to protect borrowers from being exploited by unscrupulous loan sharks.

Utility

Economist-speak for a good thing; a measure of satisfaction. (See also WELFARE.) Underlying most economic theory is the assumption that people do things because doing so gives them utility. People want as much utility as they can get. But the more they have, the less difference an additional unit of utility will make: there is diminishing MARGINAL utility. Utility is not the same as utilitarianism, a political philosophy based on achieving the greatest happiness of the greatest number.

A tricky question is how to measure utility. MONEY does not (entirely) capture it. You can get richer without becoming more satisfied. So some economists have tried to calculate broader measures of happiness. They have found that people with jobs are much happier than unemployed people. Low INFLATION also makes people happier. Extra INCOME increases happiness a bit, but not much. In many countries incomes have risen sharply in recent years, but national surveys show subjective well-being has stayed flat. Within countries, comparing people across the income distribution, richer does mean happier, but the effect is not large. Married people are often happier than single people; couples without children happier than couples with; women happier than men; white people happier than black people; well-educated people happier than uneducated people; the self-employed happier than employees; and retired people happier than economically active people. Happiness generally decreases until you are in your 30s, and then starts rising again. Other economists are dismissive of such studies. They argue that people are rational maximisers of their own utility, so, by definition, whatever they do maximises it.

" If all the economists were laid end to end, they'd never reach a conclusion.

George Bernard Shaw, Irish playwright

Value added

This usually refers to FIRMS, where it is defined as the value of the firm's OUTPUT minus the value of all its inputs purchased from other firms. It is therefore a measure of the PROFIT earned by a particular firm plus the WAGES it has paid. As a rule, the more value a firm can add to a product, the more successful it will be. In many countries, the main form of INDIRECT TAXATION is value-added tax, which is levied on the value created at each stage of production. However, it is paid, ultimately, by whoever consumes the finished product.

Another definition of value added refers to the change in the overall economic value of a company. This takes into account changes in the combined value of its SHARES, ASSETS, DEBT and other liabilities. Part of the pay of company bosses is often linked to how much economic value is added to the company under their management.

Value at risk

Value at risk models, widely used for RISK MANAGEMENT by BANKS and other financial institutions, use complex computer algorithms to calculate the maximum that the institution could lose in a single day's trading. These models seem to work well in normal conditions but not, alas, during financial crises, which is arguably when it is most necessary to know how much value is at RISK.

Variable costs

Part of a firm's production costs that changes according to how much OUTPUT it produces. Contrast with FIXED COSTS. Examples include some purchases of raw materials and workers' overtime payments. In the LONG RUN, most costs can be varied.

Velocity of circulation

The speed with which money whizzes around the economy, or, put another way, the number of times it changes hands. Technically, it is measured as GNP divided by the MONEY SUPPLY (pick your own definition). It is an important ingredient of the QUANTITY THEORY OF MONEY.

Venture capital

PRIVATE EQUITY to help new companies grow. A valuable alternative source of finance for ENTREPRENEURS, who might otherwise have to rely on a loan from a probably RISK-AVERSE BANK manager. The United States has by far the world's biggest venture capital industry. Some economists reckon that this is why more innovative new firms have become successful there. As legend has it, with a bright idea, a garage to work in and some venture capital, anybody can create a Microsoft. However, the bursting of the dotcom BUBBLE in 2000 threw American venture capital into a severe RECESSION, damaging its reputation for financing profitable INNOVATION. It later recovered somewhat, but not to bubble levels.

Vertical equity

One way to keep TAXATION fair. Vertical equity is the principle that people with a greater ability to pay should hand over more tax to the GOVERNMENT than those with a lesser ability to pay. (See EQUITY and HORIZONTAL EQUITY.)

Vertical integration

Merging with a company at a different stage in the production process, for instance, a carmaker merging with a car retailer or a parts supplier. Unlike HORIZONTAL INTEGRATION, it is likely to raise ANTITRUST concerns only if one of the companies already enjoys some MONOPOLY power, which the deal might allow it to extend into a new market.

Visible trade

Physical EXPORTS and IMPORTS, such as coal, computer chips and cars. Also known as merchandise trade. Contrast with INVISIBLE TRADE. (See BALANCE OF PAYMENTS.)

Volatility

The most widely accepted measure of RISK in FINANCIAL MARKETS is the amount by which the PRICE of a SECURITY swings up and down. The more volatile the price, the riskier is the security. Not least because there is no obvious alternative, economists often use past volatility to forecast the future risk of a security. However, as the saying goes, past results are not necessarily guides to future performance.

Voluntary unemployment

UNEMPLOYMENT through opting not to work, even though there are jobs available. This is the joblessness that remains when there is otherwise FULL EMPLOYMENT. It includes FRICTIONAL UNEMPLOYMENT as a result of people changing jobs, people not working while they undertake job search and people who just do not want to work.

Wage drift

The difference between basic pay and total earnings. Wage drift consists of things such as overtime payments, bonuses, PROFIT share and performance-related pay. It usually increases during periods of strong GROWTH and declines during an economic downturn.

Wages

The price of LABOUR. In theory, wages ought to change so that the SUPPLY and DEMAND in the labour market are always in EQUILIBRIUM. In practice, wages are often sticky, especially in a downward direction: when demand for labour falls, wages do not fall. In this situation, the fall in demand results in higher involuntary UNEMPLOYMENT. Trade UNIONS may use collective bargaining to keep wages above the market-clearing rate. Furthermore, many GOVERNMENTS impose a MINIMUM WAGE that employers must pay.

FIRMS may choose to pay above the equilibrium wage to increase the PRODUCTIVITY of workers. Such so-called EFFICIENCY WAGES may make workers less likely to join another firm, so cutting the employer's hiring and training costs. They may encourage workers to do a better job. They may also attract a higher quality of worker than wages at the market-clearing rate; better workers may have a higher RESERVATION WAGE (the lowest wage for which they are willing to work) than the market-clearing equilibrium.

In recent years, employers have tried to reduce wage stickiness by increasing the proportion of pay that is linked to the performance of their firm. Thus if falling demand reduces the employer's PROFIT, the pay of its employees falls automatically, so it does not have to lay off as many workers as it otherwise would. Performance-related wages can also reduce AGENCY COSTS by giving hired hands a stronger incentive to do a good job.

Wealth effect

As people get wealthier, they consume more. This wealth effect has important consequences for MONETARY POLICY. When there is an INTEREST RATE increase, future INCOME from ASSETS such as EQUITIES must be discounted at a higher rate than before. As a result their owners feel poorer and spend less. A cut in interest rates has the opposite effect. Economists disagree on the wealth ELASTICITY of CONSUMPTION: how much consumer spending would rise if wealth increased by, say, 1%. Different consumers may have different wealth elasticity. If most of the increase in wealth goes to poorer people, this may have a different wealth effect than if most of it went to people who are already wealthy. The source of the wealth increase may also matter. If SHARE PRICES rise or interest rates fall, consumers may be slow to spend out of their increased wealth if they think the increase may be temporary. However, if they think a sharp rise in share prices is permanent and the stockmarket then tumbles, the result may be that consumption falls by enough to cause a RECESSION. The wealth effect of rising, or falling, HOUSE PRICES is particularly uncertain.

Wealth tax

In most countries, the majority of wealth is concentrated in a fairly small number of hands. This makes a wealth tax appealing to politicians, as it should allow substantial amounts of revenue to be raised from comparatively few people, allowing the TAX BURDEN on the majority of the POPULATION to be kept down. It also appeals because it promotes meritocracy by making it harder to be born with a silver spoon in your mouth. A wealth tax reduces the disparities in wealth rather than INCOME that are the biggest determinant of how the scales are weighted for succeeding generations. What could be better than a tax that produces lots of money for the GOVERNMENT and strikes most voters as being extremely fair?

Alas, as critics point out, wealth taxes may cause inEFFICIENCY by discouraging wealth-creating economic activities. Moreover, the revenue collected may prove disappointing. The wealthiest people are often the most skilled at TAX AVOIDANCE, not least because they can afford good tax accountants. Despite the enormous concentration of wealth in a small part of the population, on average across the OECD wealth taxes account for less than 2% of total tax revenue.

A wealth tax can achieve HORIZONTAL EQUITY and VERTICAL EQUITY (so that people of similar means pay the same and those with more pay more) in ways that INCOME TAX cannot. For instance, neither a poor person nor a rich person with no income would pay income tax, and only the rich person would pay the wealth tax.

Wealth taxes come in two main forms. CAPITAL transfer taxes are levied when wealth changes hands, either at death (inheritance tax) or through donation (gift tax). Annual wealth taxes are levied each year as a fraction of the taxpayer's net worth. Some people regard CAPITAL GAINS TAX as a wealth tax, but, strictly speaking, it is a tax on the income earned on capital, rather than a wealth tax on the capital itself.

Weightless economy

At the start of the 21st century, the total OUTPUT of the American economy weighed roughly the same as it did 100 years earlier. Yet the value of that output, in REAL TERMS, was 20 times greater. Output is increasingly weightless, produced from INTELLECTUAL CAPITAL rather than physical materials. Production has shifted from steel, heavy copper wire and vacuum tubes to microprocessors, fine fibre-optic cables and transistors. SERVICES have increased their share of GDP. This weightless or dematerialised economy, most economists agree, is not just lighter but also more efficient.

Welfare

Americans use welfare as shorthand for GOVERNMENT handouts to the poor. Economists use it to describe the well-being of an individual or society, as in "Are tax cuts welfare-enhancing?". This is economist-speak for "Will tax cuts improve the overall well-being of the country?". (See UTILITY.)

Welfare economics

ECONOMICS with a heart. The study of how different forms of economic activity and different methods of allocating scarce resources affect the well-being of different individuals or countries. Welfare economics focuses on questions about EQUITY as well as EFFICIENCY.

Welfare to work

Active LABOUR market policies, in which GOVERNMENT handouts to unemployed people come with strings attached, designed to get the recipient off welfare and back to work as quickly as possible.

Windfall gains

INCOME you do not expect, such as winning a lottery prize. Economists have long argued about whether people are likely to save such windfalls or spend them. According to the PERMANENT INCOME HYPOTHESIS, favoured by most economists, people save the lion's share of windfall gains. But real life often contradicts this; ask any lottery winner.

Windfall profit

A controversial concept, often used by politicians to justify imposing a tax on PROFIT that in theory is earned unexpectedly, through circumstances beyond the control of the company concerned, and is thus deemed undeserved and ripe for the taking by the tax authorities. As the profits were neither expected nor a result of the efforts of the FIRM, taxing them should not harm the firm's incentives to maximise future profits. The problem comes when greedy politicians start claiming that profits are windfalls when in fact they are deserved and expected. Then taxing them sends a signal to firms that they should not try too hard to make profits, as if they do too well they will not get to keep the profits anyway. If this became widely believed, effort would probably decline and economic GROWTH would be slower.

Winner's curse

A surprisingly common feature of AUCTIONS, whereby the winner succeeds by bidding an amount that turns out to be more than the true value of whatever is being auctioned.

Winner-takes-all markets

No time for losers. In certain jobs, the market pays individuals not according to their absolute performance but according to their performance relative to others. The INCOME of window cleaners depends upon how many windows they clean, but investment bankers' pay may depend upon their performance ranking. Slightly more talented window cleaners will make only a small difference to the transparency of their customers' windows, but in the markets for selling BONDS that slight edge can mean everything. Rewards at the top are therefore disproportionately high, and rewards below the top are disproportionately low. People in these professions are often willing to work for very little just to have the chance to compete for the top job and the jackpot that comes with it.

This sort of ECONOMICS has long been prevalent in celebrity-dominated businesses such as entertainment and sport. But this reward structure is spreading to more and more occupations, including journalism, the law, medicine and corporate management. GLOBALISATION has expanded the market for skills, increasing the opportunities for the rich to become even richer.

In a normal market, sumptuous superstar incomes would attract COMPETITION from more applicants to do the jobs that pay them. This would then bring salaries down to less exotic levels. In a winner-takes-all market, this does not happen. An investment BANK wants the best analysts and dealers; second best will not do. It can also afford to pay. Some economists believe that because of more liberalised markets there will be growing INEQUALITY in most professions and the emergence of a winner-takes-all society.

Withholding tax

A tax that is collected at source, before the taxpayer has seen the INCOME or CAPITAL to which the tax applies. In other words, that part of the income or capital due in tax is withheld from the taxpayer, who therefore cannot easily avoid paying the tax. Withholding taxes are frequently imposed on INTEREST and DIVIDENDS.

World Bank

An institution created with the IMF at BRETTON WOODS in 1944 and opened in 1946. The World Bank has three main branches: the International Bank for Reconstruction and Development (IBRD), the International Development Agency (IDA) and the International Finance Corporation (IFC). Collectively, it aims to promote economic development in the world's poorer countries through advice and long-term lending, averaging $30 billion a year, spread around 100 countries.

Critics of the World Bank say that it often worsens the problems facing developing countries. Its advice has often been guided by economic fashion, which led it to support a centrally planned brand of DEVELOPMENT ECONOMICS in the 1960s and 1970s, before switching to PRIVATISATION and STRUCTURAL ADJUSTMENT in the 1980s and then to promoting democracy and economic TRANSPARENCY, and attacking CRONY CAPITALISM, in the late 1990s. Until recently, it has generally supported big, high-profile projects rather than more economically useful smaller schemes. It has often failed to ensure that its loans have been spent on the intended project. Its willingness to pump money into struggling countries creates a potential MORAL HAZARD, in which politicians may have little incentive to govern well because they believe that, if they do a bad job, the World Bank will come to the rescue. The increase in private-sector lending to and INVESTMENT in emerging markets has led to growing discussion of whether the World Bank is any longer needed.

World Trade Organisation

Bête noire of anti-GLOBALISATION protesters. The World Trade Organisation (WTO) is the governing body of international trade, setting and enforcing the rules of trade and punishing offenders. Established during the Uruguay Round of talks under the GENERAL AGREEMENT ON TARIFFS AND TRADE (GATT), it opened for business in 1995 with a membership of 132 countries (rising to 153 by 2009, representing 95% of world trade). Countries used to break GATT rules with impunity. They seem to be finding it harder to do so under the WTO. Even so, protestors complain that it does not promote FAIR TRADE but does promote the interests of rich countries over poorer ones. Supporters of FREE TRADE, including *The Economist*, reckon that all countries are better off as part of a well-regulated international trading system, and that the WTO is the most likely source of the good regulation that is needed. Moreover, the WTO is unusually democratic for a multilateral organisation, with every member country, however small, having an equal vote.

X-efficiency

Producing OUTPUT at the minimum possible cost. This is not enough to ensure the best sort of economic EFFICIENCY, which maximises society's total consumer plus producer surplus, because the quantity of output produced may not be ideal. For instance, a MONOPOLY can be an x-efficient producer, but in order to maximise its PROFIT it may produce a different quantity of output than there would be in a surplus-maximising market with PERFECT COMPETITION.

Yield

The annual income from a SECURITY, expressed as a percentage of the current market price of the security. The yield on a SHARE is its DIVIDEND divided by its PRICE. A BOND yield is also known as its INTEREST RATE: the annual coupon divided by the market price.

Yield curve

Shorthand for comparisons of the INTEREST RATE on GOVERN-MENT BONDS of different maturity. If investors think it is riskier to buy a bond with 15 years until it matures than a bond with five years of life, they will demand a higher interest rate (YIELD) on the longer-dated bond. If so, the yield curve will slope upwards from left (the shorter maturities) to right. It is normal for the yield curve to be positive (upward sloping, left to right) simply because investors normally demand compensation for the added RISK of holding longer-term securities. Historically, a downward-sloping (or inverted) yield curve has been an indicator of RECESSION on the horizon, or, at least, that investors expect the CENTRAL BANK to cut short-term interest rates in the near future. A flat yield curve means that investors are indifferent to maturity risk, but this is unusual. When the yield curve as a whole moves higher, it means that investors are more worried that INFLATION will rise for the foreseeable future and therefore that higher interest rates will be needed. When the whole curve moves lower, it means that investors have a rosier inflationary outlook.

Even if the direction (up or down) of a yield curve is unchanged, useful INFORMATION can be gleaned from changes in the spreads between yields on bonds of different maturities and on different sorts of bonds with the same maturity (such as government bonds versus corporate bonds, or thinly traded bonds versus highly liquid bonds).

Yield gap

A way of comparing the performance of BONDS and SHARES. The gap is defined as the AVERAGE YIELD on EQUITIES minus the average yield on bonds. Because shares are usually riskier investments than bonds, you might expect them to have a higher yield. In practice, the yield gap is often negative, with bonds yielding more than equities. This is not because investors regard equities as safer than bonds (see EQUITY RISK PREMIUM). Rather, it is that they expect most of the benefit from buying shares to come from an increase in their PRICE (CAPITAL appreciation) rather than from DIVIDEND payments. Bond investors usually expect more of their gains to come from coupon payments. They also worry that INFLATION will erode the real value of future coupons, making them value current payments more highly than those due in years to come. Moreover, the usefulness of the dividend yield as a guide to the performance of shares has declined since the early 1990s, as increasingly companies have chosen to return cash to shareholders by buying back their own shares rather than paying out bigger dividends.

Zz

Zero-sum game

When the gains made by winners in an economic transaction equal the losses suffered by the losers. It is identified as a special case in GAME THEORY. Most economic transactions are in some sense positive-sum games. But in popular discussion of economic issues, there are often examples of a mistaken zero-sum mentality, such as "PROFIT comes at the expense of WAGES", "higher PRODUCTIVITY means fewer jobs", and "IMPORTS mean fewer jobs here".